In the thirteenth century the Mongols created a vast, transcontinental empire that intensified commercial and cultural contact throughout Eurasia. One aspect of this exchange, little studied to date, was the extensive traffic in human talent; from the outset of their expansion, the Mongols systematically identified and mobilized artisans of diverse backgrounds and frequently transported them from one cultural zone of the empire to another. Prominent among those transported were Muslim textile workers, resettled in China, where they made sumptuous robes and other garments for the imperial court. In a meticulous and fascinating study, Thomas Allsen investigates the significance of cloth and color in the political cultures of Islam, Iran, the steppe peoples and China, thereby illuminating the cultural dynamics which condition the act of borrowing. His conclusion places the transmission of Muslim textiles and clothing culture to China within the broader context of the history of the Silk Road, the primary link in East–West cultural communication during the pre-modern era. The book promises, therefore, to be of interest not only to students of Middle Eastern and Asian history, but also to geographers, anthropologists, art historians and textile specialists.

Cambridge Studies in Islamic Civilization

Commodity and exchange in the Mongol empire

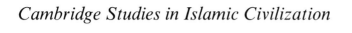

Cambridge Studies in Islamic Civilization

Titles in the series

STEFAN SPERL. *Mannerism in Arabic poetry: a structural analysis of selected texts, 3rd century AH/9th century AD–5th century AH/11th century AD*
BEATRICE FORBES MANZ. *The rise and rule of Tamerlane*
AMNON COHEN. *Economic life in Ottoman Jerusalem*
PAUL E. WALKER. *Early philosophical Shiism: the Ismaili Neoplatonism of Abū Yaʿqūb al-Sijistānī*
BOAZ SHOSHAN. *Popular culture in medieval Cairo*
STEPHEN FREDERIC DALE. *Indian merchants and Eurasian trade, 1600–1750*
AMY SINGER. *Palestinian peasants and Ottoman officials: rural administrtaion around sixteenth-century Jerusalem*
MICHAEL CHAMBERLAIN. *Knowledge and social practice in medieval Damascus, 1190–1350*
TARIF KHALIDI. *Arabic historical thought in the classical period*
REUVEN AMITAI-PRESS. *Mongols and Mamluks: the Mamluk-Īlkhānid war, 1260–1281*
LOUISE MARLOW. *Hierarchy and egalitarianism in Islamic thought*
JANE HATHAWAY. *The politics of households in Ottoman Egypt: the rise of the Qazdağlis*

Commodity and exchange in the Mongol empire

A cultural history of Islamic textiles

THOMAS T. ALLSEN
Trenton State College

CAMBRIDGE
UNIVERSITY PRESS

PUBLISHED BY THE PRESS SYNDICATE OF THE UNIVERSITY OF CAMBRIDGE
The Pitt Building, Trumpington Street, Cambridge, United Kingdom

CAMBRIDGE UNIVERSITY PRESS
The Edinburgh Building, Cambridge CB2 2RU, UK
40 West 20th Street, New York NY 10011-4211, USA
477 Williamstown Road, Port Melbourne, VIC 3207, Australia
Ruiz de Alarcón 13, 28014 Madrid, Spain
Dock House, The Waterfront, Cape Town 8001, South Africa

http://www.cambridge.org

First published 1997
First paperback edition 2002

Typeface Times 10/12 pt.

A catalogue record for this book is available from the British Library

Library of Congress Cataloguing in Publication data
Allsen, Thomas T.
Commodity and exchange in the Mongol Empire: a cultural history of Islamic
textiles / Thomas T. Allsen.
p. cm. – (Cambridge studies in Islamic civilization)
Includes bibliographical references and index.
ISBN 0 521 58301 2
1. Mongols – History. 2. Asia – Commerce – History.
3. Textile fabrics, Islamic – History. 4. Silk Road.
I. Title. II. Series.
DS22.3.A43 1997
338.4'7677'009509022–dc21 96-45214 CIP

ISBN 0 521 58301 2 hardback
ISBN 0 521 89314 3 paperback

To my Qatun Lucille Helen Allsen

Contents

Preface

The present study grew out of a larger, more comprehensive investigation of East–West cultural exchange in the period of the Mongolian Empire. Initially, my intention was to treat the Mongols' dispersal, apportionment, and resettlement of all types of artisans across Eurasia but it soon became apparent that the Chinggisids took a special interest in weavers and other textile workers, and I, too, decided to give them priority. In large part, this decision was driven by the sources, which contain extensive information on cloth and clothing, its manufacture, uses, and redistribution at the Mongolian courts. In pursuit of different research objectives, I had often read through these passages without recognizing their import; now, however, I slowly began to realize that for the Mongols cloth was central to their political culture, indeed the very stuff of their politics, and that this preoccupation explains much about the movement of textiles across Eurasia.

In previous work, I focused on the Mongols' mobilization of military manpower, war matériel and fiscal resources: here I turn to their appropriation of the cultural resources of their sedentary subjects. This, I hope, will provide a new perspective on the role of nomadic peoples in the transcontinental circulation of commodities, ideologies, technologies, and peoples that so characterizes the cultural history of the Old World.

During the years of research and writing I have incurred many debts which these acknowledgements record but hardly repay. First, my department chair for the last seventeen years, John Karras, consistently encouraged and supported my research in ways too numerous to mention. I also wish to thank JoAnn Gross, Celia Chazelle, Adam Knobler, and Alexandra Cuffel, my colleagues in the History Department of Trenton State College, who read and commented on various drafts of the manuscript. Rebecca French, Stephen Dale, and Michael Gervers also criticized, to my great benefit, these drafts. Long conversations with Peter Golden and Anatoly Khazanov about nomadic society and political culture helped me to resolve various specific problems and to sharpen my arguments. Gregory Golden checked my use of Latin sources, which I cannot read in the original.

Priscilla Soucek guided me in art historical matters, criticized an early draft, and put me in touch with Ann E. Wardwell, a textile specialist, whose careful reading and commentary greatly improved the manuscript. Carol Miklovic, the Interlibrary Loan Librarian at Trenton State provided her usual excellent service.

Last, and most specially, I would like to thank my wife Lucille Helen Allsen for long-term support and encouragement. Beyond placing her editorial and word processing skills at my disposal, she patiently listened to and expressed interest in my "latest" discovery on cloth among the nomads. For this and many other reasons, I gratefully dedicate this book to her.

Note on transliteration

For Persian and Arabic I have used the Library of Congress system. This, too, has been utilized for Russian. Chinese is in Wade-Giles, and for Mongolian I have used the system found in Cleaves' translation of the *Secret History*. Lastly, for Turkic, I have followed Nadeliaev, *et al.*, *Drevnetiurkskii slovar*.

Abbreviations used in the notes

Bar Hebraeus	Bar Hebraeus, *The Chronography of Gregory Abū'l-Faraj . . . commonly known as Bar Hebraeus*, trans. by Ernest A. Wallis Budge (London: Oxford University Press, 1932), vol. I.
Farquhar, *Government*	Farquhar, David M., *The Government of China under Mongolian Rule: A Reference Guide* (Stuttgart: Franz Steiner, 1990).
HJAS	*Harvard Journal of Asiatic Studies*
Ibn Baṭṭūṭah/Gibb	Ibn Baṭṭūṭah, *The Travels of Ibn Baṭṭūṭah*, trans. by H. A. R. Gibb (Cambridge University Press for the Hakluyt Society, 1958–71), 3 vols.
JAOS	*Journal of the American Oriental Society*
Juvaynī/Boyle	Juvaynī, ʿAṭā-Malik, *The History of the World Conqueror*, trans. by John Andrew Boyle (Cambridge, Mass.: Harvard University Press, 1958), 2 vols.
Juvaynī/Qazvīnī	Juvaynī, ʿAṭā-Malik, *Ta'rīkh-i Jahāngushā*, ed. by Mīrzā Muḥammad Qazvīnī (E. J. W. Gibb Memorial Series, vol. XVI; London: Luzac, 1912–37) 3 vols.
Marco Polo	Marco Polo, *The Description of the World*, trans. by A. C. Moule and Paul Pelliot (London: Routledge, 1938), vol.I.
Mongol Mission	Dawson, Christopher, ed., *The Mongol Mission: Narratives and Letters of the Franciscan Missionaries in Mongolia and China in the Thirteenth and Fourteenth Centuries* (New York: Sheed and Ward, 1955).
Rashīd/Boyle	Rashīd al-Dīn, *The Successors of Ghenghis Khan*, trans. by John Andrew Boyle (New York: Columbia University Press, 1971).

Rashīd/Karīmī	Rashīd al-Dīn, *Jāmiʿ al-tavārīkh*, ed. by B. Karīmī (Tehran: Eqbal, 1959), 2 vols.
Rubruck/Jackson	Jackson, Peter, trans. and David Morgan, ed., *The Mission of Friar William of Rubruck* (London: The Hakluyt Society, 1990).
SH/Cleaves	*The Secret History of the Mongols*, trans. by Francis W. Cleaves (Cambridge, Mass.: Harvard University Press, 1982).
SH/de Rachewiltz	de Rachewiltz, Igor, *Index to the Secret History of the Mongols* (Indiana University Publications, Uralic and Altaic Series, vol. CXXI; Bloomington, 1972).
Sinica Franciscana	Wyngaert, P. Anastasius van den, *Sinica Franciscana*, vol. I, *Itinera et Relationes Fratrum Minorum saeculi, XIII et XIV* (Quaracchi-Firenze: Collegium S. Bonaventunae, 1929).
YS	*Yuan shih* (Peking: Chung-hua shu-chü, 1978).
Yule, *Cathay*	Yule, Sir Henry, *Cathay and the Way Thither, being a Collection of Medieval Notices of China*, repr. (Taipei: Ch'eng-wen Publishing Company, 1966), 4 vols.

CHAPTER 1

Introduction

In the "Book of the Estate of the great Caam," a short treatise written around 1330 and attributed to William Adam, the archbishop of Sulṭāniyyah, the Mongolian capital in northwestern Iran, the author alludes to the great quantities of "cloths of silk and cloths of gold" to be found in Yuan China. Further on he elaborates on this abundance of fine textiles, noting that the

> emperor's people are very worthily arrayed . . . Although silk and gold are in great plenty, they have very little linen, wherefore all have shirts of silk; and their clothes are of Tartary cloth, and damask silk, and of other rich stuffs, oft-times adorned with gold and silver and precious stones.[1]

Similar apparel was known and extensively used in South Asia. Al-ʿUmarī, the fourteenth-century Arab encyclopedist, reports that at the court of Delhi "the sultan, the khans, princes and other military commanders wear Tatar clothes [*tatariyyāt*] . . ." A few lines later, he relates that a Muslim merchant, twice in Delhi, informed him that "most of their Tatar clothes [*aksiyah al-tatariyyah*] are brocaded with gold [*muzarkashah bi al-dhahab*]."[2]

At the western end of Eurasia, the English too, at least by the fourteenth century, were well acquainted with this type of cloth. In the reign of Edward III, 250 garters of "tarteryn ynde" (dark blue) were made for the Knights of the Garter, on each of which was embroidered the Order's motto in silk and gold.[3] More spectacularly, at the Cheapside Tournament of 1331, sixteen participants rode through the streets of London in the opening procession attired in Tartar clothes and wearing masks painted in the likeness of

[1] "The Book of the Estate of the Great Caam," in Yule, *Cathay*, vol. III, pp. 98–99.

[2] Ibn Faḍl Allah al-ʿUmarī, *Ibn Faḍlallah al-ʿOmarīs Bericht über Indien in seinem Werke Masālik al-abṣar fi mamālik al-amṣar*, ed. and trans. by Otto Spies (Sammlung orientalistischer Arbeiten, vol. XIV; Leipzig: Otto Harrassowitz, 1943), p. 35 Arabic text and pp. 61–62 German translation. On the term *tatariyyāt*, see R. P. A. Dozy, *Dictionnaire détaillé des noms des vêtements chez les Arabes*, repr. (Beirut: Librairie du Liban, n.d.), p. 94.

[3] Stella Mary Newton, *Fashion in the Age of the Black Prince: A Study of the Years 1340–1365* (Woodbridge, Sussex: Boydell Press, 1980), p. 45.

Tartars.[4] This display, Juliet Barker suggests, might have been inspired by Rusticiano's epitome of Marco Polo's travels which circulated widely in England at the beginning of the fourteenth century and which gives a detailed and informed account of Mongolian dress. The inspiration, however, may not have been entirely literary since the English monarchy at this time had direct contact with the Mongols of Iran with whom they exchanged embassies and gifts.[5] And if Mongolian diplomatic practice elsewhere in Eurasia is any guide, Tartar cloth was very likely among the articles presented on such occasions.

But whatever the precise source of the inspiration, England's familiarity with this fabric is graphically and colorfully expressed in "The Knight's Tale" in which Chaucer depicts Emetrius, an Indian king

> On a bay steed whose trappings were of steel
> Covered in cloth of gold from haunch to heel
> Fretted with a diaper. Like Mars to see.
> His surcoat in cloth of Tartary
> Studded with great white pearls; beneath its fold
> A saddle of new beaten, burnished gold.[6]

And this reference to "cloth of Tartary," it should be stressed, is only one among the many encountered in medieval West European literature. Paget Toynbee, who first investigated this matter, uncovered mentions of this textile in Dante, Boccaccio, in the works of minor French and Italian poets of the thirteenth century, and in wills and church inventories of the fourteenth century. From these frequent but laconic passages he tried to determine the type of fabric denoted by this term and came to the tentative conclusion that it described some kind of embroidered cloth.[7]

Recently, Anne Wardwell of the Cleveland Art Museum studied numerous specimens of garments and cloths designated as *panni tartarici* in the medieval inventories and demonstrated that while design and technical features vary, "Tartar cloths" were drawloom textiles typically made of silk and gold thread.[8] Her conclusion is fully sustained by the literary sources of the period, Muslim, Chinese, and European, that make it reasonably certain that the "Tartar Cloth" par excellence was a textile called *nasīj*. This term, derived from the Arabic verb, *nasaja*, "to weave," has the generic meaning

4 Juliet Vale, *Edward II and Chivalry: Chivalric Society and its Context, 1270–1350* (Woodbridge, Sussex: Boydell Press, 1982), pp. 62, 70, and 72.

5 Juliet R. V. Barker, *The Tournament in England, 1100–1400* (Woodbridge, Sussex: Boydell Press, 1986), p. 98. On the diplomatic contacts between the two courts, see Lawrence Lockhart, "The Relations between Edward I and Edward II of England and the Mongol Īl-khāns of Persia," *Iran* 6 (1968), 23–31.

6 Geoffrey Chaucer, *The Canterbury Tales*, trans. by Nevill Coghill (London: Penguin Books, 1977), p. 77.

7 Paget Toynbee, "Tartar Cloths," *Romania* 24 (1900), 559–64.

8 Anne E. Wardwell, "*Panni Tartarici*: Eastern Islamic Silks Woven with Gold and Silver (13th and 14th Centuries)," *Islamic Art* 3 (1988–1989), 95–133, especially 115–17.

of "woven stuff" or "textile" but by the Mongolian era, as Dozy rightly concludes, it was simply a shortened form of *nasīj al-dhahab al-ḥarīr*, literally "cloth of gold and silk."[9] This secondary meaning is attested in a number of contemporary texts. Pegolotti, the author of a fourteenth-century commercial manual, speaks of "pieces of *nacchetti* of silk and gold" when discussing the market prices of textiles in China.[10] Even more informative and explicit are two passages in the chapter on court dress contained in the *Yuan shih*, the official history of the Mongolian dynasty of China. Here, at the first mention of this fabric, the text adds parenthetically that "*nasīj* [*na-shih-shih*] is gold brocade [*chin-chin*]." Some pages later, another non-Chinese term is introduced, *ta-na-tu na-shih-shih*, which is defined as "large pearls basted on gold brocade."[11]

In modern usage, brocade is normally defined as a textile to which ornamental threads are added, most often in the weft. These supplementary weft weaves "have a purely decorative function and . . . partially cover the ground threads."[12] In the case of *nasīj*, obviously, the ornamental threads were of gold.

In its restricted meaning of gilded cloth or brocade, *nasīj* became a true *wanderwort*, spreading throughout the vast Mongolian imperium and beyond. In addition to the Italian and Chinese forms cited above, it is attested in Latin, Qipchaq Turkic, Persian, Arabic, and Mongolian.[13] In several sources it is paired with the Persian term *nakh* which the famed fourteenth-century Arabic traveler Ibn Baṭṭūṭah understood generally as cloth "of silk woven with gold." In one place, however, he clearly views it as a synonym for *nasīj*: in describing the mantle of one of the wives of Özbek, ruler of the Golden Horde 1313–41, he says that it was made of *nakh* and then adds that "it is also called *nasīj*."[14]

While a measure of terminological ambiguity remains, *nasīj* (and *nakh*), as used in the sources of the thirteenth and fourteenth century, most often

9 R. P. A. Dozy, *Supplément aux dictionnaires arabes*, 3rd edn. (Leiden: E. J. Brill, 1967), vol. II, p. 666.

10 Francesco Balducci Pegolotti, "La Practica della Mercatura," in Yule, *Cathay*, vol. III, p. 155, English translation. The Italian text reads "*nacchetti di seta e d'oro*." See Francesco Balducci Pegolotti, *La Practica della Mercatura*, ed. by Allan Evans (Cambridge, Mass.: Medieval Academy of America, 1936), p. 23.

11 *YS*, ch. 78, pp. 1931 and 1938. The term transcribed as *ta-na-tu* is the Mongolian *tana*, "pearl," and the adjectival suffix *tu*, that is, "pearled." This form is attested in the *Secret History* in the construction *tanatu könjile*, "pearled bed covering." See *SH*/Cleaves, sect. 133, p. 63, and *SH*/de Rachewiltz, sect. 133, p. 57.

12 Annemarie Seiler-Baldinger, *Textiles: A Classification of Techniques* (Washington: Smithsonian Institute Press, 1994), p. 98.

13 A. Bodrogligeti, *The Persian Vocabulary of the Codex Cumanicus* (Budapest: Akadémia Kiadó, 1971), p. 171; *SH*/Cleaves, sect. 274, p. 214; and *SH*/de Rachewiltz, sect. 274, p. 165.

14 Ibn Baṭṭūṭah/Gibb, vol. II, pp. 445 and 503. *Nakh* also goes back to the pre-Mongolian era. In its Georgian form, *nakhlebi*, meaning cloth of gold, it is found in Shot'ha Rust'haveli, *The Man in the Panther's Skin*, trans. by Marjory Scott Wardrop (London: Luzac, 1966), p. 106 and n.6, a work of the twelfth century.

refer to cloth woven of silk and gold, that is, to some type of brocade. And we have every reason to feel confident as well that these glittering and sumptuous textiles were the "Tartar cloths" of the medieval European texts. Further, and of greater import, this intimate association of the Mongols with a particular textile provides a point of departure for an exploration of both the setting and dynamics of trans-Eurasian cultural exchange in the Middle Ages.

For the Mongols of the thirteenth and fourteenth centuries, the family of Chinggis Qan possessed a charisma, a special good fortune which identified his particular lineage as the sole legitimate leaders of a heavenly mandated venture to bring all the known world under their sway.[15] In pursuit of this goal the Mongols fashioned the largest contiguous land empire in human history. For scholars of the nineteenth and twentieth centuries, the Mongolian Empire has always exercised a great fascination. To begin with, how did a nomadic people, numbering no more than a million, succeed in bringing populous and complex sedentary civilizations such as Iran and China under their control? Equally fascinating and far more contentious is the vexing question of the Mongolian legacy in Eurasian history. To some historians, their expansion was an unmitigated disaster that brought only destruction, death, and cultural decline, a "Tartar Yoke" that constituted a regressive force in human history. Others, on the contrary, have argued that the Chinggisids' political ambition led to a *pax mongolica* that facilitated and greatly intensified communication between East and West and thus afforded important opportunities for cultural contact, exchange, and enrichment.[16]

The debate continues, though hopefully not within the rigid parameters of the past. To make a new start, we must recognize that all premodern empires, including that of the Mongols, were possessed of "multiple personalities," in large measure because they were constantly and consciously projecting different faces to their multiple constituencies, and that they commonly pursued policies that were, by turn, destructive and constructive, brutal and paternal, exploitative and beneficent, coercive and

[15] On the political ideas of the Eurasian nomads, little studied to date, see Peter B. Golden, "Imperial Ideology and the Sources of Political Unity amongst the Pre-Činggisid Nomads of Western Eurasia," *Archivum Eurasiae Medii Aevi* 2 (1982), 37–76, and Igor de Rachewiltz, "Some Remarks on the Ideological Foundations of Chingis Khan's Empire," *Papers on Far Eastern History* 7 (1973), 21–36.

[16] As recently as the 1970s Soviet historians asserted that the Mongols had stifled the cultural and economic development of the conquered lands, while their communist Chinese colleagues argued for their progressive role in history. See Han Ju-lin, "Lun Ch'eng-chi-ssu," *Li-shih Yen-chiu* 3 (1962), 1–10; S. L. Tikhvinskii, "Tataro-mongol'skie zavoevaniia v Azii i Evrope: Vstupitel'naia stat'ia," in S. L. Tikhvinskii, ed., *Tataro-mongoly v Azii i Evrope: Sbornik Statei*, 2nd edn. (Moscow: Nauka, 1977), pp. 3–22; and Paul Hyer, "The Re-evaluation of Chinggis Khan: Its Role in the Sino-Soviet Dispute," *Asian Survey* 6 (1966), 696–705.

attractive, conservative and innovative.[17] Thus, while it is a fact that the Mongolian "peace" encouraged some cultural intermediaries – the Polo family, for example – to travel widely through Eurasia, it is also true that many cultural specialists were compelled, much against their will, to leave their homes and take up permanent residence in distant parts of the empire to better serve their Mongolian masters. Even individual events are ofttimes difficult to evaluate in absolute terms: to one scholar the act of looting a local art treasure might well be categorized as simple theft motivated by greed, while to another it might be viewed, quite legitimately, as a mechanism of cultural diffusion.[18] While balance in treating this issue is certainly desirable, selectivity, the very act of defining a problem, determines in large measure which of the multiple faces of empire will be emphasized. The present work, which examines cultural transfer within the empire, tends, of necessity, to accentuate the positive but without, I believe, ignoring or understating the coercive and destructive side of Mongolian policy in conquered lands.

To understand why the Mongols assumed such a pivotal role in trans-Eurasian exchange and to present essential background on the peoples, cultures, and locales mentioned in the text, we must first briefly describe the emergence and growth of a polity that its founders called the *Yeke Mongghol Ulus*, the "State of the Great Mongols."

In the twelfth century the eastern end of the Eurasian steppe, present-day Mongolia, was politically fragmented; tribal groupings fought one another incessantly, a condition that was actively encouraged by the Jürchens, a Tungus-speaking people from Manchuria whose dynasty, the Chin (1115–1234), ruled over most of Northern China. Such aggressive interference in the steppe zone was, however, a two-edged sword: it could divide and weaken or it might, as it did in this instance, provide an unwanted stimulus toward state formation among the feuding nomads. One of the contenders for leadership in the steppe, Temüǰin, the future Chinggis Qan, utilized this political chaos to slowly and painfully fashion a new tribal confederation. By good management, good fortune, and a real ability to attract and retain the services of talented individuals, he succeeded in unifying the eastern steppe by 1206. In that year Temüǰin took the title Chinggis Qan, "Oceanic Ruler," recast and expanded his personal retainers

[17] For the most part, the contradictory swings in Mongolian policy in subject territories have been analyzed solely in terms of court factionalism and debates over methods of exploitation. See, for example, N. Ts. Munkuev, "O dvukh tendentsiiakh v politike pervykh mongol'skikh khanov v Kitae v pervoi polovine XIII veka," in *Materialy po istorii i filologii Tsentral'noi Azii* (Trudy buriatskogo kompleksnogo nauchno-issledovatel'skogo instituta, vol. VIII; Ulan Ude, 1962), pp. 49–67.

[18] Compare the comments of Charles Singer, "East and West in Retrospect," in Charles Singer, *et al.*, eds., *A History of Technology*, vol. II, *The Mediterranean Civilizations and the Middle Ages, c. 700 B.C. to A.D. 1500* (Oxford: Clarendon Press, 1956), p. 765, who notes the technological and artistic influence of the booty brought back to Western Europe following the sack of Constantinople by the Fourth Crusade in 1204.

into an imperial guard *cum* imperial government, incorporated his newly won subjects into decimal-based military/administrative units, and commenced preparations for attacks on the sedentary peoples to the south.

As he began pressuring the Chin and its western neighbor and rival, the Tangut Hsi-hsia dynasty (990–1227) centered in Kansu and the Ordos region, some smaller states hastened to acknowledge Mongolian sovereignty. The most important to do so were the Turkic-speaking Uighurs of the eastern T'ien-shan region. Originally nomads themselves, the Uighurs left Mongolia in the ninth century and many settled amidst the oases of eastern Turkestan, where they took over much of the culture of the indigenous Indo-European-speaking peoples. Consequently, when their leader, the Iduqut, asked for Chinggis Qan's protection in 1209, he became the first ruler of a sedentary people to join the fledgling state. As such, his kingdom was ranked first among the numerous dependent states of the empire, and his subjects, systematically employed as scribes, officials, and court merchants, exercised a pronounced influence on Mongolian political culture during the empire's formative stages.

The ongoing operations in the south also produced welcome results. In 1210 the Tanguts recognized Mongolian suzerainty and in 1215 the Chin capital, Chung-tu (Peking) fell. After this triumph, Chinggis Qan withdrew to Mongolia, leaving his trusted viceroy Muqali to continue the campaign against the still resilient Jürchen regime. While in the homeland, Chinggis Qan was approached by emissaries from the Khwārazmshāh, Muḥammad (r. 1200–20), who was most curious and concerned about the intentions and capabilities of the rising power in the east. Muḥammad, who reigned over a recently and loosely constructed state centered south of the Aral Sea in western Turkestan, initially entered into peaceable commercial relations with Chinggis Qan which, however, soon soured when a Mongolian caravan was despoiled on Khwārazmian territory in 1218. After first clearing and occupying all of eastern Turkestan, the Mongols launched a large-scale invasion of the eastern Islamic world in 1219. The poorly deployed armies of the Khwārazmshāh were soon isolated and defeated and by 1224 the Mongols were in occupation of western Turkestan and Khurāsān (northern Iran and Afghanistan). The latter area was particularly hard hit; the Mongols, in reprisals for resistance and "rebellion," laid waste to many of its major cities and put part of the urban population to the sword.

Leaving garrisons and officials behind, Chinggis Qan returned to Mongolia in 1225 bent on punishing the Tanguts, erstwhile vassals who had not, in his eyes, met their obligations to the empire. The operations against the Hsi-hsia, initiated in 1226, were successfully concluded shortly after Chinggis Qan's death, from natural causes, in August 1227.

With the demise of the empire's founder, all campaigning halted and the surviving Chinggisids, their advisers and commanders, converged on Mongolia to select a successor. In 1229 they enthroned Ögödei (r. 1229–41), Chinggis Qan's third son and designated heir. He immediately restarted the campaigns of conquest on all fronts. The first success came in the east when the Chin dynasty collapsed in 1234, allowing the Mongols to occupy all Chinese territory to the frontiers of the Southern Sung (1127–1278). In the west, Mongolian forces seized the Qipchaq steppe, the Volga region, North Caucasia and the Rus Principalities between 1237 and 1241.

At Ögödei's death in 1241, campaigning again halted as discussions were held in Mongolia over the succession. After several years of wrangling the assembled princes and commanders enthroned Güyüg (r. 1246–48), Ögödei's eldest son. No blood was shed on this occasion but great bitterness was engendered by his elevation, especially among the descendants of J̌ochi, Chinggis Qan's eldest son, who controlled the western steppe and Russia. Indeed, civil war was only averted by the premature death of Güyüg, who was marching on the J̌ochid princes to settle their differences by force of arms when he conveniently met his end.

His demise, however, only delayed a confrontation among the increasingly divided princes. The Ögödeids proposed one of their own for the throne and were supported in this endeavor by the line of Chaghadai, Chinggis Qan's second son, whose territories included western and parts of eastern Turkestan. The J̌ochids, determined to prevent any Ögödeid from attaining the throne, proposed a candidate from the line of Tolui, Chinggis Qan's fourth son. Because the Toluids had more military force available in Mongolia, and because they were much the better organized of the two factions, the Toluid candidate, Möngke (r. 1251–59), prevailed.

In the end, the opposition could not accept what they perceived as an usurpation and attempted a counter-coup. This failed miserably and Möngke, a ruthless and able ruler, instituted an extensive purge in which many princes of the lines of Ögödei and Chaghadai, together with their retainers, were put to death following "show trials."

No doubt as a means of deflecting attention from his disputed succession, Möngke was eager to launch a series of campaigns of conquest to further extend the already enormous empire. To the northeast the Korean resistance was broken by 1259 and in the west large forces were dispatched to deal with the Isma'īlīs (Assassins) in western Iran and the 'Abbāsid Caliphate in Baghdad. Nominally under the command of Hülegü, Möngke's brother, these forces defeated and nearly exterminated the Assassins, occupied and sacked Baghdad in early 1258, and brought the 'Abbāsid Caliphate to an end. Meanwhile, in the south, Möngke and his brother Qubilai began operations in Yunnan and Szechuan in preparation for a large-scale attack on the Southern Sung.

The death of Möngke in southwest China in 1259 precipitated yet another contested succession, this one within the line of Tolui. The brothers Qubilai and Ariq Böke (most likely Möngke's intended heir) both proclaimed themselves emperor and a military confrontation ensued. When the dust settled in 1264, Ariq Böke was forced to recognize Qubilai's sovereignty (and was subsequently killed) but the Toluid civil war had permanently shattered the unity of the empire. The Jochids on the Volga supported Ariq Böke and refused to accept the victor's legitimacy. The Chaghadaids initially vacillated between mild support for Qubilai and an uneasy neutrality, but following Ariq Böke's submission they joined forces with the Ögödeid princes in 1269 in a concerted effort to topple Qubilai. Hülegü in Iran was Qubilai's only firm political supporter and only reliable military ally.

In place of a unified empire the Chinggisid lines now ruled over four, effectively independent qanates: Qubilai (r. 1260–94) in China, where he established the Yuan dynasty in 1271; the Chaghadai qanate in western Turkestan; the Golden Horde in control of Russia and the western steppe; and the line of Hülegü (r. 1256–65) in Iran and Iraq. These divisions, of course, slowed and finally halted the Mongols' outward expansion as increasingly their military energies were directed inward in a Chinggisid civil war that lasted into the early decades of the fourteenth century.

In characterizing the period before the breakup of the empire, the Persian chronicler Juvaynī, a mid-level bureaucrat in the Mongolian administration of Iran during the 1240s and 1250s, notes with approval and admiration that the sons of Chinggis Qan had achieved their great conquests "through concord and mutual assistance."[19] The upheavals of 1260–64, naturally, undermined this interdependency to a certain extent, but the fact that the Mongolian courts of China and Iran remained in alliance and continued to support one another ensured that the contact and exchange between East and West Asia, begun in the early years of the empire, was sustained and in certain areas intensified.

On the political-diplomatic level, Hülegü and his immediate successors, styled themselves *il-qans*, literally "subservient qans" to advertise their subordination to the emperor Qubilai from whom they sought and received patents of investiture. Even after Hülegü's great-grandson, Ghazan (r. 1295–1304) converted to Islam and ended the practice of requesting investiture, the Persian court's relations with the Yuan dynasty were still militarily important and the two remained in close partnership until the Mongolian regime in Iran collapsed in the late 1330s.[20]

The continuity in their technical and cultural contacts is nicely illustrated

[19] Juvaynī/Qazvīnī, vol. I, p. 32, and Juvaynī/Boyle, vol. I, p. 43. See also Juvaynī/Qazvīnī, vol. III, pp. 66–67, and Juvaynī/Boyle, vol. II, pp. 592–93, where he expresses these same sentiments at greater length.

[20] For an overview of this relationship, see Bertold Spuler, *Die Mongolen in Iran: Politik, Verwaltung und Kultur der Ilchanzeit, 1220–1350*, 4th edn. (Leiden: E. J. Brill, 1985), pp. 220–24; Thomas T. Allsen, "Changing Forms of Legitimation in Mongol Iran," in Gary Seaman and Daniel Marks, eds., *Rulers from the Steppe: State Formation on the Eurasian Periphery* (Los Angeles: Ethnographics Press, 1991), pp. 223–41; and Liu Yingsheng and

by the exchange of military technology. When Hülegü left for Iran in the early 1250s he was accompanied by 1,000 households of Chinese catapult operators who proved very useful in the reduction of the castles of the Assassins and the walls of Baghdad. Later, during the final phases of the Yuan campaign against the Southern Sung, the *il-qans* returned the favor. They dispatched specialists from Syria, familiar with counterweight catapults, to central China, where they materially assisted the Yuan forces during the siege of Hsiang-yang in 1272 and 1273.[21]

The field of medicine is also revealing of the nature of this relationship. Prior to the breakup of the empire, West Asian physicians, principally of Nestorian Christian background were well established in the east, while Hülegü had a contingent of Chinese doctors attached to his court in Iran.[22] Thereafter, their activities were sustained by shipments of Chinese *materia medica* to Iran and West Asian medicines to China. More spectacularly, Chinese works on physiology and sphygmology (pulse diagnosis) found their way into Persian translation.[23]

Indeed the range of these exchanges is impressive and as yet only partially explored. In addition to medicine and military technology, the two courts exchanged information and specialist personnel in the areas of historiography, cartography, astronomy, agronomy, printing, cuisine, and language, as well as in a variety of the crafts.[24] And among this latter category, weaving and textiles were by far the most visible and noteworthy, at least in the eyes of contemporary observers. Many types of fabric circulated within the empire but, as we have already noted, one class of textiles, loosely called "Tartar cloth" acquired a very special fame that rapidly spanned the whole of Eurasia.

Naturally, these "Tartar cloths" were not made by the Mongols, but rather they were made famous and popular by their extensive use among the

Peter Jackson, "Chinese–Iranian Relations, III, In the Mongol Period," *Encyclopedia Iranica* (Costa Mesa, California: Mazda Publisher, 1992), vol. IV, pp. 434–36.

21 Juvaynī/Qazvīnī, vol. III, pp. 92–93 and 128; Juvaynī/Boyle, vol. II, pp. 608 and 631; and Joseph Needham, "China's Trebuchets, Manned and Counterweighted," in Bert S. Hall and Delno C. West, eds., *On Pre-Modern Technology and Science: A Volume of Studies in Honor of Lynn White, Jr.* (Malibu, California: Undena Publications, 1976), pp. 107–45.

22 A. C. Moule, *Christians in China before the Year 1550* (London: Society for Promoting Christian Knowledge, 1930), pp. 228–34, and Rashīd al-Dīn, *Die Chinageschichte*, ed. and trans. by Karl Jahn (Vienna: Hermann Böhlaus, 1971), plate 2, Persian text and p. 21, German translation.

23 *YS*, ch. 37, p. 812; Rashīd al-Dīn, *Mukātabāt-i Rashīdī*, ed. by Muḥammad Safīʿ (Lahore: The Punjab Educational Press, 1947), pp. 285 and 286; Saburo Miyasita, "A Link in the Westward Transmission of Chinese Anatomy in the Later Middle Ages," *Isis* 58 (1967), 486–90; and Jutta Rall, "Zur persischen Übersetzung eines *Mo-chüeh*, eines chinesischen medizinischen Textes," *Oriens Extremus* 7 (1960), 152–57.

24 The best introductions to their cultural relations are Joseph Needham, *Science and Civilization in China* (Cambridge University Press, 1965), vol. I, pp. 188–90 and 214–19, and Karl Jahn, "Wissenschaftliche Kontakte zwischen Iran und China in der Mongolenzeit," *Anzeiger der phil.-hist. Klasse der Österreichischen Akademie der Wissenschaften* 106 (1969), 199–211.

ruling elite of the empire, the most powerful polity of the Middle Ages. To understand how the Mongols became so identified with this particular textile, we must address a series of interrelated questions. First, is the image, so far projected here, of Mongols draped in gilded cloth that would gladden the heart of a Liberace really true? To answer this question we need to establish the diverse uses and levels of consumption of *nasīj* in the empire at large. Second, how was the demand for this fabric met by the Mongolian rulers? This will entail an investigation of the various mechanisms of supply – booty, tribute, taxation, and court-sponsored production – used for this purpose. Third, why were the Mongols so attracted to gold brocade? Here we will examine native, nomadic cultural traditions, and the requirements of state in a multi-ethnic empire for possible answers. Lastly, did the Mongols, given the size of their empire and their penchant for moving resources and peoples about Eurasia, facilitate the diffusion of textile styles and techniques? In this instance, there is some interesting data on West Asian influences introduced into Yuan China.

From the nature of these questions, it should be evident that this study is primarily concerned with the cultural history of gold brocade within the Mongolian Empire, the principal goal of which is to elucidate the Mongols' priorities and predilections, and their role in East–West exchange. In other words, I approach this topic from the perspective of a historian of the steppe, not a specialist on textiles. But while I cannot speak to technical matters, looms, weave structures, etc., I am hopeful that those who are so qualified may find the data, arguments, and conclusions presented here suggestive in pursuing their own lines of research.

CHAPTER 2

Consumption and use

In the course of a Chinese theatrical performed for Ögödei sometime in the 1230s, the Chinese players held Islam up to ridicule. At this juncture, Juvaynī reports, the emperor called a halt to the proceedings and had Muslim and Chinese wares brought from the treasury for all to see. Included were "gold brocades [*nasīj-hā*] and garments" from Khurāsān and the two Iraqs which Ögödei pointedly extolled in contrast to the "inferior garments" coming from China.[1] While the Mongols' decided preference for *nasīj* is clearly attested in this and many other passages, reliable statistical data on their consumption of gold brocade are rare and the evidence for the most part anecdotal and circumstantial.[2] Nevertheless, an impressive array of diverse and independent sources tell a consistent and convincing story of massive demand for and consumption of this fabric throughout the imperial era.

Prior to their political unification in the early thirteenth century, the Mongols had only limited access to the luxury goods of the sedentary world, and consequently such acquisitions, usually obtained as booty from neighboring tribes, were events worthy of special mention. Rashīd al-Dīn (ca. 1247–1318), the great Persian statesman and historian whose work is based on now lost Mongolian records, recounts a revealing incident in this regard. Around 1195, Temüjin encountered and defeated the Tatar, a tribe closely allied with the Chin dynasty. And, while the victory was certainly a milestone in Temüjin's rise to power, Rashīd al-Dīn, significantly, gives equal attention to the goods seized: "And among the plunder which they found was a silver cradle and coverlets of gold brocade [*lihāfhāī zar-baftah*] and since in this era luxury articles of this type were scarce among the Mongols, they considered [this episode] important and it acquired fame."[3]

1 Juvaynī/Qazvīnī, vol. I, pp. 163–64 and Juvaynī/Boyle, vol. I, p. 207.
2 On the difficulties of finding reliable statistics on premodern textile production and consumption, see Maurice Lombard, *Études d'economie médiévale*, vol. III, *Les textiles dans le monde musulman du VIIe au XIIe siècle* (Paris, the Hague and New York: Mouton, 1978), pp. 175–206 and especially 202.
3 Rashīd/Karīmī, vol. I, p. 250. The account of this event found in the *Secret History* speaks of

The fact that the Mongols had no indigenous tradition of loom weaving, only techniques of ornamental braiding, must have made a prize of finely wrought gold cloth all the more marvelous and remarkable, and, perhaps, even portentous.[4]

Their early exposure to brocade had, evidently, a pronounced effect on the Mongols and their leader. This is reflected in two of the maxims of Chinggis Qan preserved in Rashīd al-Dīn's history. The first, dating presumably from the early stages of his career, relates that

> Once when Chinggis Qan had settled down in an upland, the name of which is the Altai, he glanced about his retinue, relations and the environs of the camps and made [the following] observations: "As my quiver bearers are black like a thick forest and [my] wives, spouses and daughters glitter and sparkle like a red hot fire, my desire and intention for all is such; to delight their mouths with the sweetness of the sugar of benevolence, to adorn them front and back, top and bottom, with garments of gold brocade [*zar-baft*], to sit them on fluid paced mounts, to give them pure and delicious water to drink, to provide verdant pastures for their herds . . . .[5]

In the second, he again speaks of his legacy but on this occasion with a certain pessimism about the likely quality and character of subsequent generations:

> After us, our posterity will wear garments of sewn gold [*zar-dūkhtah*], partake of fatty and sweet delicacies, sit well-formed horses, and embrace beauteous wives. [But] they will not say "[all] these things our fathers and elder brothers collected," and they will forget us in this great day.[6]

What is most interesting about these invocations of the good life is that all the basic elements, fine horses, pastures, and fatty foods are procurable in the steppe and clearly express traditional nomadic values, while gold brocade is the single commodity required of the outside world to complete this imagery of pastoral contentment and happiness. In many ways gold brocade came to symbolize the glorious future of the Mongolian people and perhaps became a kind of bench mark to measure their success in the quest for empire.

The maxims themselves, attributed to Chinggis Qan by later chroniclers, may well be projections on the past but the fact remains that the founder of the empire did procure for his followers the good things of the steppe and the sown, and altered in substantial ways their material circumstances and their expectations. In this connection it is noteworthy that many contemporaries from the settled regions contrast the extreme poverty of the Mongols in the pre-imperial period with their wealth following the con-

a "stomacher of gold silk [*altan torghan*]." See *SH*/Cleaves, sect. 135, p. 63, and *SH*/de Rachewiltz, sect. 135, p. 58.

4 Krystyna Chabros and L. Batčuluun, "Mongol Examples of Proto-Weaving," *Central Asiatic Journal* 37 (1993), 20–32.

5 Rashīd/Karīmī, vol. I, p. 439.

6 Rashīd/Karīmī, vol. I, pp. 437–38.

quests.[7] The Persian historian Juvaynī expresses this transformation by saying that before Chinggis Qan the Mongols' "clothing [was] from the skins of dogs and mice," while afterwards their "garments [were] of gold brocade and silk [*istabraq va ḥarir*]."[8] His testimony is fully confirmed by P'eng Ta-ya, a Sung envoy to the Mongols in 1237, who says of their garments that "formerly they used felt, fur and leather; recently they use coarse silk and gold thread [*chin-hsien*]."[9] Obviously, for these observers, expensive cloth was the most visible evidence of the Mongols' newfound prosperity and as soon as reliable supplies were secured through conquest, the Mongols, as we shall see, began to decorate themselves, their living quarters, conveyances, and transport animals in a lavish style.

One of the most spectacular uses they found for brocade was as lining for the interiors of the great tents of the qans, princes, and high officials, some of which, according to later oral tradition, which tends to exaggerate numbers, could accommodate 10,000 people.[10] The most frequently described of these impressive pavilions, which the Mongols called *ordo ger*, literally, "camp tent," is the one located at Sira Ordo, a satellite camp founded by Ögödei about fifteen to twenty kilometers southeast of Qara Qorum, the imperial capital.[11] Juvaynī, who traveled extensively in Mongolia, reports that the frame of latticed wood was constructed by Chinese and that "the ceiling was of gold brocade [*jāmahā-i muẕahhab*] and on the outside it was covered in white felt."[12] In reworking Juvaynī's data, Rashīd al-Dīn, who was never at the site, provides some sense of its size when he relates that it was "a huge tent holding 1,000 people which was never struck. Its outside," he adds, "was adorned with gold nails and its inside covered in gold brocade [*nasīj*]."[13] The Franciscan missionary, John of Plano Carpini, who visited the emperor Güyüg at Sira Ordo, confirms most of Rashīd's details. "This tent," he says, "was supported by columns covered with gold plates and fastened to other wooden beams with nails of

[7] Bar Hebraeus, p. 352, and Grigor of Akanc', "History of the Nation of Archers (The Mongols)," ed. and trans. by Robert P. Blake and Richard N. Frye, *HJAS* 12 (1949), 289.
[8] Juvaynī/Qazvīnī, vol. I, p. 15 and Juvaynī/Boyle, vol. I, pp. 21 and 22.
[9] P'eng Ta-ya and Hsü T'ing, *Hei-ta shih-lüeh*, in Wang Kuo-wei, ed., *Meng-ku shih-liao ssu-ching* (Taipei: Cheng-chung shu-chü, 1975), p. 479. For a German translation, see Erich Haenisch and Yao Ts'ung-wu, trans. and eds., *Meng-ta pei-lu und Hei-ta shih-lüeh: Chinesische Gesandtenberichte über die frühen Mongolen* (Wiesbaden: Otto Harrassowitz, 1980), p. 121.
[10] This figure was recorded by Robert Shaw, who traveled in eastern Turkestan in the late 1860s. See his *Visits to High Tartary, Yarkand and Kashgar* (Hong Kong: Oxford University Press, 1984), pp. 239–40.
[11] On the Mongolian term, see *SH*/Cleaves, sect. 123, p. 54 and sect. 230, p. 168, and *SH*/de Rachewiltz, sect. 123, p. 51 and sect. 230, p. 133. On Sira Ordo and other satellite camps, see John A. Boyle, "The Seasonal Residences of the Great Khan Ögedei," *Central Asiatic Journal* 16 (1972), 125–31.
[12] Juvaynī/Qazvīnī, vol. I, p. 194, and Juvaynī/Boyle, vol. I, pp. 238–39.
[13] Rashīd/Karīmī, vol. I, p. 478, and Rashīd/Boyle, p. 63.

gold, and the roof above and the sides on the interior were of brocade, but outside they were of other materials."[14] Finally, William of Rubruck, another Franciscan traveler to Mongolia, had an audience with Möngke Qaghan in an unnamed camp outside of Qara Qorum in which there was a huge tent of felt that "was completely covered inside with cloth of gold."[15] This, too, is very likely a reference to Sira Ordo.

These opulent palace tents were by no means limited to the great qans in Mongolia and were indeed found everywhere in the empire. Ibn Baṭṭūṭah, for instance, had an audience with Tarmasharin (r. 1326–ca. 1334), the ruler of the Chaghadai Qanate in Turkestan, in a tent "lined with silken cloth of gold."[16] More informative is the description of Clavijo, the Spanish ambassador who visited Temür's court at Samarqand in 1405. Here he encountered huge pavilion tents, square in shape, the sides of which measured 100 paces in length. The interiors were lined with silk cloth worked with gold thread. The tents themselves were surrounded by walls of silk cloth again decorated with gold thread. So, too, were the doorways in the wall and the elaborate archways over these portals.[17]

Princely status demanded such tents and even non-Chinggisids, if sufficiently powerful, enjoyed similar accommodations. Maḥmūd Yalavach, the head of the regional chancellery of North China in the 1240s and 1250s, worked out of a pavilion swathed in *nasīj*, as did his son Masʿūd Beg, who held a similar position in Turkestan; and the chief administrator of Khwārazm in the 1320s, Qutlugh Temür, was ensconced in a wooden audience hall whose ceiling was covered in "gold-embroidered silk."[18]

As for the manufacturing of these brocades, we are given a brief glimpse of the process in the description of the tent Möngke had prepared to honor his brother Hülegü on the latter's arrival in Khurāsān. According to Juvaynī, an eyewitness, the tent in question, made entirely of *nasīj*, required special measures and careful planning:

> The master craftsmen of the workshop [*kār-khānah*] gathered and consulted and in the end determined that the pavilion should be fashioned of a single, double-faced [cloth]. . . . The back and front were uniform and its inside and outside, in the correspondence of the pictures and colors, were true to one another [*mutasāvī*, literally, "parallel"] like the pure-hearted.[19]

[14] *Mongol Mission*, p. 63 and *Sinica Franciscana*, p. 119. Ibn Baṭṭūṭah also saw in Özbek's palace tent a framework of "wooden rods covered with plaques of gold," Ibn Baṭṭūṭah/Gibb, vol. II, p. 483.

[15] *Mongol Mission*, p. 153; Rubruck/Jackson, p. 177; and *Sinica Franciscana*, p. 249.

[16] Ibn Baṭṭūṭah/Gibb, vol. III, p. 558.

[17] Ruy González de Clavijo, *Embassy to Tamerlane, 1403–1406*, trans. by Guy Le Strange (New York and London: Harper Brothers, 1928), pp. 238, 239, and 251–52.

[18] Juvaynī/Qazvīnī, vol. III, pp. 33–34 and 98; Juvaynī/Boyle, vol. II, pp. 570 and 612; Rashīd/Karīmī, vol II, p. 688; and Ibn Baṭṭūṭah/Gibb, vol. III, p. 345.

[19] Juvaynī/Qazvīnī, vol. III, pp. 103–4, and Juvaynī/Boyle, vol. II, p. 616.

This, clearly, is the famous *dū-rūy*, the production of which required a number of weavers and special, complex looms.[20] While certainly dazzling, a tent of this material, in the absence of a felt exterior, was hardly practical and was evidently made primarily for display. But, by this time, the Mongols had immense resources, could call upon the best artisans in Eurasia and could therefore indulge their passion for beautiful textiles.

Some idea of the time and labor invested in such tents can be gleaned from Rashīd al-Dīn's account of Ghazan's quarters at Ūjān in southern Azerbaijan. Here a huge garden was laid out and when construction commenced Ghazan further ordered "distinguished masters and expert engineers to make a golden pavilion [*khar-gāh-i zarīn*]," to which end, he continues, "a large workforce busied themselves with its fabrication for a period of three years." When the royal party arrived in Ūjān in 1302 to view the facilities, the assembled tenters and engineers were only "able to pitch the tent in the course of a month because of its great size."[21]

Even while traveling, the ruling strata, particularly the imperial family, surrounded themselves in gold brocade on special occasions. Here it must be remembered that in contrast to the sedentary world the horse in and of itself conferred no special prestige in nomadic society because almost everyone, poor or rich, old or young, female or male, rode regularly. Consequently, as several contemporaries noted, social distinctions could only be communicated by differences in trappings or by the use of elaborate and special conveyances.[22] For example, Qubilai, the founder of the Yuan dynasty, who suffered from gout, was carried about in a palanquin borne by elephants.[23] This imposing structure is briefly mentioned in the Chinese and Persian sources and in greater detail by Marco Polo, who describes it as "a great wooden castle, full of crossbowmen and archers, very well arranged on four elephants all covered with boiled leather very hard, and above were cloths of silk and gold."[24] The more traditional nomadic conveyance, the *ger tergen*, literally, "tent cart," was sometimes similarly adorned. Each of Özbek's four principal wives had "wagons covered in silk fabrics gilded."[25] Transport animals, too, were exquisitely caparisoned on special occasions. Carpini saw forty or fifty camels "decked with brocade" at Güyüg's coronation, and Marco Polo, attending a New Year feast at Qubilai's court, claims to have seen 5,000 elephants "all covered with beautiful cloths

[20] John Chardin, *Travels in Persia, 1673–1677*, repr. (New York: Dover Publications, 1988), pp. 278–80, briefly describes the weaving of "*d'ouroye*."

[21] Rashīd/Karīmī, vol. II, pp. 947 and 948.

[22] Bar Hebreaus, p. 352; Juvaynī/Qazvīnī, vol. I, p. 15; and Juvaynī/Boyle, vol. I, p. 22.

[23] Called an "elephant litter [*hsiang-chiao*]" in Chinese, *YS*, ch. 11, p. 227; *Ming shih* (Peking: Chung-hua shu-chü, 1974), ch. 65, p. 1597; and a *miḥaffah*, "litter," in Persian, Rashīd/Karīmī, vol. I, p. 657, and Rashīd/Boyle, p. 298.

[24] Marco Polo, p. 197. See also p. 231 for a slightly different description.

[25] Ibn Baṭṭūṭah/Gibb, vol. II, p. 494. For the Mongolian term, see *SH*/Cleaves, sect. 124, p. 56, and *SH*/de Rachewiltz, sect. 124, p. 52.

worked artificially and richly in gold and silk . . ." and, finally, Ibn Baṭṭūṭah reports that the wagons of Özbek's wives were drawn by horses "caparisoned with cloths of silk gilt."[26] Chinggisid princes and their retinues lived, worked, played, and, as noted later, died, in a world filled with gold brocade.

From the standpoint of consumption there is little doubt that clothing placed the greatest demands on gilded textiles. Any appearance at court or other ceremonial occasions required proper attire, and in Mongolian views of style gold brocade was clearly the fabric of choice.

To begin at the top, headgear, especially for women, was an important indicator of social status and wealth in the nomadic world. The standard for married women was a spectacular framed construction that had deep roots in steppe culture. The first references are in the Greek and Old Persian sources which note the tall, pointed caps of the Scythians.[27] The oldest extant example of such a hat was recently retrieved from the grave of a mummified female found at Toyuq, east of Turfan. The deceased and her two-foot conical cap were interred, by all indications, around 300 BC.[28] In the reconstruction of the historical ethnographers T. A. Zhdanko and S. K. Kamalov, such hats had their origin among the early Iranian nomads, first as headgear for soldiers, then as a crown for rulers, pictured on Bactrian coinage from the beginning of the Christian era, and finally as the headdress of married women.[29] The earliest literary description of the latter comes from the Buddhist pilgrim Sung Yün, who in 519 traveled through the territory of the Hephthalites in southern Turkestan. Here he encountered the Hephthalite queen wearing "a cornered [turban] eight Chinese feet in length and three Chinese feet in the diagonal. It was adorned," he continues, "with pearls in rose and five other colors on top." As for the wives of high officials, he notes that "each seemed to wear a cornered turban that was round and trailing," presenting "the appearance of a gem-decorated canopy of precious materials."[30] Such elaborate headdresses, called *ku-ku* in Chinese, became so popular at the Sung court that their material composition and size were subjected to detailed regulation from the throne.[31] While

[26] *Mongol Mission*, p. 64; *Sinica Franciscana*, p. 120; Marco Polo, p. 223; and Ibn Baṭṭūṭah/Gibb, vol. II, p. 485. See also p. 494.

[27] Herodotus, *The Persian Wars*, trans. by George Rawlinson (New York: Modern Library, 1942), vii.64; and Roland G. Kent, *Old Persian: Grammar, Texts, Lexicon*, 2nd edn. (New Haven: American Oriental Society, 1953), p. 134.

[28] Victor H. Mair, "Mummies of the Tarim Basin," *Archaeology* 48/2 (1995), 29 and photo, 33.

[29] T. A. Zhdanko and S. K. Kamalov, *Etnografiia Karakalpakov, XIX-nachalo XX veka (Materialy i issledovaniia)* (Tashkent: Fan, 1980), pp. 94–97.

[30] Yang Hsüan-chih, *A Record of Buddhist Monasteries in Lo Yang*, trans. by Yi-t'ung Wang (Princeton University Press, 1984), p. 226.

[31] G. Schlegel, "Hennins or Conical Lady's Hats in Asia, China and Europe," *T'oung-pao* 3 (1892), 426–27. The term *ku-ku*, in the past wrongly associated with the Mongolian *kükül*, "tress of hair," is as yet unexplained. Since, however, conical hats clearly predate the Turks and Mongols, and are associated originally with Scythians and Tokharians, the origin of the Chinese transcription *ku-ku* ought to be sought in the Indo-European or Iranian languages, not the Altaic. On this word, see Paul Pelliot, "Le mots mongols dans le *Korye sǎ*," *Journal*

for the Chinese this was a passing fashion, for the peoples of the steppe such hats became a permanent cultural trait which lasted down to the twentieth century.[32]

In the Mongolian era elongated headdresses are much in evidence; they are depicted in a native rock carving and in Chinese portraiture,[33] and attracted favorable comment from outsiders who were otherwise hostile to the Mongols.[34] Called *boghta*, they were two to three feet in length, and like their prototypes, gave ample scope for elaboration and decoration.[35] We are fortunate in having two eyewitness accounts of the *boghta* from the year 1221 and one from 1237 which reveal the changing notions of fashion among the Mongols. The first, by Li Chih-chang, who accompanied the Taoist monk Ch'ang Ch'un to central Asia on his visit to Chinggis Qan, says that the "headdress of married women is made of birch [for the frame], reaching a height of two feet. Most often they cover it with coarse black wool [but] the wealthier ones use plain, red silk."[36] The second, from Chao Hung, a Sung ambassador, relates that headgear of women of the ruling strata consists of an iron wire frame "about three feet in length, adorned with red and blue[37] brocade [*chin-hsiu*] or with pearls."[38] Some fifteen years later, Hsü T'ing, another Sung envoy, who personally witnessed the fabrication of *ku-kus*, reports that the frames were now wrapped "with red silk or with gold brocade [*chin-pai*]."[39] Clearly, at the time of these observations, a

Asiatique 217 (1930), 259, and Antoine Mostaert," A propos de quelques portraits d'empereurs mongols," *Asia Major* 4 (1927), 154–55.

32 The archaeological evidence on the continuity of use of such headdresses is summarized by V. A. Ivanov and V. A. Kriger, *Kurgany kypchakskogo vremeni na Iuzhnom Urale (XII–XIV vv.)* (Moscow: Nauka, 1988), p. 18. For the modern Kazakh version, the *säukele*, see Nina P. Lobachëva, "Clothing and Personal Adornment," in Vladimir N. Basilov, ed., *Nomads of Eurasia* (Seattle: University of Washington Press, 1989), pp. 112–13. Conical hats were also worn by dervishes in nineteenth-century eastern Turkestan. Shaw, *Visits to High Tartary*, p. 369.

33 A. P. Okladnikov, "Drevnemongol'skii portret, nadpisi i risunki na skale y podnozh'ia gory Bogdo-Uula," in S. V. Kiselev, ed., *Mongol'skii arkheologicheskii sbornik*: *Posviashchaetsia slavnomu XL-letiiu Mongol'skoi Narodnoi Respubliki* (Moscow: Izdatel'stvo akademii nauk SSSR, 1962), pp. 68–72 and p. 70 for reproduction; and Zhou Xun and Gao Chunming, *5,000 Years of Chinese Costumes* (San Francisco: China Books and Periodicals, 1987), p. 141, plate 24.

34 Grigor of Akanc', "Nation of Archers," 295.

35 *SH*/Cleaves, sect. 74, p. 21, and *SH*/de Rachewiltz, sect. 74, p. 28. On the Mongolian form of this word, see Larry V. Clark, "The Turkic and Mongol Words in William of Rubruck's Journey," *JAOS* 93, 2 (1973), 183–84.

36 Li Chih-chang, *Hsi-yü chi*, in Wang, *Meng-ku shih-liao*, p. 269, and Li Chih-chang, *The Travels of an Alchemist*, tr. Arthur Waley (London: Routledge and Kegan Paul, 1963), p. 67.

37 The phrase "red and blue" [*hung ch'ing*] might be read as "plum colored." This is supported by the discovery of a silk brocade covering for headgear in Qara Qorum which is described by one of the Russian excavators as *krasnovato-korichnevyi*, "red-brown." See L. A. Evtiukhova, "Izdeliia razlichnykh remesel iz Kara Koruma," in S. V. Kiselev, *et al.*, eds., *Drevnemongol'skie goroda* (Moscow: Nauka, 1965), plate XXX, 1, following p. 291.

38 Chao Hung, *Meng-ta pei-lu*, in Wang, *Meng-ku shih-liao*, p. 454, and Haenisch and Yao, *Chinesische Gesandtenberichte*, p. 79.

39 P'eng and Hsü, *Hei-ta shih-lüeh*, p. 479, and Haenisch and Yao, *Chinesische Gesandtenberichte*, p. 119.

transition was taking place from plain native materials to more elegant and expensive ones made available by the Mongolian occupation of North China and the eastern Islamic world. Thereafter, as the empire continued its expansion, a wide variety of decorative materials bedecked the *boghtas* of Mongolian women, including velvet, buckram, gold embroidery, pearls, and bird feathers.[40]

There are various indications that this arresting Mongolian headgear enjoyed considerable visibility, if not currency, in the late medieval West. First of all, there is explicit testimony that at least one "Mongolian original" found its way to Europe, for we know from an inventory of Marco Polo's property at the time of his death that he possessed a "*bochta* of gold with stones and pearls."[41] More fancifully, there are the not infrequent portrayals of conical hats in European art. One fourteenth-century Italian painting contains numerous representations of such hats, some of which are worn by Tartars, some by Hungarians and Qipchaqs, and some by native Italians. Further, Parisian illuminators of the early fifteenth century, basing themselves on the literary descriptions of Marco Polo and other travelers to the East, depict the courtiers of the Grand Qan of China, both men and women, in cone-shaped hats.[42] In the opinion of one scholar, this fascination with the *ku-kus* of the nomads explains the great popularity of hennins, the elongated female headgear of Renaissance Europe.[43]

Girdles were another element of dress important to the Mongols. The evident favorites were those "of silk threaded with gold" which Carpini saw in great abundance at the coronation of Güyüg.[44] Such belts, termed *altan büse*, "golden girdle," in Mongolian, were regularly granted to court functionaries and notables.[45] Rashīd al-Dīn relates that Ghazan once bestowed "fifty bejewelled belts and three hundred gold belts [*kamar-i zar*]" on his retainers, and the Franciscan friar Odoric of Pordenone, who was at the Yuan court in the 1320s, says that at the emperor's feasts each of his barons, or commanders, "wears a golden girdle of a half a span in breadth."[46] Marco Polo, more descriptively, notes that these belts were of

[40] *Mongol Mission*, pp. 7–8 and 102; Rubruck/Jackson, p. 89; *Sinica Franciscana*, pp. 34 and 83; Ibn Baṭṭūṭah/Gibb, vol. II, p. 485; and Odoric of Pordenone, "The Eastern Parts of the World Described," in Yule, *Cathay*, vol. II, p. 222.

[41] Marco Polo, p. 586, and Leonardo Olschki, *Marco Polo's Asia: An Introduction to his* "Description of the World" *called* "il Milione" (Los Angeles: University of California Press, 1960), pp. 105–06 and note 23.

[42] Stella Mary Newton, "Tomaso da Modena, Simone Martini, Hungarians and St. Martin in Fourteenth Century Italy," *Journal of the Warburg and Courtauld Institutes* 43 (1980), 234–38 and plates 30a–b and 31a–d; and Millard Meiss, *French Painting in the Time of Jean de Berry: The Boucicault Master* (Kress Foundation Studies in the History of European Art, no. 3; New York and London: Phaidon, 1968), pp. 42–46 and fig. 83.

[43] Schlegel, "Hennins or Conical Lady's Hats," 422–24.

[44] *Mongol Mission*, p. 64, and *Sinica Franciscana*, p. 120.

[45] Francis W. Cleaves, "The Sino-Mongolian Inscription of 1362 in Memory of Prince Hindu," *HJAS* 12 (1949), 66–67, Mongolian text and 90, English translation.

[46] Rashīd/Karīmī, vol. II, p. 981; A. P. Martinez, "The Third Portion of the Story of Gāzān

"crimson cunningly worked with threads of gold and of silver, very rich and very beautiful and of great value."[47] The Venetian's account of these objects, as are most of his statements on material culture, is fully substantiated in the *Yuan shih*, which lists among the court's ceremonial and sacrificial wear "red silk gilded girdles," then adds parenthetically that "red silk gilded [girdle] translated is called *nasīj* [*na-shih-shih*]; each girdle has two pendants of precious stone."[48] So extensive was their use that a special agency, the Imperial Belt Treasury (*Yü-tai k'u*), was founded to "tend imperial use and make ready bestowals."[49]

Even shoes, at least for ceremonial occasions, were fashioned from gold brocade. According to the *Yuan shih*, the emperor's footwear, festooned with "two pair of side flaps, buckles and adorned with pearls" were "by regulation made of *nasīj* [*na-shih-shih*]."[50] Further, according to Marco Polo, high-ranking military officers, to mark their authority and power, carried "a golden canopy which is called an umbrella."[51]

The hats, belts, etc., however beautiful, attracted far less attention and comment than did the dazzling ceremonial robes found in great numbers everywhere in the Mongolian domains. Outer garments came in a variety of textiles – buckram, velvet – and furs – sable, ermine, vair, and fox. Individual options in robes were of course conditioned by season, wealth, and social status, but little affected by gender, male and female clothes, except in hats, being "made in the same style."[52] For all state occasions, however, there was a special garment, called a *jisün* in Mongolian, and *chih-sun* in Chinese transcription, which the *Yuan shih* defines as "a robe of one color."[53] The word itself simply means "color" in Mongolian and by later extension during the imperial era came to denote ceremonial robes. In such garments, presumably, the supplemental gold threads partially covered the ground weave composed of threads of a uniform color.

The classic description of these vestments is found in Marco Polo, who speaks at length of their characteristics, function, value, and numbers:

For on the day of his birth the great Kaan [Qubilai] is drest in the most noble cloth of purest beaten gold that he has. And quite twelve thousand barons and knights who are called the faithful companions of the Lord are dressed afterwards with him in a color and in a fashion like that of the robe of the great lord; not that they are so

Xān in Rašīdu 'd-Dīn's *Ta'rīx-e mobark-e Gāzānī*," *Archivum Eurasiae Medii Aevi* 6 (1986 [1988]), 69–70; and Odoric of Pordenone, "Eastern Parts of the World Described," in Yule, *Cathay*, vol. II, pp. 237–38.

47 Marco Polo, p. 225.
48 *YS*, ch. 78, p. 1935.
49 *YS*, ch. 90, p. 2295, and Farquar, *Government*, p. 95.
50 *YS*, ch. 78, p. 1931.
51 Marco Polo, p. 204.
52 *Mongol Mission*, p. 7; *Sinica Franciscana*, p. 33; and Marco Polo, p. 171.
53 *YS*, ch. 78, p. 1938. See also Cleaves, "The Sino-Mongolian Inscription of 1362," 66, Mongolian text and 90, English translation, and 125, note 212; and Paul Pelliot, "Les mots mongols dans le *Korye sǎ*, 264–65.

dear robes as those of the king, but they are of one color and all are cloth of silk and gold, and all those who are robed have great girdles of great value, of leather worked with thread of gold and silver very cunningly, given them, and a pair of shoes of leather worked with silver thread very skillfully. And the great lord gives them all these robes which are of very great value. Moreover, I tell you that, although the king's robe is more costly, yet there are some of these robes which are worth, the precious stones and pearls which were on them are worth, more than 10,000 bezants [coins] of gold. And there are many like this, as are those of the barons who for loyalty are nearest to the lord and are called *quesitan* [*kesigten* = Mongolian, "imperial guardsmen"]. And you may know that thirteen times a year, solely for the thirteen solemn feast days which the Tartars keep with great ceremony according to the thirteen moons of the year, the great kaan gives rich robes adorned with gold, pearls and precious stones with girdles and shoes aforesaid, altogether to the number of 156,000, to those twelve thousand barons and knights, and he clothes them all with a like clothing with himself and of great value, so that when they are dressed and thus richly adorned they all seem to be kings. And when the lord wears any robe these barons and knights are likewise dressed in one of the same colour; but those of the lord are of more value and more costly ornament. And the said robes of the barons are always ready; not that they are made each year, on the contrary, they last ten years more or less. And so for each time one color is distinct from the other. And from this you can see that it is a very great thing, the great excellency of the great kaan, for there is no other lord in all the world who could do this nor continually keep it up, but he alone.[54]

What is to be made of this picture of kingly munificence and extravagance? To test the general accuracy of Marco Polo's recollections we need to survey the history of this tradition as recorded in other sources.

Robes of one color are first mentioned in Chinggis Qan's day. To the best of my knowledge, the earliest dates to 1209, when the Uighurs submitted to the emerging empire. Bilge Buqa, an Uighur official who was instrumental in persuading his sovereign to seek Mongolian protection, was handsomely rewarded by Chinggis Qan, who bestowed upon him a badge of authority, a seal, silver ingots and "gilded clothing of one color [*i-chin chih-sun*]."[55] Grants of such clothing were by no means limited to great events and important personages. The Mongolian ruler also presented *jisün* robes to lesser figures for more mundane services; for example, Mai-ko, a Qitan official at the imperial court, received his robe of one color for services as an interpreter and parasol holder.[56] The latter grant, it should be emphasized, strongly implies that *jisün* robes were widely distributed from the early days of the empire.

Information on robes of one color is, however, more frequent and more

[54] Marco Polo, p. 221. The essentials are repeated on pp. 225–26. On the basis of Marco Polo's description, French artists of the fifteenth century depicted Qubilai's dispensation of "robes of one color." See Biblioteque Nationale, *Le Livres des Merveilles* (Paris: Berthand Frères, n.d.), vol. I, folio 41.

[55] *YS*, ch. 124, p. 3050.

[56] *YS*, ch. 150, p. 3550.

detailed from the reign of Ögödei, who assumed the throne in 1229. On this occasion Juvaynī relates that those attending "for a full forty days donned each day a new robe of a different color."[57] Nor was this an isolated occurrence, for Rashīd al-Dīn states that when the qaghan left his winter quarters in central Mongolia for Qara Qorum he would stop at Tuzghu Baliq, another satellite camp fifteen kilometers to the east of the capital, for a celebration. There, "on the next day, all people would don clothes of one color, and he [Ögödei] would go to Qarshi [his palace in Qara Qorum] . . . and for a period of a month devote himself to pleasure."[58] From the context of this passage, the celebrations sound as if they were recurring, annual affairs such as those described by Marco Polo. And as regular features of court life their use was controlled by specific rules and requirements, which are outlined in one of the ordinances issued prior to a diet of princes (*quriltai*) held in 1234:

> All women making garments for the *jisün* [*chih-sun*] feast not conforming to regulations as well as those who are jealous [of others attire?], will be made to ride around the center of the district on an unsaddled cow as punishment and then have [their] valuables collected so that [their husbands have the bride price] to remarry.[59]

Dress codes, it is fair to conclude, were a serious matter for the imperial court, indicating again that clothing in general and *jisün* robes in particular held deep significance for Mongolian political culture.

Ögödei's successors kept up the tradition. At a celebration leading up to Güyüg's elevation, Carpini reports that for four days running the retinue of the heir apparent was clothed in raiment of one color.[60] More helpful, however, is the information furnished by Benedict the Pole, who accompanied Carpini on his journey and dictated his remembrances to another cleric in Cologne after his return. In describing the actual coronation ceremony this account states the following:

> And the same Brother Benedict the Pole related to us by word of mouth how they had both [Benedict and Carpini] seen about 5,000 princes and great men who were all clad in cloth of gold on the first day when they assembled for the election of the king. . . . And among them were the aforesaid Friars who wore brocade over their habit as needs must, for no envoy is allowed to see the face of the elect and crowned king, unless he is correctly dressed.[61]

Möngke, as well, adhered to all the precedents regarding *jisün* robes and feasts. At his elevation in 1251, Juvaynī tells us, all those in attendance daily "donned a robe of another color," and that they did so "in conformity to

57 Juvaynī/Qazvīnī, vol. I, p. 147, and Juvaynī/Boyle, vol. I, p. 186.
58 Rashīd al-Dīn, *Jamiʿ al-tavārīkh*, ed. A. A. Alizade (Moscow: Nauka, 1980), vol. II, pt. 1, pp. 146–47, and Rashīd/Boyle, p. 64.
59 *YS*, ch. 2, p. 33.
60 *Mongol Mission*, p. 61, and *Sinica Franciscana*, p. 117.
61 *Mongol Mission*, pp. 81–82, and *Sinica Franciscana*, p. 139.

the apparel of the emperor of the world."[62] Further, Möngke marked Hülegü's departure for Iran in 1253 with an elaborate drinking party at which the participants donned "robes of one color" and a few years later at another, apparently annual, feast they did the same: "On each of the four days," Rubruck writes, "they changed their clothes, which they [the court] gave to them on each day all of one color, from shoes to the headdress."[63]

This testimony, particularly that of Carpini, Benedict the Pole and Rubruck, all reliable eyewitnesses, lends credence to Marco Polo's account: Mongolian rulers, from Chinggis Qan to Toghan Temür (r. 1332–68), the last Yuan emperor, did in fact give large numbers of *jisün* robes and hats, some made of textiles and some of furs, including ermine, to their retinues, guards, and officials to celebrate important events, some of an annual nature, and they did so on a regular basis as an integral feature of court life.[64] In short, such bestowals were not the exception but the rule.

Furthermore, it should be stressed that the wide use of expensive cloth was common practice within the regional qanates. In Iran, for example, Vardan, an Armenian monk and historian who visited Hülegü's court in July 1264 during the course of a month-long festival, relates that "with all their nobles they put on new clothes, each day changing into a different color, whatever they regarded as appropriate."[65] And in the Golden Horde, Ibn Baṭṭūṭah reports that Özbek's four principal wives had six slave girls, each of whom had "a robe of silk gilt which is called *nakh*," and fifteen male pages "dressed in robes of silk gilt." And in a later passage he records that when Bayalun, the qan's third wife, a Byzantine princess, visited her father in Constantinople, she was accompanied by "her *mamlūks* [guards], her slave girls, pages and attendants, about five hundred, wearing robes of silk embroidered with gold and jewels."[66]

Before assessing the reliability of the numbers recorded above, other uses of gold brocade deserve mention. Besides the court robes, bestowed collectively for public occasions, there were frequent grants of raiment to individuals that, cumulatively at least, contributed to the high demand for this cloth. These were given out for a wide variety of reasons, most commonly as rewards to military and civil officials for some particular service to the state. In 1256, for instance, Möngke granted Uriyangqadai, his senior commander in the East, "one elegant suit of clothes woven from

[62] Juvaynī/Qazvīnī, vol. III, pp. 37–38, and Juvaynī/Boyle, vol. II, p. 573.

[63] Juvaynī/Qazvīnī, vol. III, p. 95; Juvaynī/Boyle, vol., II, p. 611; Rashīd/Karīmī, vol. II, p. 687; *Mongol Mission*, p. 201; Rubruck/Jackson, p. 246; and *Sinica Franciscana*, p. 306.

[64] Grants of *jisün* robes are frequently noted in the Chinese sources. See, for example, *YS*, ch. 128, p. 3132; ch. 132, p. 3209; ch. 147, p. 3477; ch. 176, p. 4117; and ch. 177, p. 4125. For examples of *jisün* robes made of ermine, weasel and squirrel, see ch. 9, p. 187; ch. 127, p. 3113; ch. 149, p. 3517; ch. 202, p. 4521; and Francis W. Cleaves, "The Biography of Bayan of the Barīn in the *Yuan shih*," *HJAS* 19 (1956), 258–59.

[65] Robert W. Thompson, "The Historical Compilation of Vardan Arewelc'i," *Dumbarton Oaks Papers*, no. 43 (1989), 220.

[66] Ibn Baṭṭūṭah/Gibb, vol. II, pp. 485–86 and 503.

gold threads" for defeating a Sung army.[67] And beyond this, the sources affirm that Chinggisid princes bestowed such raiment as acts of charity, vestments for clerics, peace offerings, prizes in athletic contests, and diplomatic gifts.[68] And if Juvaynī and Rashīd al-Dīn are to be believed, forty young maidens dispatched in 1229 to join the spirit of the deceased Chinggis Qan were decked out in "precious robes embellished with gold [*muraṣṣ'at*]."[69] Whether factual or not, it is nonetheless revealing that these chroniclers, both intimately familiar with Mongolian customs, deemed it fitting and proper for sacrificial victims to meet the founding father in gilded cloth.

To conclude this survey of the Mongolian court's lavish expenditure on gold brocade, we must take into account as well the many grants of uncut cloth. Like the bestowals of robes, bolts and pieces were given to officials, clerics, envoys, and foreign rulers.[70] Amounts are not always indicated but in some cases they were substantial. Qubilai once gave an Alan military officer "nine pieces [*tuan*] of *nasīj* [*na-shih-ssu*]" and a wife of Möngke offered Rubruck "a *nasic* [*nasīj*]" that was "as wide as a bedcover and very long."[71] More vaguely but even more generously, Ögödei, on a visit to Maḥmūd Yalavach, is said to have "carpeted the outside of his [i.e., Maḥmūd's] tent with all kinds of gold brocades [*nasīj va zar-baft*]."[72]

The analysis of quantitative data found in medieval narrative sources, both east and west, is always a thorny problem and the assumption that figures on population, size of armies, battle casualties, etc., are greatly inflated is most often justified. Our suspicion is naturally aroused as well by the repeated claims of vast amounts of "political" clothing in circulation. It is easy to dismiss, for example, the assertion of the Georgian chronicler, Juansher Juansheriani, that the Sasanian court once granted Vakhtang Gorgasal (r. ca. 446–510) "a thousand kingly garments" and other "valuable textiles," or Bar Hebraeus' report that the Caliph Mustarshid (r. 1118–35) reputedly carried in his military train "five thousand camel loads

67 *YS*, ch. 3, p. 49. For examples of grants to civil servants, see Francis W. Cleaves, "The Fifteen 'Palace Poems' by K'o Chiu-ssu," *HJAS* 20 (1957), 421 and 446–47, note 90.

68 Juvaynī/Qazvīnī, vol. I, pp. 176 and 184; Juvaynī/Boyle, vol. I, pp. 220 and 228; Ernest A. Wallis Budge, trans., *The Monks of Kūblāi Khān* (London: The Religious Tract Society, 1928), p. 202; Bar Hebraeus, p. 495; Grigor of Akanc', "Nation of Archers," 345; and John de Marignolli, "Recollections of Travel in the East," in Yule, *Cathay*, vol. III, pp. 215 and 232.

69 Juvaynī/Qazvīnī, vol. I, p. 149; Juvaynī/Boyle, vol. I, p. 189; Rashīd/Karīmī, vol. I, p. 454; and Rashīd/Boyle, p. 31.

70 *YS*, ch. 9, p. 193 and ch. 123, p. 3034; Li Chih-chang, *Hsi-yü chi*, p. 327; Li Chih-chang, *Travels of an Alchemist*, p. 94; *Mongol Mission*, p. 203; Rubruck/Jackson, p. 249; *Sinica Franciscana*, p. 308; Ibn Baṭṭūṭah, *Travels in Asia and Africa*, trans. by H. A. R. Gibb (London: Routledge and Kegan Paul, 1929), p. 214; and Abū'l Fidā, *The Memoirs of a Syrian Prince*, trans. by P. M. Holt (Wiesbaden: Franz Steiner, 1983), p. 84.

71 *YS*, ch. 132, p. 3212; *Mongol Mission*, pp. 162–63; Rubruck/Jackson, pp. 190–91; and *Sinica Franciscana*, p. 249.

72 Juvaynī/Qazvīnī, vol. I, p. 174, and Juvaynī/Boyle, vol. I, p. 218.

and four hundred mule loads of bales of cloth and apparel . . ." as well as "forty thousand turbans and head coverings, and sewed tunics with sleeves."[73] But in evaluating these reports or those on the consumption of gold brocade in the Mongolian domains our ready scepticism should be modified. Two general considerations can be cited in justification. First, in the particular case of textiles, the amounts produced, collected, stored and dispensed in pre-industrial societies are frequently far higher than expected. In the Inka state, for example, the huge volume of textiles in circulation astounded contemporary European observers.[74] Even more telling, for our immediate purposes, are the numbers reported by western travelers in western and central Asia in the post-Mongolian era. Clavijo, who visited the court of Temür, whose state was a direct continuation of the Chaghadai qanate, testifies to the great frequency of robing ceremonies. He was so honored on sixteen different occasions during his progress through this domain. Indeed, at every major city, or whenever princes or court officials were encountered, Clavijo and his fellow envoys received sumptuous robes. Finally, at their destination, Samarqand, they were robed four additional times.[75] Another sober and discerning witness, Anthony Jenkinson, a factor of the Moscovy Company with wide experience in Russia and central Asia, provides a detailed inventory of Ottoman ceremonial dress. Present at the entry of Sulaiman into Aleppo in 1553, he relates the marching order of the emperor's army, identifies individual formations, and minutely describes their distinctive uniforms. In all, he states, 88,000 troops and retainers, richly clad in velvets, silks and "cloth of golde" paraded through the city.[76] Certainly less spectacular but in some respects equally illuminating, is the testimony of Robert Shaw, an English tea-planter who traveled through eastern Turkestan in 1868–69 just after Yaq'ūb Beg established his short-lived state in Kashgar. During his stay there as a guest of the court, Shaw, like Clavijo, was robed on sixteen different occasions, acquiring in the process about twenty robes, many of which were made of the finest Chinese stuffs.[77] In the political life of these societies, cloth was essential and ubiquitous, a kind of medium of exchange by which political valuations were made, and it was the responsibility of the government to keep large stocks in circulation. Second, in considering the issue of numbers, it must

[73] Dzhuansher Dzhuansheriani, *Zhizn Vakhtanga Gorgasala*, trans. by G. V. Tsulaia (Tbilisi: Izdatel'stvo "Metsnierba," 1986), pp. 82 and 83, and Bar Hebraeus, p. 259.

[74] John V. Murra, "Cloth and its Function in the Inka State," in Annette B. Weiner and Jane Schneider, eds., *Cloth and Human Experience* (Washington: Smithsonian Institution Press, 1988), pp. 285–91.

[75] Clavijo, *Embassy to Tamerlane*, pp. 158, 167, 169, 175, 182, 184, 195, 197, 198, 203, 217, 232, 233, 236, and 276.

[76] E. Delmar Morgan and C. H. Coote, eds., *Early Voyages and Travels to Russia and Persia by Anthony Jenkinson and Other Englishmen*, repr. (New York: Burt Franklin, n.d.), vol. I, pp. 1–5.

[77] Shaw, *Visits to High Tartary*, pp. 117, 140, 180–81, 186, 188, 191, 211, 219, 229, 263, 332, 358, 361, 373, 382, and 407.

also be remembered that by the mid-thirteenth century the Mongolian Empire, even when compared to the Inka, Temürid, or Ottoman states, was an immense polity, stretching from Poland to Vietnam and from Korea to Syria. Within its frontiers there were abundant human and material resources to produce opulent fabrics in great quantities. This is not to say, however, that specific figures should always be taken at face value but rather that the exaggerations are best viewed as symbolic yet meaningful statements about the actual levels of consumption.

We have, fortunately, at least one case, the *jisün* robes bestowed at the Yuan court, in which the imperial largesse alluded to by Marco Polo can be substantiated in broad outline by independent sources. In speaking of the *chih-sun* robes of the "Son of Heaven," the *Yuan shih* states that

> when there was a great feast in the palace, then they wore them. . . . As for all the meritorious relatives, great ministers, and personal attendants, when [the emperor] bestowed [these garments], then they wore them. Down to the musicians and guards, all had their garments.[78]

No numbers are given but this passage does indicate that the imperial household, including the guard, were indeed granted robes of a single color. Moreover, the same source affirms elsewhere that the guard was about 14,000 strong, a figure also used by Odoric of Pordenone in the 1320s as the proximate number of the Yuan emperor's "barons and coronets," each of whom, he adds, attended banquets in a coat "such that the pearls in it alone are worth some fifteen thousand florins."[79] Thus Marco Polo's recollection of the size and attire of the guard is quite accurate.

In assessing the overall numbers involved, it is crucial to note that the household and guard were not the only recipients of these robes. This is made clear in an edict issued in late 1332 during the brief reign of the Yuan emperor Irinjibal which states that "the hundred officials and guardsmen have *jisün* [*chih-sun*] clothing" and then reminds all that "whenever taking part in imperial feasts everyone is to wear [such clothing] in order to attend."[80] Further, in the section devoted to the dress of the "Hundred Officials," that is, officialdom collectively, the *Yuan shih* specifies in tabular form twenty-three robes of one color, nine for winter wear and fourteen for summer. Listed first in the former category is "one [robe] of crimson gold brocade [*na-shih-shih*]" while the latter begins its enumeration with "one

[78] *YS*, ch. 78, p. 1938.

[79] *YS*, ch. 99, p. 2525; Hsiao Ch'i-ch'ing, *The Military Establishment of the Yuan Dynasty* (Cambridge, Mass.: Harvard University Press, 1978), p. 94; and Odoric of Pordenone, "The Eastern Parts of the World Described," in Yule, *Cathay*, vol. II, pp. 224–25. The size of the imperial guard fluctuated over time; the figure 14,000 is the only one given, unfortunately, without a date.

[80] *YS*, ch. 37, p. 812. See also ch. 67, on "Rites and Music," p. 1669, which also affirms *jisün* garments were required at feasts.

[robe] of plain [*su*] gold brocade."[81] The approximate size of the Yuan bureaucracy, which was large by Chinese standards, is known from the *Yuan tien-chang*, a compilation of raw administrative documents published in 1322. According to this source, the "Hundred Officials" in the early fourteenth century numbered 22,490 with "rank and title" and 4,208 "without rank and title," for a total of 26,698.[82] If each official had all the prescribed robes, then in principle the bureaucracy alone accounted for over 50,000 gold brocade *jisün*. The problem with this formulation is that there is no way of knowing if each of the "Hundred Officials" actually had, or was actually intended to have, all these robes. As a further complication, there are at least hints that robes were provided to individuals for specific events and then taken back, much like the "loaner" ties and jackets made available by expensive restaurants so that casually dressed patrons can temporarily be fitted out to meet the establishment's dress code. This is certainly implied in Benedict the Pole's account of Güyüg's enthronement, where he and Carpini, as well as other envoys, were given brocaded robes to wear so that they could attend the festivities properly attired.

Thus, while firm figures remain elusive, taking into consideration its wide uses in tenting and conveyances and in robes for officialdom and the guard, there can be little doubt that the Mongolian courts consumed and dispensed gold brocade on a vast scale. I have no difficulty in believing that the Chinggisids mobilized the 5,000 garments of "cloth of gold" Benedict saw at Güyüg's coronation. And since Marco Polo says himself that the robes given to the "barons and knights" lasted about ten years, and therefore only some 15,000 were actually granted on an annual basis, I do not think his numbers are a wild or meaningless exaggeration, especially in light of the supporting evidence in the Chinese sources. But even if halved to be conservative, the numbers of gold brocade robes in circulation remain impressively high.

81 *YS*, ch. 78, p. 1938. Also listed under summer wear is a garment called a "gathered thread *pao-li* [*chü-hsien pao-li*] of gold brocade." *Pao-li* appears to represent the Mongolian *ba'uri*, a word derived from the stem *ba'u*, "to fall," "descend," and should perhaps be understood as long flowing garment. The primary meaning of *ba'uri* is, however, "a place where one descends from a horse." On this problematical term, see Pelliot, "Le mots mongols dans le *Korye să*," 264 and note 2.

82 *Ta-yuan sheng-cheng kuo-ch'ao tien-chang* (Taipei: Kuo-li ku-kung po-wu yuan, 1976, reprint of the Yuan edn.), ch. 7, 27a. These numbers almost certainly under-report the size of the Yuan bureaucracy, since they include, apparently, only North Chinese and foreigners, the *se-mu-jen*, and exclude South Chinese and Mongols. For analysis, see Elizabeth Endicott-West, *Mongolian Rule in China: Local Administration under the Yuan* (Cambridge, Mass.: Harvard University Press, 1989), pp. 13–14.

CHAPTER 3

Acquisition and production

That gold brocade was utilized on the scale indicated is further borne out by an examination of the Mongols' efforts to secure a reliable supply. There is every evidence that they took special care to acquire this highly valued commodity at the desired levels. Methods of acquisition varied in time and space, and for purposes of presentation can usefully be divided into four categories – booty, taxation/tribute, trade, and court-sponsored production.

In the early, expansionist phase of the empire, plunder, sytematically organized, was the principal source of the luxury goods produced in the sedentary world, and textiles of various types are mentioned prominently among the prizes taken from defeated and surrendering states.[1] In 1215 when the Chin capital of Chung-tu fell, the Mongols seized "satins [Mongolian *a'urasun*] having gold and having patterns," and in 1234, at the time of the Chin's final defeat, more of the same fabric came into their possession.[2] In West Asia a similar pattern prevails. Juvaynī succinctly points up Mongolian priorities when he says that in their numerous operations in Khurāsān they regularly carried off "all the cattle and textiles [*aqmishah*]" that came to hand.[3] In Transcaucasia, according to Ibn al-Athīr, the Mongols demanded and received money and clothing (*al-māl wa al-thiyāb*) from the inhabitants of Ganja, well known for its cloth of gold.[4]

[1] Even before their incursions into the sedentary zone the Mongols were gathering up cloth in a systematic fashion. In 1204, in the campaign against the Naiman, certain units were assigned the task of stripping their fallen foes of their "bloody clothing [*chisutu tonoq*]" and taking their "treasure and clothing [*üb tonaq*]." See *SH*/Cleaves, sect. 195, p. 126 and *SH*/de Rachewiltz, sect. 195, p. 104.

[2] *SH*/Cleaves, sect. 252, p. 188 and sect. 273, p. 214; and *SH*/de Rachewiltz, sect. 252, p. 148 and sect. 273, p. 165. Cf. Rashīd/Karīmī, vol. I, p. 329, who lists "gold brocade garments [*jāmah-hā-yi zar-baft*]."

[3] Juvaynī/Qazvīnī, vol. II, p. 269, and Juvaynī/Boyle, vol. II, p. 533.

[4] Ibn al-Athīr, *Al-Kāmil fī al-ta'rīkh*, ed. by C. J. Tornberg, repr. (Beirut, 1966), vol. XII, p. 383. In the pre-Mongolian era, the city of Ganja presented the Georgian Queen T'amar (r. 1184–1212) "fabrics of various colors, gold stuffs and priceless garments." See Katherine Vivian, trans., *The Georgian Chronicle: The Period Giorgi Lasha* (Amsterdam: Adolf M. Hakkert, 1991), p. 71.

And in Asia Minor, following the defeat of the Seljuqs of Rum in 1243, the victors acquired the sultan's "large and beautifully colored tents" and "gathered in rich booty in gold, silver and garments."[5] One of their richest prizes, of course, was the ʿAbbāsid capital, Baghdad, which fell in 1258. Here, according to the anonymous Georgian Chronicle, the booty was so great that the Mongols and their Georgian allies "sank under the weight of the gold, silver, gems and pearls, the textiles and precious garments, the plates and vases of gold and silver, for they only took those two metals, the gems, the pearls, the textiles and the garments."[6] The Mongols, of course, actually took other items of use, especially riding and pack animals, but the common thread running through all the inventories of plunder is rare and colorful textiles, tenting, and clothing. The more exquisite finds went, naturally, to the princes and commanders, while the ordinary troopers took the remainder. In consequence of this practice, diverse types of fabrics from all over Eurasia began to circulate widely from the very inception of the empire.

Even before actual conquest the Mongols pressured targeted states for tribute and once in occupation demanded endless exactions from the subject population. Initially these imposts tended to be irregular and arbitrary and were only partially standardized in the course of time. But, whatever form these exactions took, the sources reveal a continuing preoccupation with textiles. From the Uighurs of Turfan, who submitted voluntarily in 1209, Chinggis required tribute of gold brocade (*nachit*), damasks (*dardas*), silks and satins; three years later the Tangut state of Kansu, attacked but still unoccupied, sent the Mongols woolen garments and satins.[7] To the northeast, the Mongols, displeased with the quantity and quality of the Koreans' first shipment of tribute, dispatched envoys to their court in 1232 demanding "one million military uniforms," "ten thousand pieces of genuine purple gauze," and "twenty thousand of the best otter skins."[8] And at the other end of the empire, the Armenians, following their conquest in 1236, were, according to contemporary observers, subjected on one occasion to a demand for "gold cloth" and on another for "precious garments and horses, since," the text continues, "they very much love them."[9] A good steed and fine raiment were high on the Mongols' list of priorities.

[5] Grigor of Akancʿ, "Nation of Archers," 311, and M. Brosset, trans., *Histoire de la Géorgie*, 1re partie, *Histoire ancienne, jusqu'an en 1469 de J.C.* (St. Petersburg: Académie des sciences, 1850), p. 519.

[6] Brosset, *Histoire de la Géorgie*, p. 544. Cf. Grigor of Akancʿ, "Nation of Archers," 333.

[7] *SH*/Cleaves, sect. 238, p. 172 and sect. 249, p. 186, and *SH*/de Rachewiltz, sect. 238, p. 136 and sect. 249, p. 146. On the production of wool and satin in the Tangut kingdom, see A. P. Terent'ev-Katanskii, *Materialnaia kul'tura Si Sia* (Moscow: Vostochnaia literatura, 1993), pp. 13, 19, 164, and 165.

[8] Gari Ledyard, "Two Mongolian Documents from the *Koryŏ Sa*," *JAOS* 85 (1963), 234.

[9] Grigor of Akancʿ, "Nation of Archers," 321, and Kirakos Gandzaketsi, *Istoriia Armenii*, trans. by L. A. Khanlarian (Moscow: Nauka, 1976), p. 168.

This priority is well reflected, too, in Ögödei's orders to Chormaqan, his commander in West Asia in the early 1230s, to compel the Caliph of Baghdad to pay annual tribute in gold and pack animals, and in *naqud* (Persian *nakh*), *nachitud* (Arabic *nasīj*), and *dardas* (damask), all of which were to be adorned with yellow gold and big and small pearls.[10] Following increased military pressure in 1238, the caliph finally responded and by the mid 1240s, according to Carpini, the amounts delivered were substantial: "Every day," he says, "they pay them [the Mongols] as tribute four hundred bezants, in addition to brocades and other gifts."[11] These orders of submission, a kind of shopping list, not only reveal the Mongols' preferences but also their detailed knowledge of the clothing materials available in a particular region. The empire was both demanding and remarkably well informed.

The result of these persistent efforts everywhere in the empire was a steady supply of elegant clothing for the conquerors. Rubruck, in speaking of Mongolian garments in the 1250s, records that from the northern climes, Siberia, and the Russian lands, they acquired precious furs for winter attire, while "from Cathay and other countries to the east, and also from Persia and other districts of the south, came cloths of silk and gold and cotton materials which they wear in the summer."[12]

Tributes and taxes account for part of this flow of textiles but some traveled along the intercontinental trade networks which the Mongols now controlled and actively encouraged.[13] The close connection between their interest in long-distance trade and the desire for luxury textiles is frequently mirrored in the sources. In one of his maxims, Chinggis Qan extols the virtues of merchants who "come with garments of gold brocade" and even proclaims them as role models for his military officers![14] More concretely, this sentiment was expressed in policies designed to attract merchants to the imperial camp. The first, Juvaynī informs us, were two Bukharan traders who arrived in 1217/18 with a large store of merchandise including "robes worked with gold thread [*muẕahhab*]." When one of the merchants offered his fabrics to Chinggis Qan at exorbitant prices the Mongol leader, greatly ired, pointedly showed him the rich array of textiles already in his treasury to demonstrate to the offender that he was not dealing with the unsophisticated. Soon afterwards, however, his anger abated and he "commanded that for each garment of gold brocade [*jāmah-i zar*] one gold ingot should be paid and for every two of cotton or *zandanīchī* [a textile from Zandān,

[10] *SH*/Cleaves, sect. 274, p. 214, and *SH*/de Rachewiltz, sect. 274, p. 165.

[11] *Mongol Mission*, p. 32, and *Sinica Franciscana*, p. 76. See also Bar Hebraeus, p. 404, for the attack on Baghdad.

[12] *Mongol Mission*, p. 101; Rubruck/Jackson, pp. 85–86; and *Sinica Franciscana*, p. 181.

[13] On the Mongols' positive attitudes toward, and heavy investment in, transcontinental trade, see Thomas T. Allsen "Mongolian Princes and Their Merchant Partners," *Asia Major*, 3rd series, 2/2 (1989), 83–126.

[14] Rashīd/Karīmī, vol. I, p. 437.

near Bukhara] one silver ingot."[15] Chinggis Qan's policies were continued by his immediate successors, who, if anything, were even more encouraging to merchant interests providing, as they did, subsidized transport and above market prices for most goods. The consequence was an immense influx of valuable textiles to Mongolia. Juvaynī, speaking of his own time, says that the Mongols' "everyday apparel [is] studded with jewels and woven with gold [*zar-baft gashtah*]" and then continues, stating that so many opulent garments have been shipped east that the markets are much depressed and concludes that taking fabrics (*qumāsh*) there is like presenting "caraway-seeds to Kirmān or offering [sea] water to Oman," that is, taking coals to Newcastle.[16] His statement is not mere hyperbole but a reflection of an important transition that was taking place in the mid thirteenth century, one with interesting cultural implications. By this point in time, the Mongolian court in the east was no longer dependent upon imports or tributes of West Asian textiles, especially gold brocade, and was now capable of producing its own supplies of these fabrics in imperially sponsored and controlled textile centers. To adequately account for this new state of affairs we must first explore the Mongols' policy toward artisans.

Wherever they campaigned, the Mongols took special care to identify and mobilize individuals possessing useful skills or talents for service to the empire. Of equal importance, artisans once in their hands were shared out like other forms of booty and widely distributed throughout the domain, thereby creating numerous opportunities for artistic and technological transfer. This phenomenon has often been noted in passing but never studied in depth and thus constitutes a major and as yet unwritten chapter on the cultural history of Eurasia. What follows is only an outline of the problem designed to provide background for a particular instance of transfer: the dispatch of West Asian textile workers to East Asia.

Like other nomads, whose pastoral mode of existence requires the even dispersal of their small human and large animal populations over a wide territory, the Mongols were generalists equally versed in a variety of skills, from riding and herding to felting and saddle-making. With the partial exception of shamans, blacksmiths, and bards, who at times might withdraw from direct participation in subsistence activities and earn a living offering a single service, occupational specialists possessing a distinct social identity and a degree of economic autonomy are seldom encountered among the nomads.[17] While this adaptation was well suited to life in the steppe, once in control of agricultural and urban societies in which there is a far more

[15] Juvaynī/Qazvīnī, vol. I, pp. 59–60, and Juvaynī/Boyle, vol. I, pp. 77–78.
[16] Juvaynī/Qazvīnī, vol. I, pp. 15–16, and Juvaynī/Boyle, vol. I, p. 22.
[17] Cf. the comments of S. E. Tolybekov, *Kochevoe obshchestvo Kazakhov v XVII-nachale XX veka* (Alma Ata: Izdatel'stvo 'nauka' Kazakhskoi SSR, 1971), pp. 601–02.

elaborate division of labor, the Mongols soon realized that they needed the services of numerous specialists to help consolidate their conquests. And to acquire sufficient quantities of such personnel, which for cultural and demographic reasons they could not supply from their own ranks, the Mongols turned to outsiders, principally their sedentary subjects, for assistance. Administrative systems, for example, were usually refashioned from indigenous institutions and staffed by both local and foreign-born officials with a Mongol to monitor their activities. In addition to professional bureaucrats, the conquerors also regularly recruited merchants and coopted religious hierarchies, two groups whose literacy, knowledge of accounts, communication networks, and ideological influence proved most useful in controlling and exploiting subject populations.[18] And they quickly appreciated as well that to fully enjoy the fruits of their military success they needed artisans to provide them with the rich array of products and services available in the sedentary zone of their domain.

The practice of sparing the lives of artisans is first noted during their campaigns against the Chin dynasty. One of the earliest instances came in 1216 at Tung-p'ing in Shantung where, following the Mongolian victory, the "rebel" forces, a euphemism for the Jürchen and Chinese resistors, were put to the sword "with the exception of the artisans and actors."[19] By the time Chinggis Qan led his armies into western Turkestan and northern Iran in 1219 this had become a firmly established pattern: everywhere they encountered strong resistance a slaughter ensued but only after the artisans were identified and separated out. This procedure, reported in grisly detail, was applied at Ūtrār, Fanākat, Samarqand, Khwārazm and Marv in Turkestan, at Ghazna, Nīshāpūr, and Tūn in Khurāsān, at Ani in Transcaucasia, at Mosul in Iraq, and Aleppo in Syria.[20]

What happened to those so spared is related by various authors. In reference to Samarqand, taken in 1221, Rashīd al-Dīn reports that

> when the city and fortress were reduced to ruins [the Mongols] killed many notables and military officers, and the next day counted the survivors and from this group they identified 3,000 artisans [*pīshah-varī*] and they apportioned them among the officers, commanders and wives and in this manner they assigned the same quantity to the levy [*ḥashar*].[21]

Describing the situation in the mid 1240s, Carpini notes that "in the land of the Saracens and other nations the Tartars, who live among them as their

[18] Anatoly M. Khazanov, *Nomads and the Outside World* (Cambridge University Press, 1984), pp. 225–26.
[19] *YS*, ch. 119, p. 2932.
[20] Juvaynī/Qazvīnī, vol. I, pp. 66, 70–71, 95, 100, 127 and 140; Juvaynī/Boyle, vol. I, pp. 85, 92, 122, 127, 135, 162 and 177; Rashīd/Karīmī, vol. II, p. 691, 719 and 730; and Kirakos, *Istoriia Armenii*, p. 165.
[21] Rashīd/Karīmī, vol. I, p. 364. Juvaynī says 30,000 artisans were identified. See Juvaynī/Qazvīnī, vol. I, p. 95, and Juvaynī/Boyle, vol. I, p. 122.

lords and masters, take all the best craftsmen and employ them in their own service, while the rest of the artificers pay tribute out of their work."[22] From this data three broad categories of artisans can be discerned: those assigned to the military levy, those paying taxes in kind, and those directly attached to the princes and notables. These divisions are more clearly articulated in the Chinese sources, which supply much fuller information on population registration. In the Yuan realm the Mongols classified the subject population as a whole into four basic categories – civilian, military, postal relay, and artisan households (*chiang-hu*) for purposes of census taking. The artisan households in turn were divided into three sub-categories:

> Government artisans (*kuan-chiang*), who were permanently attached to court workshops and who received compensation in the form of rations.
>
> Civil artisans (*jen-* or *min-chiang*), who sustained themselves through private trade and manufacture and provided services and goods to the government through taxes and corvée.
>
> Military artisans (*chün-chiang*), who were permanently attached to the army, where they served in labor, engineering, and artillery units and, like other soldiers, received rations.

From the Chinese data it is evident that once enrolled on the registers all artisans and their descendants became hereditary servitors, a status from which it was difficult to escape. It is noteworthy, however, that in the Yuan the artisanate had to be purged on occasion to eliminate incompetents who had entered their ranks under false pretenses in order to gain the protection and support afforded by this status.[23] As producers of valued commodities, artisans were treated in a manner that other segments of the population found attractive.

The Mongolian equivalents of the Chinese terminology for the three categories of artisans is not known. The general term was *uran*, "artisan" or "craftsman," and those distributed to the notables were called *ger-ün köbegün*, "sons of the yurt," a usage reflecting the Mongols' patrimonial notions about society and government.[24] The Persian sources are similarly vague in this regard. They describe in a general way the threefold division of artisans but apply no consistent terminology to them. It seems clear,

[22] *Mongol Mission*, p. 42, and *Sinica Franciscana*, p. 91.

[23] These matters are discussed at length by Chü Ch'ing-yuan, "Government Artisans of the Yuan Dynasty," in E-tu Zen Sun and John De Francis, eds. and trans., *Chinese Social History: Translations of Selected Studies*, repr. (New York: Octogon Books, 1966), pp. 234–46; and Ōshima Ritsuko, "The *Chiang-hu* in the Yuan," *Acta Asiatica* 45 (1983), 69–95.

[24] Antoine Mostaert, *La matérial Mongol du Houa i i iu de Houng-ou (1398)*, ed. by Igor de Rachewiltz (Mélanges chinois et bouddhiques, 18; Brussels: Institut belge des hautes études chinoises, 1977), vol. I, p. 106; and Francis W. Cleaves, "The Sino-Mongolian Inscription of 1335 in Memory of Chang Ying-jui," *HJAS* 13 (1950), 26, 74, 75, 99, and 51–52, note 170.

however, that those craftsmen employed in the court workshops in Iran, called a *kār-khānah*, held the same status as the *kuan-chiang*, "government artisans" of Yuan China.[25]

The formal organization of artisans on a wide scale took place in the 1230s and 1240s in conjunction with systematic population registration. Once identified and classified, artisans of all types were set to work under imperial commissioners and new workshops were founded. Officials who seized the initiative and produced results gained stature and praise.[26] In Iran there are scattered references to such workshops in Herat, Nīshāpūr, Ṭūs, and Isfarāyin, as well as to a seemingly special manufactory in Baghdad, called the "Paradise Workshop [*kār-khānah-i firdaws*]" which made "rare clothing [*jāmah-i tansūq*]."[27]

That a specialized workshop was located in Baghdad is hardly unexpected, since prior to the Mongolian conquest the ʻAbbāsid capital had been a major manufacturing center, producing high-quality textiles for court consumption. An anonymous geographical compilation of the early thirteenth century notes that under the direction of a court-appointed master three hundred workshops (*kār-gah*) making atlas, brocade, linen, etc., "worked continually on behalf of the imperial treasury" during the reign of the Caliph Nāṣir al-Dīn (r. 1180–1225). The same text adds, intriguingly, that one of the products of Baghdad were "instruments for drawing gold thread [*ālāt-i zarkashīdah*]."[28] Such talent and technology was unlikely to escape the notice of the Mongols. Indeed, throughout the empire, textile workers were in particular demand and apparently accorded special status. This is evident from a passage in the *Yuan shih* which relates that in 1235 when a selective draft of Chinese, Tangut, and Muslim artisans was ordered, only craftsmen working on the imperial palaces at Qara Qorum and weavers (*chih-chiang*) were exempted.[29] To the best of my knowledge, textile workers were rarely if ever assigned to military units, by far the most dangerous and onerous duty that befell the artisanate.

The vast majority were certainly classified as government or civil artisans, and it is most likely that the latter category, dispersed in villages, cities, and special colonies throughout the realm, contained the greatest number of weavers. In any event, the fact that among Möngke's "pillars of the state" there were those, according to Juvaynī, who "collect and care for the

25 On the organization of workshops in Iran, see A. G. Kiknadze, "Iz istorii remeslennogo proizvodstva (Karkhane) v Iran XIII–XIV vv.," in A. I. Falina, ed., *Blizhnii i Srednii Vostok* (Moscow: Izdatel'stvo vostochnoi literatury, 1962), pp. 47–55.

26 Juvaynī/Qazvīnī, vol. II, pp. 229–30 and 247; and Juvaynī/Boyle, vol. II, pp. 493 and 511.

27 Rashīd/Karīmī, vol. II, p. 792; Sayf ibn Muḥammad ibn Yaʻqub al-Havarī, *Taʻrīkh nāmah-i Harāt*, ed. by M. Ṣiddīqī (Calcutta: Baptist Mission Press, 1944), pp. 285–87; and Abū al-Qasīm al-Qāshānī, *Taʻrīkh-i Ūljaytū*, ed. by Mahin Hambly (Tehran: B.T.N.K., 1969), pp. 121–22.

28 L. P. Smirnova, trans. and ed., *ʻAjā'ib al-dunyā* (Moscow: Nauka, 1993), pp. 492–93, Persian text and p. 184 Russian translation.

29 *YS*, ch. 98, pp. 2509–10.

garments which are assigned on the provinces," suggests that the weavers in the civil artisan category were a major source of court textiles.[30] We know little, unhappily, about the organization of production aside from the fact that in court workshops the government provided subsidies, imposed quotas, and demanded high technical standards and top quality raw materials. In the extant Chinese records such specifications are expressed in the weight of the yarn or thread in pounds (*chin*) used to produce a square foot (*ch'ih*) of fabric or carpet.[31]

While our data are incomplete, it is nonetheless clear that Mongolian rulers had sufficient skilled weavers at their beck and call to produce large special orders on short notice. This is exemplified in Bar Hebraeus's account of the preparations for an embassy from Tegüder, the Mongolian ruler of Iran (r. 1281–84), to the Mamlūk ruler of Egypt. As diplomatic presents, the court decided to send gems, silver, gold, apparel "and bales of stuffs wherein much gold was woven." Teguder's envoy, a certain ʿAbd al-Raḥmān, then went to Tabrīz, where he spent a month. And there, Bar Hebraeus continues, "he gathered together handicraftsmen of all kinds, jewelers, and sewers, and others, and he made everything to a royal pattern."[32]

As a result of the measures undertaken in preceding decades, the empire's production of textiles, particularly those woven with gold, was truly impressive by the latter half of the thirteenth century. Marco Polo, with a merchant's keen eye for commercial possibilities, provides a partial inventory of the centers producing "cloth of gold" he saw or heard of in the course of his extensive travels: Baghdad, Tabrīz, Georgia, and Lesser Armenia in the West, and Cuigiu (Hsu-chou) and Chinghianfu (Chen-chiang) in the East. Such cloth, according to the Venetian, was even produced in Tibet where, interestingly, the Persian *zar-bāf*, "gold brocade," passed into the indigenous language in the form of *zar-babs*.[33] Tartar cloth, to be sure, was not a Mongolian product but it is nonetheless well named, for its great fame and wide dissemination in medieval Eurasia was a direct byproduct of Mongolian priorities, policies, and organizational abilities.

The general mobilization of craftsmen also entailed, as already remarked, the wholesale transfer of artisan populations from one cultural zone of the empire to another. The capital, Qara Qorum, is a case in point. Built by Chinese and Muslim craftsmen in the reign of Ögödei, its architecture and decor betray, not unexpectedly, a mixture of East,

[30] Juvaynī/Qazvīnī, vol. III, p. 88, and Juvaynī/Boyle, vol. 2, p. 606.

[31] These data emerge from Rashīd al-Dīn's discussion of the effectiveness of Ghazan's administrative and fiscal reforms. See Rashīd/Karīmī, vol. II, p. 980, and Martinez, "The Third Portion of the Story of Gāzān Xān," 67–68. On Chinese technical specifications, see *Ta-yuan chan-chi kung-wu chi* (Hsüeh-shu ts'ung-pien ed.; Taipei, 1971), pp. 10b-11a.

[32] Bar Hebraeus, pp. 467–68.

[33] Marco Polo, pp. 98, 101, 104, 272, 300 and, 323, and Bertold Laufer, "Loan Words in Tibetan," *T'oung-pao* 17 (1916), 477, no. 119.

Central, and West Asian influences.[34] Archeological investigation has also revealed that its artisans' quarters contained metalsmiths, ceramicists, bead-makers, bone-carvers, and weavers drawn from such diverse regions as China, Tibet, Khwārazm, Volga Bulgaria, Uighuristan, and southern Siberia.[35] Temür's famed draft of artisans to embellish Samarqand had a well-established precedent.[36]

From literary sources there is evidence as well that at least two other urban sites in Mongolia contained foreign craftsmen: Chinqai's City in west central Mongolia, first established as a military colony in 1212, later housed a contingent of Chinese artisans, some of whom returned home in 1265.[37] Bai Baliq or "Rich Town" on the Selenge River, originally built by Sogdian and Chinese workers in 757 on orders of the Uighur qaghan Moyun Chur (r. 747–59), became in the Mongolian era a center for goldsmiths and jewelers. The ethnic affiliations of the artisans stationed there is not known, but like their counterparts in Chinqai's City, many were relocated to China in the 1260s.[38]

The forced resettlement of artisans, a regular feature of imperial policy, commenced immediately after the initial campaigns of conquest. Li Chih-chang, who arrived in Samarqand in the winter of 1221/22, less than a year after the fall of the city, encountered Chinese craftsmen living amongst the locals. And on his return trip to China he heard reports of many Chinese artisans settled in the Upper Yenesei region of Siberia who were "weaving thin silk, gauze, brocade and open-work silk."[39] The traffic in human skills flowed in the opposite direction as well. Juvaynī, in one place speaks generally of the large levies of Muslim artisans settled in "the farthest countries of the East" following the conquest of Turkestan and northern Iran, and later on more specifically of Khwārazmian artisans sent to the countries of the East, where "at present there are many localities in those climes that are cultivated and well-peopled by its [Khwārazm's] inhabi-

34 For a summary of the excavations at Qara Qorum, see Thomas T. Allsen, "Archeology and Mid-Imperial History: The Chin and Yuan," in Gilbert Rozman, ed., *Soviet Studies of Premodern China: Assessments of Recent Scholarship* (Ann Arbor: Center for Chinese Studies, The University of Michigan, 1984), pp. 88–90.

35 On the artisans quarter and the textile finds, see *Mongol Mission*, p. 184; Rubruck/Jackson, p. 221; *Sinica Franciscana*, p. 286; and Evtiukhova, "Izdeliia razlichnykh remesel iz Kara-Koruma," pp. 289–93.

36 Clavijo, *Embassy to Tamerlane*, pp. 134, 286, and 287–88.

37 *YS*, ch. 6, p. 105 and ch. 120, p. 2964; Li Chih-chang, *Hsi-yü chi*, p. 284; and Li Chih-chang, *Travels of an Alchemist*, pp. 72–73.

38 S. E. Malov, trans., *Pamiatniki drevnetiurkskoi pis'mennosti Mongoli i Kirgizii* (Moscow-Leningrad: Izdatel'stvo akademii nauk SSSR, 1959), p. 43; and Su T'ien-chüeh, *Yuan wen-lei* (Taipei: Shih-chiai shu-chü ying-hsing, 1967), ch. 42, pp. 16a–17b. The text has Pai Li-pa, an obvious error for Pai Pa-li. For a brief archaeological description of Bai Baliq, see Yu. S. Khudiadov, "Pamiatniki uigurskoi kul'tury v Mongoli," in V. E. Larichev, ed., *Tsentral'naia Aziia i sosednie territorii v srednie veka* (Novosibirsk: Nauka, Sibirskoe otdelenie, 1990), pp. 85–87.

39 Li Chih-chang, *Hsi-yü chi*, pp. 327 and 366–67, and Li Chih-chang, *Travels of an Alchemist*, pp. 93 and 124.

tants."[40] The arrival of the Muslims in the East can be dated by a passage in the biography of Liu Min, a Chinese official in Mongolian employ, which relates that in 1223 he was given "over 1,000 artisans of the Western Region [*Hsi-yü kung-chiang*] as well as troops from Shantung and Shansi to organize into two military units."[41] In this case the lapsed time between military occupation and resettlement is at most two years.

Prominent among the levies dispatched to the East were textile workers from various parts of the "Western Region," all of whom Qubilai inherited when he came to the throne in 1260. During his tenure the Mongolian regime adopted many of the trappings of Chinese-style government, which resulted in the reorganization of cloth production. A more centralized administrative structure was elaborated to better direct and control the activities of both the foreign imports and the locally mobilized weavers. The *Specimens of Yuan Literature*, a miscellany of private writings, official documents and biographies, gives a generalized picture of the measures utilized to achieve this end. Once the Mongols, it states, had created an orderly administration in China, "then they gathered the artisans from All-Under-Heaven [i.e., the known world], assembled them at the capital [now Peking], classified and distributed them to offices [*chü*]."[42] No date is provided, but another passage in the same work, specifically devoted to weaving, states that the reorganization of textile workers commenced in 1274 at the capital and that subsequently in each circuit (*lu*) of the country "they established an office [*chü*] to direct them."[43] The Yuan regime, Ōshima rightly remarks, took care to exert more control over artisan households than over the bulk of the population, the civilian, peasant households.[44]

The Mongolian governments' direct involvement in and organization of textile production is hardly surprising. In all preindustrial societies large-scale manufacturing efforts, whether of armaments or textiles, are typically coordinated by the state with the assistance of merchants, guilds, and so on. As the principal consumer of such goods, the state took an active role in the creation and staffing of manufacturing facilities and in production and distribution.[45] Given the Mongols' penchant for expensive cloth and robes, the open market was hardly an option and served only as a supplementary source. As Willem Floor has argued in the case of the Safavids, also avid consumers of sumptuous textiles, production on the scale desired was simply out of the question for private weavers. They lacked, among other

40 Juvaynī/Qazvīnī, vol. I, pp. 9 and 101, and Juvaynī/Boyle, vol. I, pp. 13 and 128.

41 *YS*, ch. 153, p. 3609.

42 Su T'ien-chüeh, *Yuan wen-lei*, ch. 42, p. 19a.

43 Su-T'ien-chüeh, *Yuan wen-lei*, ch. 42, pp. 18a–b. For further evidence of the reordering and renaming of offices and bureaus concerned with cloth and clothing in Qubilai's reign, see *YS*, ch. 88, pp. 2228–29, and Farquhar, *Government*, pp. 86–87.

44 Ōshima, "The *Chiang-hu* in the Yuan," pp. 92–93.

45 My comments are based on the discussion of Jane Schneider and Annette B. Weiner, "Introduction," in *Cloth and Human Experience*, p. 12.

things, the requisite amounts of capital and raw materials, quantities that the court alone could supply.[46]

For the manufacture of the Mongols' favored textile, *nasīj*, great quantities of silk and gold were required. Inasmuch as China was still the major center of silk production in the world, the Mongols had ready access to one of the essential raw materials. Even before the Mongols completed the conquest of the south, they received regular tributes of silk from the Sung.[47] Thereafter, the Yuan court consistently encouraged the planting and cultivation of mulberry trees inasmuch as silk backed their paper currency and was a critical item in their revenue system. High officials of the regime were frequently assigned the proceeds from silk-producing households and taxes paid the central government were partially collected in silk. The amounts generated were enormous. In 1263, for example, the silk fibers received totaled 425 tons and in 1328 the figure reached 655 tons.[48]

The supply of gold, the other essential ingredient, is more problematical and less fully reported in the sources. Some, of course, came from the "Western Region" in the form of booty and tribute, particularly in the early years of the empire. Within China itself this metal is not particularly abundant but the Yuan government organized the panning and mining of the available sources through various state agencies and monopolies.[49] While there are no hard data on gold production in the Yuan, it seems probable that the court's major supplies came from its frontier provinces. In the southwest, Marco Polo's Caragian, the area of the former Ta-li kingdom, much gold was found in alluvial deposits and was panned rather than mined. Tibet, too, had considerable quantities of "grains of gold," a fact well known to outsiders both before and after the Mongols.[50] Further, the Upper Yenesei and the Altai or "Gold" Mountains, an integral part of the Yuan state, was an early and fabled center of gold production known to the ancient Greeks through legendary tales of ore-mining ants and guardian griffins which, in fact, were a common decorative motif in the early art of

[46] Willem Floor, "Economy and Society: Fibers, Fabrics, Factories," in Carol Bier, ed., *Woven from the Soul, Spun from the Heart: Textile Arts of Safavid and Qajar Iran, 16th–19th Centuries* (Washington, DC: Textile Museum, 1987), p. 23.

[47] *Mongol Mission*, p. 144; Rubruck/Jackson, p. 162; and *Sinica Franciscana*, p. 237.

[48] The Chinese data are conveniently assembled in Dieter Kuhn, *Textile Technology: Spinning and Reeling*, part 9 of *Science and Civilization in China*, vol. V, *Chemistry and Chemical Technology*, ed. by Joseph Needham (Cambridge University Press, 1988), pp. 286–89.

[49] Farquhar, *Government*, pp. 184–85 and 186, and Herbert Franz Schurmann, *Economic Structure of the Yuan Dynasty* (Cambridge, Mass.: Harvard University Press, 1967), pp. 152–53 and 154–55. I have found no data on the location of these operations during the Yuan. In Ming times, however, gold was panned and mined in Szechuan, Yunnan, Kuangtung, Hunan, and Honan. See Sung Ying-hsing, *T'ien-kung k'ai-wu: Exploitation of the Work of Nature* (Taipei: China Academy, 1980), pp. 336–37.

[50] Marco Polo, pp. 272 and 278; Vladimir Minorsky, ed. and trans., *Hudūd al-ʿĀlam*, 2nd edn. (London: Luzac and Co., 1970), pp. 92–93 and 257; and Muḥammad Haidar, *A History of the Moghuls of Central Asia*, trans. by E. D. Ross and ed. by N. Elias, repr. (New York: Praeger, 1970), pp. 422–12.

the area.[51] From antiquity through the Middle Ages, the indigenous smiths, as documented in the archeological records, fashioned well-executed earrings, goblets, plates, etc., from the locally obtained gold.[52] But unlike silk fiber and thread, which tens of thousands of peasants could readily produce in the countryside, the preparation of metallic thread was a highly specialized craft under the control of the Gold Thread Office (*Chin ssu-tzu chü*). Three such offices existed at various times during the Yuan, and they, presumably, supplied some of the gold thread used by the weavers of *nasīj*.[53]

In concluding the discussion of gold supply, it should be noted that the actual levels of consumption were not as extravagant as it might appear. In the first place, much of the gold used in textiles was readily recycled by the simple expedient of placing worn-out cloth in a fire and retrieving the melted metal. Second, we must bear in mind the unique properties of gold. It is extremely malleable: a troy ounce can be beaten into a sheet 100–feet square. And more to the point, it is highly ductile: a troy ounce can be transformed into a thin wire, 50 miles long, and the same amount in the form of gold foil wrapped around a substrate, will produce a thread 1,000 miles in length.[54]

Despite the trend toward administrative centralization, the production of *nasīj* in the Yuan realm was never concentrated in a single place nor in a specific government agency. There was, it is true, a Gold Brocade Office (*Na-shih-shih chü*) but the sources provide nothing beyond its name and the fact that it was under the Ministry of Works. The date of its establishment, its location, and, most importantly, its responsibilities – whether it operated as a coordinating body, storage and distribution center, or production facility – are unknown.[55] Whatever its actual functions, the available information makes it clear that much of the *nasīj* produced for the Yuan court came from communities of civil artisans dispersed throughout the realm and not exclusively from government artisans working at court factories in the capital. And, most interesting from the perspective of cultural transmission, is that at least three of these civil artisan colonies were settled by imported West Asian weavers, colonies whose individual histories can be reconstructed in broad outline.

The first of these communities was located in Besh Baliq, the Uighur

[51] See Adrienne Mayor, "Guardians of the Gold," *Archaeology* 47/6 (1994), 53–59; Adrienne Mayor and Michael Heaney, "Griffins and Arimaspeans," *Folklore* 104 (1993), 40–65; and N. S. Polos'mak, *Steregushchie zoloto grify* (*Ak-Alakhinskie kurgany*) (Novosibirsk: Nauka, 1994), pp. 7–10 and 49–54.

[52] L. R. Kyzlasov, *Istoriia Tuvy v srednie veka* (Moscow: Izdatel'stvo Moskovskogo universiteta, 1969), pp. 46–47, 119, and 154.

[53] *YS*, ch. 88, pp. 2226–27, and Farquhar, *Government*, pp. 83–84.

[54] These data are taken from C. H. V. Sutherland, *Gold, its Beauty, Power and Allure* (London: Thames and Hudson, 1959), pp. 19–20.

[55] *YS*, ch. 85, p. 2150, and Farquhar, *Government*, p. 211.

summer capital on the northern slopes of the T'ien-shan Mountains, which had its origins in the city of Herat. The Mongols invaded Afghanistan in early 1221, wreaking great devastation on its major cities. Herat, initially, was spared destruction when its inhabitants peaceably surrendered to Tolui, Chinggis Qan's fourth son, in the spring of that year. In December, however, the population revolted and successfully drove out the Mongolian garrison and officials. The invaders, preoccupied with other operations, did not return until the summer of 1222, at which point, following fierce resistance, they regained the city and in retribution put the entire populace to the sword. For the next fifteen years Herat remained a ghost town, inhabited by a few survivors, until Ögödei decided to rebuild the cities of Khurāsān as a means of increasing the flow of monies and goods to the imperial coffers.[56]

Herat, long a center of textile production, was particularly famed for its gold brocades. When, for example, the Khwārazmshāh Muḥammad took possession of the city ca. 1206–07, the inhabitants, desirous of securing the goodwill of their new sovereign "decorated the main thoroughfare with all sorts of gilt garments [*s̱iyāb-i muẕahhab*] and hung up pictures and engravings."[57] The close connection between its weaving tradition and its subsequent restoration is related at length by Sayf, a resident of Herat who wrote a history of his hometown between 1318–22, one based on both literary and oral sources. His discussion of Ögödei's decision to rebuild the city throws welcome light on the transport of Muslim textile specialists to the East. In the first of two versions of this event provided by Sayf, it is recounted that once Ögödei's advisers had convinced the qaghan that restoration was advisable he queried them as to the means and they in response memorialized, saying "As for the weavers [*jāmah-i bāfān*] of Herat, there are 1,000 households [*khānah-vār*] of people residing in Bīshbālīgh [Besh Baliq] whom we sent." Sayf then resumes his narrative:

> They [then] brought before emperor Ögödei Amīr ʿIzz al-Dīn, the headman of Herat, who in ability and administrative skill excels all, and [whose] understanding is supreme,[58] and they said that "this is the person who, before the taking of Herat the first time [Spring 1221], came out of Herat, in [the course of] two days with two hundred weavers, each one with ten expensive garments, and begged imperial prince Tolui qan for quarter. From that time on, by the order of imperial prince Tolui qan he has been in Bīshbālīgh."[59]

[56] This is described in M. G. Pikulin, "Chingiskhan v Afganistane," in Tikhvinskii, *Tataro-Mongoly v Azii i Evrope*, pp. 140–49.

[57] Juvaynī/Qazvīnī, vol. II, p. 64, and Juvaynī/Boyle, vol. I, p. 331. For a summary of the textile and weaving industries of Herat, see R. B. Serjeant, *Islamic Textiles: Material for a History up to the Mongol Conquest* (Beirut: Librairie du Liban, 1972), pp. 93–95.

[58] ʿIzz al-Dīn was in fact the head of the weavers guild, an appointment he received just prior to the Mongols arrival. See note 59 for the reference.

[59] Sayf, *Taʾrīkh nāmah-i Harāt*, pp. 106–07. See also p. 81, where ʿIzz al-Dīn's appointment as head of the weavers of Herat and his subsequent approach to Tolui is briefly mentioned.

Following his audience, ʿIzz al-Dīn, on the recommendation of the imperial advisers, was assigned administrative responsibility for Herat, and Ögödei ordered him home with one hundred households of Heratis with instructions to gather up people from diverse regions and to restore the desolate city to its former glory.

In an alternative explanation of the emperor's decision to rebuild Herat, derived from other, unnamed historians, Sayf recounts that one day Qutlugh Ishi,[60] a wife of the deceased Chinggis Qan, brought before Ögödei "several garments of gold brocade with regal pictorial decorations [*jāmah-i zar-baft muṣavar-i bādshāhanah*]," The garments, Sayf continues,

> pleased Ögödei and he asked Qutlugh Ishi "who is the weaver [*nāsij*] of these cloths [*nasj-hā*], the illustrator [*muṣauvir*] of these pictures [*ṣūrat-hā*], and the maker [*muṭarriz*] of these embroidered garment borders [*ʿalam-hā*]?" Qutlugh Ishi said that "in the time when Tolui qan personally apportioned the captives of the city of Herat among the elder and younger brothers [i.e., the Chinggisids collectively], he bestowed the weavers on me. These garments woven of gold [*aṣwāb az mansūjāt*] and works of art are theirs." Emperor Ögödei said that "[if] these weavers are given to me then I will give to thee in compensation whatever thy heart desires." Qutlugh Ishi conferred the weavers on Ögödei and she received five flourishing villages in Turkestan. Emperor Ögödei treated these weavers with a special princely kindness and civility and ordered that each year they were to receive a substantial sum from the revenues of Bīshbālīgh and that they were to send 1,000 garments to [his] flourishing treasury.[61]

According to this version, ʿIzz al-Dīn, several years after this exchange, brought before Ögödei several garments with gold embroidered inscriptions (*muṭarraz-i zar-nikār*) which greatly impressed the emperor by their beauty. By subsequent presentations, ʿIzz al-Dīn gradually persuaded Ögödei to authorize the restoration of Herat under his charge. Finally, in 1236 ʿIzz al-Dīn returned to Afghanistan with fifty Heratis to begin this project, and in 1239 the Mongolian court, to facilitate its successful completion, sent another 200 households back home.[62]

Whichever tradition reported by Sayf is the correct one, the common feature, and for our immediate purposes the crucial point, is that a large number of Herati weavers were transported to Besh Baliq in 1221 and that while a portion, 10 or 25 percent, returned home between 1236 and 1239, the majority remained in the Uighur lands where they came under the general control of the imperial court in Mongolia.

We lose sight of these weavers for several decades, though Juvaynī, who passed through Besh Baliq in the early 1250s, in all likelihood alludes to

[60] The text gives Alshī, but the variant Īshī, the Turkic *ishi*, "wife of a noble," is certainly the correct reading. See V. M. Nadeliaev, *et al.*, eds., *Drevnetiurkskii Slovar* (Leningrad: Nauka, 1969), p. 214; and Sir Gerard Clausen, *An Etymological Dictionary of Pre-Thirteenth-Century Turkish* (Oxford: The Clarendon Press, 1972), p. 256.

[61] Sayf, *Taʿrīkh nāmah-i Harāt*, pp. 107–9. Quote is on p. 107.

[62] Sayf, *Taʿrīkh nāmah-i Harāt*, p. 122.

them indirectly when he reports that the Uighurs' summer capital, whose native inhabitants were predominantly Buddhists and Nestorians, also had a thriving Muslim community and a Friday Mosque.[63] The weavers are next noted in 1276 when the Yuan government, clearly as part of its overall efforts to reorganize the artisans of the realm, established a Besh Baliq Office (Pieh-shih Pa-li *chü*) headed by a High Commissioner and an Assistant Commissioner. Their responsibility, the *Yuan shih* informs us, was to "superintend the weaving and preparation of collars, sleeves, gold brocade [*na-shih-shih*], and other garments for imperial use."[64] We may even have some specimens of their handiwork, for fragments of ceremonial tunics found in graves near Besh Baliq are described by Wang Ping-hua, who examined these finds, as a kind of gold brocade (*chin-chin*). He, too, sees a possible connection with the *nasīj* produced at the Uighur summer capital.[65]

The final fate of this community is not known. The Uighur lands became a battleground between the Yuan and the rival Chaghadai line of central Asia during the latter part of the thirteenth and early decades of the fourteenth centuries. Gradually the Chaghadai armies gained the upper hand and drove the Yuan forces out of the region by 1316 or 1317 and became the predominant presence there in succeeding years. Presumably, the community of Muslim textile workers either fell under the control of the Chaghadai qans or, what is more likely in my view, these weavers, a prized asset of the Yuan court, retreated eastward into Chinese territory when the Uighur ruling house set up a government-in-exile in the Kansu Corridor around 1283.[66]

The second colony of deported weavers in Yuan China was situated to the north of Ta-tu (Peking) along one of the three major routes leading to Qubilai's summer palace of Shang-tu, the fabled Xanadu of Coleridge's poem. This community has already been studied in depth by Paul Pelliot,[67] but for reasons of completeness, and as a basis for comparison with other West Asian textile colonies, I will recapitulate in full the evidence he brought forward, to which I can contribute a few additional details and observations.

The foundation of this textile center, called variously Hsin-ma-lin, Hsün-ma-lin, and Sīmālī, is related in the biography of Ha-san-na, a Mongol of the Kereyid tribe. He accompanied Chinggis Qan on the campaign in

63 Juvaynī/Qazvīnī, vol. III, p. 60, and Juvaynī/Boyle, vol. II, p. 589.
64 *YS*, ch. 85, p. 2149, and Farquhar, *Government*, p. 208.
65 Wang Ping-hua, "Yen-hu ku-mu," *Wen-wu*, no. 10 (1973), 28–34, and especially 28–30.
66 On the struggle over Uighuristan, see Thomas T. Allsen, "The Yuan Dynasty and the Uighurs of Turfan in the 13th Century," in Morris Rossabi, ed., *China among Equals: The Middle Kingdom and its Neighbors, 10th–14th Centuries* (Berkeley: University of California Press, 1983), pp. 248–61.
67 Paul Pelliot, "Une ville musulmane dans la Chine du Nord sous les Mongols," *Journal Asiatique* 211 (1927), 261–79.

central Asia, where he participated in the assaults on Samarqand and Bukhara. During Ögödei's reign (1229–41) he was placed in command of the Arghun Army, a unit composed of Mongolian tribesmen, and then

he united 3,000 households of Muslim civil artisans and stationed [them] at Hsün-ma-lin. Subsequently, he was made imperial agent [*darugachi*] of the two circuits of P'ing-yang and Tai-yuan [in Shansi] and concurrently supervisor of sundry civil artisans [*kuan chu-se jen-chiang*].[68]

Though Ha-san-na's biography is mute on the point, it is quite evident that Hsün-ma-lin became an important garrison town; by 1261, according to the *Yuan shih*, it housed elements of the Arghun and Hsi-hsia Armies under the overall command of Ang-chi-erh, a Tangut general in Qubilai's service.[69]

From Rashīd al-Dīn's account of China we learn further that along the Sangīn (Sang-kan) River in a region abounding in grapes and other fruit, there is "a town whose name is Sīmalī, of which the majority of the people are Samarqandis and they have fashioned many gardens in the manner of Samarqand."[70] Rashīd al-dīn's comment on the "abundance of grapes" in the vicinity is confirmed by the *Yuan shih*, which reports, *sub anno* 1298, that "they abolished the surplus wine tax [levied] on Hsün-ma-lin."[71] This underscores the fact that the colony in question was peopled by civil artisans (*jen-* or *min-chiang*) who were expected to be largely self-sufficient.

The general administration of the community was vested in the Hsin-ma-lin Civil Artisans Superintendency (*jen-chiang t'i-chü-ssu*).[72] Apparently subordinate to this body was the Hsün-ma-lin Gold Brocade Office (*na-shih-shih chü*) over which presided a Commissioner and Assistant Commissioner of the "Gold Brocade [Weavers] of Hsün-ma-lin."[73] From indications in a variety of sources, it is apparent that many of the weavers in question were those Samarqandi craftsmen apportioned among Chinggis Qan's "sons and kinsmen" in 1221.[74]

The location of Hsin-ma-lin on the banks of the Sang-kan River, the modern Hun-ho, means that it is to be found to the northwest of Peking. Pelliot has identified the Hsün/Hsin-ma-lin of the Yuan texts with the modern town of Hsi-ma-lin in the neighborhood of Kalgan.[75] To my knowledge, this site has not yet been subjected to archeological investigation.

68 *YS*, ch. 122, p. 3016, and Pelliot, "Une ville," 266.
69 *YS*, ch. 4, p. 75, and ch. 123, p. 3027.
70 Rashīd/Karīmī, vol. I, p. 641, and Rashīd/Boyle, p. 271. Boyle has Sinali.
71 *YS*, ch. 19, p. 419, and Pelliot, "Une ville," 264.
72 *YS*, ch. 85, p. 2152; Pelliot, "Une ville," 264; and Farquhar, *Government*, p. 214.
73 *YS*, ch. 89, p. 2263; Farquhar, *Government*, p. 319, who reads *Hsün* as *Ch'ien*; *Yuan tien-chang*, ch. 7, pp. 19b and 25a; and Pelliot, "Une ville," 269–70.
74 Juvaynī/Qazvīnī, vol. I, p. 95, and Juvaynī/Boyle, vol. 1, p. 122. On the textile industry of Samarqand, see Serjeant, *Textiles*, pp. 101–03.
75 Pelliot, "Une ville," 273–76, and Pelliot, *Notes on Marco Polo*, 2 vols. (Paris: Libraire Adrien-Maisonneuve, 1959–63), vol. II, p. 812.

The variant forms of the name found in Chinese and Persian sources have been satisfactorily explained by Pelliot who points out that the characters *hsün* and *hsin*, graphically very similar, were actually pronounced *sim* in the thirteenth century. As for the Persian form, Sīmalī, this poses no problem since Rashīd al-Dīn's information on China usually came from Mongolian speakers who often drop terminal consonants, particularly "n."[76] The original word underlying this toponym has not, however, been identified. Tentatively, I would suggest the Manchu *simelen*, "marsh," "mire," or "lake."[77] Several reasons can be advanced in support of this supposition: (1) phonetically, *simelen* can explain either the Chinese or Persian forms; (2) prior to the Mongolian occupation, the region in question was for over one hundred years under the control of the Chin dynasty whose ruling strata, the Jürchen, spoke Old Manchu; and (3) Hsin-ma-lin was situated on the banks of a large river where, of course, marshes and mires are commonplace.

What finally became of the Samarqandi weavers and wine-makers settled there is unknown. Although Hsin-ma-lin certainly survived as a town into the Ming era, and quite possibly well beyond, all references to textile production at this locale date to the thirteenth century.

The third of our colonies was located in Hung-chou in west central Hopei, the present-day Hsi-ch'eng which lies about 180 kilometers directly west of Peking. The founding of the Hung-chou textile center is related in the biography of Chinqai, the head of the central chancellery under Ögödei and Güyüg:

> Prior to this [i.e., the elevation of Ögödei in 1229], they gathered together young boys, young girls and artisans from All-Under-Heaven and established an office [*chü*] at Hung-chou. Lastly, they obtained some 300 weavers, goldsmiths, twill and figured textile weavers [*chih chin ch'i wen kung*] from the Western Region [Hsi-yü] and 300 weavers and coarse woolen cloth-makers from Pien-ching [K'ai-feng], all [of whom] were attached to the Hung-chou [Office]. Chinqai [Chen-hai] was ordered to hereditarily superintend [them] in that place.[78]

It is most interesting, of course, that this colony, from the beginning contained both Chinese and West Asian weavers, creating obvious opportunities for technical and artistic exchange.

Like its counterpart Hsin-ma-lin, only some 100 kilometers distant, Hung-chou was the site of a Civil Artisans Superintendency (*Jen-chiang t'i-*

[76] Pelliot, "Une ville," 270–73, and Nicholas Poppe, *Introduction to Mongolian Comparative Studies* (Helsinki: Suomalais-Ugrilainen Seura, 1955), pp. 166–70.

[77] Jerry Norman, *Manchu-English Lexicon* (Seattle: University of Washington Press, 1978), p. 242, and V. I. Tintsius, ed., *Sravnitnel'nyi slovar Tunguso-Man'chzhurskikh iazykov: materialy k etimologicheskomu slovariu* (Leningrad: Nauka, 1977), vol. II, p. 87.

[78] *YS*, ch. 120, p. 2964. The biography of Chinqai (T'ien Chen-hai) found in Hsü Yu-jen, *Kuei-t'ang hsiao-kao* (Ying-yin wen-yuan ko-ssu k'u-ch'uan-shu ed.), ch. 10, p. 7b, mentions the establishment of the office at Hung-chou but is less informative on the origins and specialities of the foreign artisans sent there.

chü-ssu) and a Gold Brocade Office (*Na-shih-shih chü*), the latter established in 1278. Additionally, it housed a Clothing and Brocade Bureau (*I-chin yuan*] which was under the supervision of the Bureau for the Empress' Administration.[79] Lastly, Hung-chou was also the site of an Agricultural Superintendency, at least until 1301 when it was abolished and its responsibilities transfered to other, unnamed authorities. Down to this date, and very likely even after, Hung-chou supplied cooking oil and flour to the imperial court and to the Food Stuffs Storehouse located in Shang-tu, the summer palace.[80]

Again, the later history of the West Asian community at Hung-chou is not known but presumably they continued to produce until the collapse of the dynasty in the latter half of the fourteenth century. In any event, both Hsin-ma-lin and Hung-chou were extremely active in the 1270s and 1280s when Marco Polo was resident in China. In relating his route through the "province of Tenduc," actually a city situated just to the north of the great loop of the Yellow River, the Venetian says that

> when one rides through this province [i.e., Tenduc] seven days marches by sunrising [i.e., the east] one draws toward the borders of Catai [Cathay]; so that riding these seven marches one finds many cities and villages in which there are people who worship the law of Mahomet and there are also many idolaters [Buddhists] and some Nestorian Turkish Christians also. And they live by trade and by crafts, for there are made cloths of silk and of gold which one calls *nascici* [*nasīj*], very fine, and another kind of cloth which is called *nac* [*nakh*], and cloth of silk of many different kinds. For just as we have the woolen cloths in our countries of many kinds, just so they have cloths of gold and of silk of many kinds. And they are all subject to the great kaan [Qubilai].[81]

No place names are provided, but the direction of Marco Polo's march from Tenduc "toward the borders of Catai" would have taken him quite close to our two colonies. To my mind, in any event, this passage, which accords in all essentials with the data of the Chinese and Persian sources, is a further, if somewhat oblique, reference to Hsin-ma-lin and Hung-chou.

Examples of the textile produced by the artisans of these colonies may well have come down to us. In 1978, a gold brocade robe of one color was recovered from a tomb not far distant from Tenduc. Its exact place of manufacture cannot of course be determined but one might reasonably connect this garment of *nasīj* with the looms of Hsin-ma-lin and Hung-chou.[82]

79 *YS*, ch. 85, p. 2150 and ch. 89, pp. 2259 and 2261, and Farquhar, *Government*, pp. 211, 319, and 336.

80 *YS*, ch. 6, p. 109, ch. 20, p. 438, and ch. 87, pp. 2203 and 2206; and Farquar, *Government*, pp. 76–77 and 81.

81 Marco Polo, p. 183.

82 Adam T. Kessler, *Empires beyond the Great Wall: The Heritage of Genghis Khan* (Los Angeles: Natural History Museum of Los Angeles County, 1993), pp. 158 photo, and 160–61 text.

In comparing the histories of the three colonies of West Asian weavers within the Yuan domain, a number of common features are clearly evident. All were initially populated with artisans taken during the campaign of 1219–22 in Turkestan and Khurāsān, all were first organized as textile production centers under Chinggis Qan and Ögödei, and all were reorganized in the 1270s under Qubilai. Moreover, each produced *nasīj* under the supervision of an office (*chü*) and each colony was in an area of, or was initially composed of, an ethnically mixed population: Muslims, Turkic-speaking Nestorians, and Chinese in the cases of Hsin-ma-lin and Hung-chou, and Muslims and Uighurs, who had their own well-developed weaving traditions, in the instance of Besh Baliq.[83]

The three colonies of imported weavers, in conjunction with other local sources of gold and silk cloth located in the capital and in cities along the Yangtze River provided a productive capacity that allowed the Yuan court to supply, domestically, its great demand for *nasīj*.[84] Thus, by the latter half of the thirteenth century, bringing West Asian gold brocades to China was indeed like taking coals to Newcastle.

[83] On textile production in the Uighur state, see D. I. Tikhonov, *Khoziaistvo i obshchestvennyi stroi uigurskogo gosudarstva* (Moscow-Leningrad: Nauka, 1966), pp. 82–83.
[84] Marco Polo, pp. 237, 300, and 323.

CHAPTER 4

Clothing and color

The explanation for the Mongols' strong attraction to and extensive use of *nasīj* is intimately linked to indigenous cultural values, most of which, it is important to stress, are in evidence prior to the advent of empire. For the Mongols and other nomadic peoples of the Eurasian steppes, cloth, clothing, and color had great symbolic significance that was regularly used to communicate a wide range of ideas about society, ethnicity, political authority, and personal relationships. And it is these notions, some with a very long history in the steppe, that best account for the Mongols' receptivity to cloths of gold and why Muslim weavers and other elements of the West Asian textile tradition were transported to China during the Yuan.

The basic components of Mongolian dress in the Middle Ages, which we know from ethnographic, art historical, literary, and archaelogical sources, were an ankle-length robe cut of one piece of cloth, a wide belt of soft fabric, trousers, very likely a nomadic innovation, and leather boots. Clothing was made of a wide variety of materials – fur, leather, wool, camel's hair, felt, and on occasion cotton and silk obtained from sedentary neighbors. All elements of their dress had deep roots in nomadic tradition and most are documented in the eastern end of the steppe long before the Mongols emerged as an identifiable ethnic group. While there was considerable continuity and a large measure of uniformity in nomadic attire, variations in design, ornamentation and cut, and differences in color and material typically revealed important information about an individual's status, wealth, tribal affiliation, or ethnic identity.[1] This point is well illustrated in Constantine Porphyrogenitus' account of those Pechenegs who remained in the Volga-Ural region after the majority of their kindred

[1] The most recent discussions of nomadic and Mongolian attire are found in Lobachëva, "Clothing and Personal Adornment," pp. 111–26; Henny Harald Hansen, *Mongolian Costumes* (London: Thames and Hudson, 1993), pp. 131–38; L. L. Viktorova, *Mongoly: Proiskhozhdenie naroda i istoki kul'tury* (Moscow: Nauka, 1980), pp. 30–48; Sechin Jagchid and Paul Hyer, *Mongolia's Culture and Society* (Boulder, Colorado: Westview Press, 1979), pp. 46–56; and D. Baiar, "Kammennye izvaianiia Sukhe-Batorskogo Aimaka (Vostochnaia Mongolia)," in R. S. Vasil'evskii, ed., *Drevnie kul'tury Mongolii* (Novosibirsk: Nauka, Sibirskoe otdelenie, 1985), pp. 148–59.

fled west in the early ninth century under Oghuz pressure. The remnants, he notes, joined the victors but henceforth carefully marked their ethnic origins with a special tunic, the sleeves of which were cut off near the shoulder "to indicate that they had been cut off from their own folk and those of their race."[2] And at the other end of the steppe, the fastening of garments on the left served as a basic ethnic marker; for over two millenia the Chinese identified its use with their nomadic neighbors and with the acceptance of barbarian political authority.[3]

While design features and material were the basic markers and communicators, even more dramatic messages could be conveyed by the transfer and physical manipulation of clothes, messages that relayed basic information concerning individual intentions as well as social and political aspirations. When, for example, Hö'elün, the mother of Chinggis Qan, made fast her *boghta* and tightened her belt, she signaled her determination to begin a difficult enterprise, and when Arghun, the ruler of Iran (1284–91) "placed a *bughtāq* on Tudai Qatun," all understood that he took her as wife. And when Chinggis Qan, at the outset of his career, presented a black sable coat, itself a wedding gift of his in-laws, to Ong Qan, the powerful ruler of the Kereyid tribe, both parties understood that protection and assistance were expected in return.[4]

The practice of giving clothing was widespread and indeed prescribed in certain social situations. In 1249 Sorqaghtani Beki, the wife of Tolui and mother of Möngke, Ariq Böke and Qubilai, sent to Oghul Qaimish, the recently widowed wife of Güyüg, "counsel and condolences, a garment and a *bughtāgh*." In actuality the two were bitter rivals but Sorqaghtani Beki, in order to maintain her public posture as defender of Mongolian and Chinggisid traditions even while laying plans to depose the line of Ögödei and Güyüg, had to conform to this particular convention, which, as Juvaynī states, "is an established custom [*rasm-i maʿhūd*]."[5] Similarly, presentations of clothing were an essential part of the process of political reconciliation among the Mongols. Thus in 1317, when the Herati Amir Yasa'ul negotiated a rapprochment with the Chinggisid prince Yasaʿur following a bitter clash, he did so with a peace offering of "gold, gems, gilded bejewelled hats [*kālah-hāi muraṣṣaʿ*] gilded tunics [*qabā-hāi nigār*] . . . etc."[6] Further, the presentation of cloth was prescribed at the birth of royal children. In the

[2] Constantine Porphyrogenitus, *De Administrando Imperio*, rev. edn., ed. by Gy. Moravcsik and trans. by R. J. H. Jenkins (Dumbarton Oaks Texts, 1; Washington, DC: Dumbarton Oaks and Harvard University, 1967), p. 169.

[3] *The Analects of Confucius*, trans. by Arthur Waley (London: George Allen and Unwin, 1938), xiv.18 (p. 185).

[4] *SH*/Cleaves, sect. 74, p. 21, sect. 96, pp. 32–33, and sect. 254, p. 193; *SH*/de Rachewiltz, sect. 74, p. 28, sect. 254, p. 151; and Rashīd/Karīmī, vol. II, p. 740.

[5] Juvaynī/Qazvīnī, vol. I, p. 217, and Juvaynī/Boyle, vol. I, p. 262.

[6] Ḥāfiẓ-i Abrū, *Ẕayl jāmiʿ al-tavārīkh-i Rashīdī*, ed. by Khānbābā Bayānī (Salsatat-i intishārāt-i anjuman-i aṡār millī, no. 88: Tehran, 1971), p. 124. See also Sayf, *Ta'rīkh nāmah-i Harāt*, p. 650.

section on "National Customs" the *Yuan shih* notes that "If an imperial son or grandson is born, then they confer on the hundred officials gold and silver multi-colored satins [*chin-yin ts'ai-tuan*]"; this, the text continues, "is called *sa-ta-hai*."[7] Unfortunately, the text gives no explanation for this problematical transcription. Paul Ratchnevsky has suggested that *sa-ta-hai*, which he reconstructs as **sadaghai*, is connected with the Mongolian *sadu[n]*, "friend" or "relative."[8] A more likely possibility, in my opinion, is the Arabic *ṣadaqah*, "alms." While its primary meaning is certainly the prescribed charitable offering of Islamic law, it also acquired the extended meaning of "gift" or "act of kindness"; moreover, in some Turkic languages it came to express the idea of "royal favor."[9] In any event, *sadaqa* is registered as a Mongolian word meaning "alms" or "gift" in the *Muqaddimah al-adab*, a multi-lingual dictionary of the fourteenth century.[10]

Putting on and taking off articles of clothing also had great cultural meaning for the Mongols. In certain circumstances this was used to establish equality and partnership. When Chinggis Qan and his friend and future rival, J̌amugha, renewed their oaths as sworn brothers (*anda*), they exchanged golden belts (*altan büse*), obvious representations of the ties that bound them together.[11] Although the belt seems an obvious choice for this particular purpose, other nomads achieved the same end with different articles of clothing, robes, for instance.[12] In most cases, however, the manipulation of clothing was used to establish hierarchy and dependence. Once, when Chinggis Qan was on the run, hiding from his enemies, before praying to the sun he removed his belt (*büse*) and hat (*maqalai*) to symbolize his present powerlessness and his need for heavenly assistance. Some years later, when Chinggis Qan suspected his brother J̌ochi Qasar of treachery, he forcibly removed his sibling's hat and belt as a sign that he no longer trusted him. Only after the intervention of Hö'elün, their mother, were their differences settled and the items restored to J̌ochi Qasar.[13]

7 *YS*, ch. 77, p. 1925. The Chinese *ts'ai-tuan* answers to the Mongolian *önggeten a'urasun*. See Francis W. Cleaves, "The Sino-Mongolian Edict of 1453 in the Topkapi Sarayi Müzesi," *HJAS* 13 (1950), 437, 439, note 10, and 442, 445, note 25.

8 Paul Ratchnevsky, "Über den mongolischen Kult um Hofe der Grosskhane in China," in Louis Ligeti, ed., *Mongolian Studies* (Amsterdam: Verlag B. R. Grüner, 1970), p. 433 and note 90.

9 Dozy, *Supplément aux dictionnaires arabes*, p. 825, and A. Z. Budagov, *Sravnitel'nii slovar Turetsko-Tatarskikh narechii* (St. Petersburg: Imperatorskoi akademii nauka, 1869), vol. I, p. 697.

10 N. N. Poppe, trans., *Mongol'skii slovar Mukaddimat al-Adab* (Moscow-Leningrad: Akademii nauk SSSR, 1938), p. 314, col. b.

11 *SH*/Cleaves, sect. 103, p. 37, and *SH*/de Rachewiltz, sect. 103, p. 40. On *anda*, see Fujiko Isono, "A Few Reflections on the *Anda* Relationship," in Larry V. Clark and Paul Alexander Draghi, eds., *Aspects of Altaic Civilization, II* (Indiana University Uralic and Altaic Series, vol. CXXXIV; Bloomington, 1978), pp. 81–87.

12 Karl A. Wittfogel and Feng Chia-sheng, *History of Chinese Society, Liao (907–1125)* (Philadelphia: American Philosophical Society, 1949), p. 239.

13 *SH*/Cleaves, sect. 117, pp. 49–50, and sect. 244, pp. 177–78, and *SH*/de Rachewiltz, sect. 117, p. 48, and sect. 244, p. 140.

Finally, Rashīd al-Dīn reports that before his major campaigns against the Chin in 1211 and Khwārazm in 1219, Chinggis Qan removed his hat and belt and requested heavenly support and sanction. In the latter instance

> he proceeded alone to the top of a small hill, slung his belt around his neck, uncovered his head and placed his face on the ground. [For] three days and nights he abased himself and lamented before God, and [then] said: "Oh great Lord! Oh Creator of Tajiks [Persians] and Turks! I have not provoked this trouble; give me, through your assistance, the power to extract vengeance!"[14]

As Jean-Paul Roux has pointed out, among the nomads the removal of one's hat and belt before another, whether human or divinity, is to give up one's rights, standing, and liberty, while the act of replacing them establishes ties of subordination and constitutes an acknowledgment that the privileges and benefits thus gained (or regained) are derivative and contingent.[15] This is why at the accessions of Ögödei, Güyüg, Möngke, and many later Chinggisid rulers, all those present, whether blood kin, officials or dependent rulers, stood before the throne, removed their hats and slung their belts over their shoulders.[16] This ceremony served as an act of political reorientation, an effort to fit one's self into a new regime, a new reign, and thereby acquire or reacquire position and status in the new order.

In most contexts, then, the removal of clothing signalled subordination and/or the reduction of one's social and political standing and was therefore employed in certain circumstances as a kind of punishment or form of demotion. This latter usage is exemplified by the penalty exacted for stepping on the threshold of the emperor's tent, a strong taboo among the Mongols. In response to such an infraction, the imperial guard, in Marco Polo's words "take away [the offender's] clothes, and to have them again he must redeem them."[17] Obviously, in this case, the loss of one's robes meant, in effect, the loss of one's access to court, a situation that could only be rectified by the payment of the appropriate fine.

Given these practices, it is not surprising that clothing was a key feature of the Mongols' political culture, the importance of which is clearly reflected in their political language. This is brought out in the *Secret History*'s account of the Uighur ruler's petition for protection of 1209, in which he expresses his willingness to submit to Chinggis Qan by requesting a golden belt and a red robe (*al de'el*).[18] In this case the request was granted and the

14 Rashīd/Karīmī, vol. I, p. 344. See pp. 438–39 for the events of 1211.

15 Jean-Paul Roux, "Quelques objects numineux des Turcs et des Mongols. I, Le bonnet et la ceinture," *Turcica* 7 (1975), 50–51.

16 Juvaynī/Qazvīnī, vol. I, pp. 147 and 206–07, and vol. III, p. 30; Juvaynī/Boyle, vol. I, pp. 187 and 251, and vol. II, p. 568; Rashīd/Karīmī, vol. I, pp. 453, 569, and 583, and vol. II, p. 807; Rashīd/Boyle, pp. 31, 182, and 202; and Al-Qāshānī, *Ta'rīkh-i Ūljaytū*, p. 150.

17 Marco Polo, p. 219.

18 *SH*/Cleaves, sect. 238, p. 172, and *SH*/de Rachewiltz, sect. 238, p. 136. This message is repeated almost verbatim in Rashīd al-Dīn, Rashīd/Karīmī, vol. I, p. 320, and in the *Sheng-*

Uighurs became the first and most honored dependent state of an empire that gathered up many.

Princely favor could be communicated in a number of ways and clothing, in one form or another, regularly played a central role. The West Asian and Chinese sources report a practice, reserved for very special occasions, in which the qan himself removes articles of his own dress and bestows them directly on favored subjects. The Persian historian Jūzjānī reports on one so dignified, the unnamed son of Malik Shihāb al-Dīn Ghāzī, who held territories in northern Iraq. This noble youth visited the court of Möngke in the late 1250s, where he received an imperial robe of honor (*tashrif-i khaṣṣ*):

> The reason for this [Jūzjānī continues] was that during a drinking party [the emperor] ordered the son of Shihāb al-Dīn Ghāzī [to partake of] wine but he abstained and did not do so. Möngke Qaghan asked the reason for his refusal and he replied that "it is forbidden by the Muslim religion and I will not offend my faith." Mongke Qaghan was pleased with this speech and at that very gathering bestowed upon him a tunic he was wearing and showed him honor.[19]

Further instances are noted in Iran where Abagha (r. 1265–81) similarly honored the son of the king of Lesser Armenia, and Abū Saʿīd (r. 1316–35), gave his own clothes to a qāḍī of Shīrāz.[20] Lastly, the *Yuan shih* relates that in 1262 Hoqu, a son of Güyüg, removed his own "gold-bound belt" and presented it to a civil official.[21] In each case the specific reasons differ but all seem to be spontaneous acts motivated by the courage, loyalty, and character of the recipient. The sharing out of a prince's wardrobe, in whatever form it was manifest, created special personal ties and was a common feature of all the Mongolian courts, early and late, east and west.

Besides clothing, textiles in general had symbolic significance within nomadic society. Nor did a cloth have to be beautiful or expensive to make a statement. In medieval and early modern times the West European preference for locally produced black woolens was a means of demonstrating moral and economic opposition to the luxurious polychrome silks of Byzantium and the Islamic East. Moreover, simple fabrics, such as the shroud of Turin, can become the symbol of past values and of humble origins that gave rise to greatness and majesty, whether spiritual or political.[22]

For the nomads, felt, wool that has been beaten, wetted, and rolled, was

wu ch'in-cheng lu, in Wang, *Meng-ku shih-liao*, pp. 156–57. All three go back to a common source, presumably some version of the original petition in Uighur or Mongolian.

19 Jūzjānī, *Ṭabaqāt-i Nāṣirī*, ed. by ʿAbd al-Ḥayy Habībī (Kābul: Anjuman-i tārīkh-i Afghānistān, 1963), vol. II, pp. 200–01.

20 Stephannos Orbelian, *Histoire de la Siounie*, trans. by M. Brosset (St. Petersburg: Academie imperiale des sciences, 1864), p. 236, and Ibn Baṭṭūṭah/Gibb, vol. II, p. 304.

21 *YS*, ch. 180, pp. 4160–61.

22 Jane Schneider, "Peacocks and Penguins: The Political Economy of European Cloth and Color," *American Ethnologist* 5 (1978), 413–47, and Jane Schneider, "The Anthropology of Cloth," *Annual Review of Anthropology* 16 (1987), 414.

just such a material.[23] Developed in the steppe, felt was widely used in everyday life – for tenting, wagon covers, clothes, blankets, riding gear, etc. – and was a visible element in native religious practice.[24] So visible, in fact, that virtually all medieval European travelers among the Mongols took notice of the idols fashioned in felt to which the common people regularly made ceremonial offerings of fermented mare's milk (kumys).[25] Particularly important among the deities so honored was the earth god *nachighai* which Marco Polo describes at some length.[26] Equally revealing, in the preparation of black, that is, "pure" kumys for court use, the emperor, the imperial princes, and high officials all spread out *tologh* felts on the floor of an extended tent in which the mares were milked.[27] This return to roots on special occasions is seen, too, in the custom, recorded in the *Yuan shih*, that "whenever the empress or a concubine became pregnant, she was transferred, when the month of confinement arrived, to a felt tent outside [the imperial palace]."[28] To meet the Yuan court's needs, an elaborate production and supply system was created; this included a Special Directorate (*Ts'ung kuan-fu*) established in 1260 to oversee 29,000 households assigned to felt-making, a Directorate of Felt Manufactures, four regional Felt Offices, and a Storehouse for Felts. One of the major consumers of this product was the Tent Office (*Ch'a-tieh-erh chü*), whose fabrication and construction activities extended far beyond that implied by its official name.[29]

Given the place of felt in steppe culture, it is hardly surprising that this homely fabric came to play an important symbolic role in their political life as well. Chinggis Qan called his fellow nomads "those who live in felt-walled tents" and Mongolian qans, like their Toba and Türk predecessors,

23 András Róna-Tas, "Felt-making in Mongolia," *Acta Orientalia Academiae Scientiarum Hungaricae* 16 (1963), 199–215.

24 The place of felt in steppe society is nicely summarized in Leonardo Olschki's small booklet, *The Myth of Felt* (Berkeley: University of California Press, 1949), and in Bertold Laufer, "The Early History of Felt," *American Anthropologist* 32 (1930), 1–18. The most recent discussions of the subject are Veronica Gervers, "Felt in Eurasia," in Anthony N. Landreau, ed., *Yörük*: *The Nomadic Weaving Traditions of the Middle East* (Pittsburgh: Museum of Art and Carnegie Institute, 1978), pp. 16–22, and E. J. W. Barber, *Prehistoric Textiles*: *The Development of Cloth in the Neolithic and Bronze Ages* (Princeton University Press, 1991), pp. 215–22.

25 *Mongol Mission*, pp. 9 and 95–96; Rubruck/Jackson, p. 75; *Sinica Franciscana*, p. 36 and 174–75; and Odoric of Pordenone, "The Eastern Parts of the World Described," in Yule, *Cathay*, p. 261.

26 Marco Polo, pp. 170 and 469, and Antoine Mostaert, "Le mot *natigay/načigay* chez Marco Polo," in *Oriente Poliano* (Rome: Instituto Italiano per il Medio ed Estremo Oriente, 1957), pp. 95–101.

27 *YS*, ch. 100, p. 2554. On the term *tologh*, Chinese *t'o-lo*, see Henry Serruys, *Kumiss Ceremonies and Horse Races*: *The Mongolian Texts* (Wiesbaden: Otto Harrassowitz, 1974), p. 4 and note 15.

28 *YS*, ch. 77, p. 1925.

29 *YS*, ch. 85, p. 2146, ch. 89, p. 2256, ch. 90, p. 2294, and Farquhar, *Government*, pp. 94, 203 and 314; and *Ta-yuan chan-chi kung-wu chi*, pp. 7a and 9a–b.

were quite literally "elevated" to high office on felt blankets which represented the nomadic roots of their state and celebrated its ethnic and political core.[30]

Both the plain and the sumptuous can communicate and are sometimes very effectively combined to intensify and extend their individual symbolic power. In medieval Japan, for example, accession rituals made use of both "rough cloth" and "smooth cloth" to symbolize the emperors' ability to harmonize the old and the new, the native and the foreign.[31] In the Mongolian case, the two textiles used in the large pavilion tents contained a message that all the nomads could readily read. Their felt exteriors evoked the cultural past and their gold brocade interiors the political present, and the contrast between the two served as a dramatic reminder of the historical path trod by the Mongols in realizing their imperial ambitions.[32]

To complete this discussion of clothing in nomadic society, we must explore the patrimonial principles that gave the Mongolian Empire its basic structure and produced its political style. These principles, concerning the proper relationship between rulers and ruled, shed essential light on the Mongols' extensive political use of cloth and clothing, and on their openness to certain foreign textile traditions.

In the late 1180s when Chinggis Qan first proclaimed his political pretensions and began the prolonged struggle to unify the nomadic peoples of the eastern steppe, he formed a household establishment composed of cooks, doorkeepers, wagon masters, sheep herders, etc. During the first decade of the thirteenth century, while completing his subjugation of these tribes, he twice enlarged and recast his household into an imperial guard (*kesig*). Once sedentary people fell under his control the guard assumed the functions of a central government, keeping records, establishing legal precedents, collecting taxes, and distributing the spoils of war. Throughout the next five decades the guard continued to exercise these multiple functions and served at the same time as the principal recruiting ground for most military and government personnel. Typically, members of the guard, *kesigten*, were detached for service further afield and then rotated back to the court to renew their ties to the ruler by taking up their former household duties which required them to work, live, eat, and drink in close proximity

30 *SH*/Cleaves, sect. 202, p. 141, and sect. 203, p. 144; and *SH*/de Rachewiltz, sect. 202, p. 113, and sect. 203, p. 115. In the *Secret History* felt is *sisgei* and *isgei*. For the elevation of rulers on felt blankets, see Peter A. Boodberg, "Marginalia to the Histories of the Northern Dynasties," *HJAS* 4 (1939), 242–46, reprinted in Alvin P. Cohn, comp., *Selected Works of Peter Boodberg* (Berkeley: University of California Press, 1979), pp. 308–12.

31 Louise Allison Cort, "The Changing Fortunes of Three Archaic Japanese Textiles," in Weiner and Schneider, *Cloth and Human Experience*, pp. 383–86. See also the comments of Mary Ellen Roach and Joanne Bubolz Eicher, "The Language of Personal Adornment," in Justine M. Cordwell and Ronald A. Schwarz, eds., *The Fabric of Culture: The Anthropology of Clothing and Adornment* (The Hague: Mouton, 1979), p. 17.

32 The Qitan, nomadic founders of the Liao, also had a pavilion made of felt and brocade. See Wittfogel and Feng, *History of Chinese Society*, p. 133.

to the qaghan. This institution, which has a long history among the steppe peoples, has rightly been compared to the *comitatus* of the early Germanic tribes.[33]

The essential characteristic of this system of governance was the highly personalized nature of politics within the empire. There were no disinterested, apolitical bureaucrats loyal to the Chinggisid dynasty at large, only retainers with personal ties to specific princes of the blood. When a prince became a qaghan his own guard/household establishment became the new central government, replacing, and sometimes eliminating, the guard of the previous emperor. The Mongols' patrimonial notions of government also explain why the highest officials of the realm bore titles such as cook, parasol-holder, etc., that sound quite menial to modern ears. In the Mongolian scheme of things, however, these titles proclaimed and advertised the bearer's closeness to the center of power, his trustworthiness in the eyes of the qaghan, and, therefore, his authority to carry out imperial policy. The ties that bound retainers to a prince or qaghan were forged by the military discipline of the guard and further reinforced by daily social interaction with their patron.

The qaghan in his turn had obligations to his immediate retainers, chief among them being the regular supply of clothing, drink, and food. The intimate linkage between the supply of sustenance and clothing and individual political commitment is well exemplified in an episode reported in the *Secret History*. In 1203, following the defeat of the Kereyid leader, Ong Qan, his son, Senggüm, fled into the Gobi with his equerry (*aqtachi*), Kököchü, and the latter's wife. Kököchü, concluding that the future lay with Chinggis Qan, decided to depart. As he rode off, his wife called to him: "At the moment when [thou] wast wearing raiment having gold, at the moment when [thou] wast eating [meats] having savor, he was wont to say 'my Kököchü.' How art thou going, so forsaking and abandoning Senggüm, thy qan?" Kököchü, the text continues, ignored this rebuke and went to Chinggis Qan whom he told of his decision to defect. The Mongolian ruler, hearing this story, pointedly praised the wife's behavior and then denounced Kököchü, saying he "is come thus forsaking his proper qan. Such a man now by whom if he became a companion [*nökör*], will be trusted? Cut [him] down and abandon him."[34] The message imparted here is self-evident: So long as a ruler supplies his retainers with clothing and food he can expect and demand unflinching service and complete loyalty.

Such notions, which permeated Mongolian politics throughout the

33 For details and documentation on the evolution of this governmental apparatus, see Thomas T. Allsen, "Guard and Government in the Reign of the Grand Qan Möngke, 1251–59," *HJAS* 46 (1986), 495–521. For its pre-Mongolian roots, see C. I. Beckwith, "Aspects of the Early History of the Central Asian Guard Corps in Islam," *Archivum Eurasiae Medii Aevi* 4 (1984), 29–43.

34 *SH*/Cleaves, sect. 188, pp. 115–16, and *SH*/de Rachewiltz, sect. 188, pp. 96–97.

imperial era, exercized a pronounced effect on the personnel policies of the Yuan regime, which, as is widely known, differed greatly from those of Chinese dynasties. This is brought out in a debate in 1335 between the Mongolian general Bayan the Merkid and the Chinese official Hsü Yu-fen on recruitment to high office. For Hsü, of course, appropriately trained scholars dedicated to good government should form the core of officialdom, whereas Bayan championed aspirants from diverse occupational and ethnic backgrounds "who desire beautiful clothing and delicious food."[35] For Bayan, such men understood and embraced Mongolian notions of service and were thus the only kind of officials a qaghan could really trust.

Given the principles that framed their political expectations and behavior, it is hardly surprising that Mongolian qans expended substantial resources to acquire and sustain their "companions." Odoric of Pordenone relates that when he was in China in the mid 1320s, he "made diligent inquiry" of all the qaghan's courtiers about the size and organization of the imperial establishment and they told him that all these officials, some 14,000 in number, "have from the king's court whatever provision they require." A few sentences later Odoric adds that "the court is truly magnificent, and the most perfectly ordered that there is in the world, with barons, gentlemen, servants, secretaries, Christians, Turks and idolators, *all receiving from the court* what they have need of."[36]

The Mongols' patrimonial ethos is typified, too, by the fact that even those officials discharging duties at a distance were brought back to court for their rations. Rubruck relates that Möngke held annually two great drinking festivals at Qara Qorum, one in the spring and one in the summer. "The second," he says, "is the more important for on that occasion there assemble at his court all nobles [high officials] anywhere within a two-months journey; and then he bestows on them garments and presents and displays his great glory."[37] These nobles, despite their separation from the court, were still members of the household and as such were expected, if logistically practical, to come home for the holidays to participate in the feasting and presentations. In other words, besides allowing the ruler to "display his majesty," such occasions, which might last for several months, were also a means of reasserting his control over distant officials and retainers by reintroducing them into his extended, political family.[38]

The patrimonial principles, so visibly applied to the imperial household *cum* government, were also extended to the qaghan's subjects as a whole, a feature of nomadic polities that long precedes the Mongolian Empire. The Orkhon inscriptions, prepared for the rulers of the Second Türk Qaganate,

35 *YS*, ch. 142, p. 3405.

36 Odoric of Pordenone, "The Eastern Parts of the World Described," in Yule, *Cathay*, vol. II, pp. 225–26. My italics.

37 *Mongol Mission*, p. 175; Rubruck/Jackson, p. 209; and *Sinica Franciscana*, p. 276.

38 The spring festival of 1256 was "sixty-odd days" in length, according to the *YS*, ch. 3, p. 49.

founded in eighth-century Mongolia, clearly articulate such principles. Bilge Qaghan (r. 716–34), in one inscription says he inherited a people "foodless on the inside and clothless on the outside," and then asserts that owing to his unstinting efforts he "furnished the naked people with clothes." In another, Bilge justifies his many campaigns by saying he undertook them "for the benefit of my Türks and my people," and then notes that he "won and acquired their [i.e., the enemies'] yellow gold and white silver, their hemmed silk cloth and hemstitched fabric, their saddle horses . . . etc."[39] The inscriptions are essentially ideological statements and on one level this language, some of which is reminiscent of phrasing found in Middle Persian Manichaean texts,[40] is certainly a metaphor for benevolent government, and therefore a claim of legitimacy and an evocation of loyalty; on another level, however, the distribution of food and clothing is a prescription for practical politics. This is brought out clearly by Yūsuf Khāṣṣ Ḥājib, the eleventh-century author of a mirror for princes in Turkish, who reminds his sovereign, the Qarakhanid ruler of Turkestan, that a "prince must give good reward for service, clothing the naked and feeding the hungry."[41] This is not to say that a qaghan fed and clothed all his people all of the time, but that he was obliged to feed and clothe part of his people, his immediate entourage, most of the time, and to provide succor, in the form of life's basic necessities, to any of his people who found themselves in distressed circumstances. If he failed to do so, a nomadic leader could not retain a following for long.

The giving of clothes was therefore an essential element of nomadic statecraft, and one with a long history behind it. When, for example, the Uighur qaghan, Moyun Chur (r. 747–59), received a bride and wedding gifts from the T'ang court in 758 he immediately distributed the silks and multicolored cloths and garments brought by the Chinese envoys "down to the last one among his officials, chiefs and others."[42] Even more explicit is the statement of the Arabic chronicler Ṭabarī, who relates that in 738 Kursūl, the leader of Türgesh Turks, paid each of his 15,000 men "per month one piece of silk, which at that time was worth twenty-five dirhams." This is why nomadic leaders, when selling their military services to sedentary powers, often took payment in cloth and clothing.[43]

[39] Talāt Tekin, *A Grammar of Orkhon Turkic* (Indiana University Publications, Uralic and Altaic Series, vol. LXIX; Bloomington, 1968), pp. 267–68 and 281.

[40] Hans-Joachim Klimkeit, trans, *Gnosis on the Silk Road: Gnostic Parables, Hymns and Prayers from Central Asia* (San Francisco: Harper, 1993), pp. 243 and 249, note 2.

[41] Yūsuf Khāṣṣ Ḥājib, *Wisdom of Royal Glory* (*Kutudgu Bilig*): *A Turko-Islamic Mirror for Princes*, ed. and trans.by Robert Dankoff (University of Chicago Press, 1983), p. 138. This is a theme to which the author continuously returns, pp. 93, 116, 137, 142, 160, 167, 180, 181, 188, 208, and 210.

[42] Colin Mackerras, ed. and trans., *The Uighur Empire according to the T'ang Dynastic Histories: A Study in Sino-Uighur Relations* (Canberra: Australian National University Press, 1972), p. 64.

[43] Al-Ṭabarī, *The History of al-Ṭabarī*, vol. 26, *The Waning of the Umayyad Caliphate*, trans.

Such practices are much in evidence in the Mongolian Empire as well. Chinggis Qan had his night guards distribute satin to his followers and Ögödei did the same. In addition, Ögödei gave precious robes to the indigent at Qara Qorum and Güyüg clothed all attending his coronation according to their rank. Möngke, too, distributed robes to his officials and their servants, contributed precious garments to help celebrate a Muslim festival, and gave clothing to his brother Hülegü and all his retainers on the eve of the latter's departure for Iran. And Qubilai established agencies to supply clothing and food to the poor in his capital of Ta-tu. Similar efforts were made as well on behalf of impoverished Mongolian herders, whom the Yuan court regularly assisted throughout the thirteenth and fourteenth centuries with grants of money, food, and cloth.[44] Travelers and envoys were treated in like fashion. When Marignolli and his companions wintered at Özbek's court they, by the friar's own testimony, were "well fed, well clothed [and] loaded with handsome presents."[45] Last, and most revealingly, Rashīd al-Dīn records that "following his elevation to the throne of the qanate [in 1265], Abagha Qan presented immeasurable amounts of money, gems and precious garments [*jāmah-hāi-girān-mayah*] to the wives, princes and commanders so that *all the soldiers* received benefit from that [dispensation]."[46]

As P'eng Ta-ya correctly observed, Mongols in imperial service received no regular salary or stipends.[47] Their recompense came rather from shares in the booty, through provision of food, drink, and clothing associated with court-sponsored feasts and celebrations, and by the generosity of the ruler, whose acts of largesse were ofttimes carefully staged affairs. Thus, when Güyüg proclaimed his intention to surpass his father's record for munificence by withdrawing large quantities of luxury goods from the imperial warehouses and then ordering his ministers to give "all of it to the army and the common people," he was engaging in a form of redistribution, the trickle-down economics common to tribal societies.[48]

But for whatever specific purpose it was done – political posturing, rewards, charity, affirmation of friendship, or celebration of native or foreign festivals – the distribution of garments had the effect of displaying

by Carole Hillenbrand (Albany: State University of New York Press, 1989), p. 25, and Constantine Porphyrogenitus, *De Administrando Imperio*, p. 53.

44 *SH*/Cleaves, sect. 234, p. 171, and sect. 279, p. 224; *SH*/de Rachewiltz, sect. 234, p. 135, and sect. 279, p. 171; Juvaynī/Qazvīnī, vol. I, pp. 173, 174, and 209, vol. II, pp. 255–56, vol. III, pp. 80 and 95–96; Juvaynī/Boyle, vol. I, pp. 217, 218, 254–55, vol. II, pp. 519, 601, and 611; Marco Polo, pp. 247–48 and 251; and N. Ts. Munkuev, "Novye materialy o polozhenii mongol'skikh aratov v XIII–XIV v.v.," in Tikhvinskii, *Tataro-Mongoly v Azii i Evrope*, pp. 413–31.

45 de Marignolli, "Recollections of Eastern Travel," in Yule, *Cathay*, vol. III, p. 212.

46 Rashīd/Karīmī, vol. II, p. 742. My italics.

47 P'eng and Hsü, *Hei-ta shih-lüeh*, p. 496, and Haenisch and Yao, *Chinesische Gesandtenberichte*, p. 161.

48 Juvaynī/Qazvīnī, vol. I, pp. 214–15; and Juvaynī/Boyle, vol. I, pp. 259–60.

the majesty and power of the ruler and at the same time encouraged loyalty to and a very personal identification with the reigning qaghan. The critical importance of clothing to the politics of Chinggisid courts is dramatically illustrated by an episode that occurred in the struggle between Tegüder (Aḥmad, r. 1281–84) and Arghun (r. 1284–91) for control of the throne in Iran. According to Rashīd al-Dīn's recounting, an advanced patrol of Tegüder's troops went to Varāmīn, to the south of Ray, where

> they seized all three hundred households of artisans who belonged to Arghun, plundered their homes and returned to the [main] army. When Arghun became aware of this situation he sent envoys to the treasury of Gurgān in order to make ready all that was on hand and he sent to the workshops [*kār-khānah-hā*] of Nīshāpūr, Ṭūs and Isfarāyin [all towns in Khurāsān] to bring garments [*jāmah-hā*]; and in the course of twenty days they conveyed sums of ready money of gold, objects adorned with gold and gems, jewels and garments to ʿĀdiliyyah in Jūrjān [Gurgān] and [Arghun] distributed these things to the military commanders.[49]

Obviously, by Arghun's own calculation, his ability to prosecute a successful war against his rival turned in part on his ability to "display majesty" and distribute clothing.[50] This is why Mongolian rulers often imposed sumptuary laws to secure a monopoly on the right to bestow certain kinds of "political fabrics," such as *jīsün* robes, on their subjects.[51] This is why, too, the Mongols tended to measure their wealth and power by reference to both precious metals and textiles, which they assiduously stockpiled in their treasuries.[52] Like other pre-modern rulers, particularly in West Asia, financial reserves were not exclusively in the form of coin or bullion but in prestige goods which often served as collateral for loans or as liquid capital.[53]

Cloth and clothing imparted much social and political information to the Mongols and so did color. In the Eurasian steppe colors carried a multitude of meanings that in a given historical period were generally comprehensible to all its nomadic inhabitants regardless of tribal, ethnic, or linguistic differences. Colors were used, most prominently, as indicators of directional orientation. Among the Uighurs in the pre-Mongolian era, east was correlated with blue/green, west with white, south with red, and north with

49 Rashīd/Karīmī, vol. II, p. 792.

50 Cf. the comments of Bar Hebraeus, p. 505, concerning Baidu's efforts to win political support through incessant robing and those of Clavijo, *Embassy to Tamerlane*, p. 327 about Prince ʿUmarī, a grandson of Temür, who in preparation for an anticipated succession struggle demanded 3,000 robes from Tabrīz and Sultāniyyāh to bestow on his followers.

51 *YS*, ch. 12, p. 247, and ch. 39, p. 835.

52 Rashīd/Karīmī, vol. II, pp. 1092 and 1094.

53 For textiles as a standard category of wealth, see Benjamin of Tudela, *The Itinerary*, trans. by M. N. Adler, repr. (Malibu, California: Pangloss Press, 1987), pp. 71 and 97, and Bar Hebreaus, p. 219. For prestige goods as financial reserves, see Grahame Clark, *Symbols of Excellence: Precious Materials as Expressions of Status* (Cambridge University Press, 1986), p. 101.

black.[54] Color terms are frequently encountered, too, as elements in personal, ethnic, and topographical names. According to one recent estimate, over 14 percent of Turko-Mongolian place names contain color words.[55] Colors are also used as a means of marking social distinctions and defining political status; for instance, the term "black," *qara* in Turkic and Mongolian, was widely used to convey the notion of subordination and to designate the common people. White, on the other hand, is consistently used to denote the well-born.[56] This sensitivity to clothing and color was still very much alive in this century. Traveling in eastern Turkestan in the late 1920s, Owen Lattimore soon discovered that to the locals a red sash communicated pro-Soviet sympathies, while a yellow coat demonstrated sympathy for the fallen Tsarist regime.[57]

The Mongols, following the precedents of their Turkic predecessors, retained the basic symbolic categories and in some cases adapted the system to more specific ends.[58] Their classification of food, for instance, was (and is) expressed by color symbolism: white for dairy products, red for blood and meat, black for tea and soup, yellow for butter, and green for seasonings such as wild onion and rhubarb.[59]

Color, however, was more than a classifying device for the nomads: certain properties inhered within certain colors, the spiritual force of which was regularly and powerfully felt in human affairs. White, in this regard, had interesting associations that reveal the power attributed to color in Mongolian culture. Most importantly, white was (and is) associated with good fortune. At the birth of Muqali, later Chinggis Qan's viceroy in North China, "there was white vapor that arose from the tent's interior" to inform all that this was a child with a brilliant future.[60] The white vapor, however, not only signaled that the newborn infant would be fortunate, it induced or created his "luck." As one Chinese source puts it, the Mongols "take white to be the cause of good fortune."[61]

Such beliefs explain the rationale underlying other Mongolian customs. Marco Polo tells of a herd of "mares white as snow [numbering] more than ten thousand" that belonged to the qaghan. From these animals a special type of kumys was produced which was called, somewhat unexpectedly,

[54] A. N. Kononov, "Semantika tsvetooboznachenii v Tiurkskikh iazykakh," *Tiurkologicheskii sbornik, 1975* (Moscow: Nauka, 1978), pp. 159–79 and especially p. 160.

[55] O. T. Molchanova, "Zheltye tsveta v altaiskom onomastike," *Turcologica, 1986* (Leningrad: Nauka, 1986), p. 192.

[56] Peter B. Golden, "The Černii Klobouci," in Á. Berta, *et al.*, eds., *Symbolae Turcologicae* (Swedish Research Institute in Istanbul, Transactions, vol. VI: Uppsala, 1996), pp. 104–07.

[57] Owen Lattimore, *High Tartary* (Boston: Little, Brown and Co., 1930), p. 28.

[58] Omeljan Pritsak, "Orientierung und Farbsymbolik: Zu den Farbenbezeichnungen in den altaischen Volkernamen," *Speculum* 5 (1954), 376–83, and Nicholas Poppe, "The Use of Colour Names in Mongolian," *The Canada-Mongolia Review* 3/2 (1977), 118–34.

[59] N. L. Zhukovskaia, *Kategorii i simvolika traditsionnoi kul'tury mongolov* (Moscow: Nauka, 1988), pp. 154–57, and Viktorova, *Mongoly*, pp. 21–22.

[60] *YS*, ch. 119, p. 2929.

[61] Su T'ien-chüeh, *Yuan wen-lei*, ch. 57, p. 12a.

"black kumys." This black, that is, "pure," kumys, was ceremonially sprinkled on specific occasions so "that all [Qubilai's] things may prosper."[62]

While these efforts were exclusively devoted to the interests of the qaghan, there were also public ceremonies geared to the enhancement of everyone's good fortune. This is described at length by Marco Polo:

It is true that the Tartars . . . make their solemn feast which they name white at the beginning of the year in the month of February, on the kalends, that is, the first day of the year, by the Tartar computation. And the great Lord [i.e., Qubilai] and his clan and all those who are subject to him, throughout their districts, wherever they are, make of it such a feast as I shall tell you. It is the custom that the kaan with all his subjects dress themselves all in white robes, so that on that day both men and women, small and great, when they have the power to do it, are all dressed in new and white clothes and they do it because white dress seems to them lucky and good, and therefore they wear it at the beginning of their year so that they may take their good and have joy and comfort all the year.[63]

The White Festival was celebrated elsewhere in the empire and is still observed today in Mongolia as a national holiday.[64]

White, naturally, had clear political associations as well, since special good fortune or charisma was an essential attribute of kingship in steppe ideology.[65] Thus in 1206, at the proclamation of the Mongolian state, they also, according to the *Secret History*, set up the "white standard [*chagha'an tuq*] with the nine feet [i.e., tails]" or as Juvaynī rightly calls it, "the banner of Chinggis Qan's good fortune."[66] Thereafter, as Chao Hung states, the presence of the royal household was "made known by erecting a pure white banner."[67] In subsequent centuries this identification with Chinggis Qan's charisma, which was seen to inhere in his standard, was so complete that its original name, borrowed from the Turkic *tugh*, was gradually replaced by *sülde*, a Mongolian term meaning "soul," "prosperity," and "good fortune."[68]

The power attributed to this color predates the Chinggisid era. Animals

62 Marco Polo, pp. 187–88, and Odoric of Pordenone, "The Eastern Parts of the World Described," in Yule, *Cathay*, vol II, p. 239.

63 Marco Polo, p. 222.

64 Budge, *The Monks of Kūblāi Khān*, pp. 250–51; Bar Hebreaus, pp. 466 and 480; Jagchid and Hyer, *Mongolia's Culture and Society*, pp. 116–17; and N. L. Zhukovskaia, "Mongoly," in R. Sh. Dzharylgachinova and M. V. Kriukov, eds., *Kalendarnye obychai i obriady narodov Vostochnoi Azii: Novyi god* (Moscow: Nauka, 1985), pp. 179–87.

65 On white as good fortune, see Zhukovskaia, *Kategorii*, pp. 158–59. On the notion of good fortune or charisma in the nomads' political ideology, see Alessio Bombaci, "Qutluγ Bolzun!" *Ural-Altaische Jahrbücher* 36 (1965), 284–91 and 38 (1966), 13–43.

66 *SH*/Cleaves, sect. 202, p. 141; *SH*/de Rachewiltz, sect. 202, p. 114; Rashīd/Karīmī, vol. I, p. 307; Juvaynī/Qazvīnī, vol. I, p. 15; and Juvaynī/Boyle, vol. I, p. 22.

67 Chao Hung, *Meng-ta pei-lu*, p. 452, and Haenisch and Yao, *Chinesischen Gesandtenberichte*, p. 72.

68 T. D. Skrynnikov, "Sülde – The Basic Idea of the Chinggis Khan Cult," *Acta Orientalia Academiae Scientiarum Hungaricae* 46/2 (1992/93), 55–56.

sacrificed or consecrated to secure good fortune were usually white among the Parthians, Sasanians, and early Turks, as well as the Mongols of later times.[69] White is also closely associated with Manichaeanism, which moved from Iran to East Asia in the early Middle Ages. The Chinese sources regularly identify the "Religion of Light" with white dress and white-clad Manichaean electi are often portrayed in the art of Turfan.[70] The Uighurs, who converted to Manichaeanism in the eighth century, are, as is so often the case, the connecting link between the early Turks and Mongols. According to the Uighurs' own account of their rise to political dominance, recorded by Juvaynī in the thirteenth century, Būqū Khān (Bögü Qaghan), the ruler who converted to Manichaeanism, had a dream in which he saw an elderly man dressed in a white robe and carrying a white staff who informs him of his forthcoming political success. Later, his chief adviser has the same dream and Būqū Khān, confident of his good fortune, launches his campaigns of conquest.[71] This is not to argue that the Manichaeans were responsible for introducing white as a "political color" into the steppe. As others have pointed out, the Manichaeans had no monopoly on white; many other priestly estates – Brahmins, Magi, etc. – made extensive use of white apparel.[72] What is more likely is that the Uighur adoption of Manichaeanism simply reinforced an existing native equation of white, good fortune, and political charisma.

In all steppe cultures colors often represented key political concepts and most significantly for our immediate theme, gold was systematically equated with imperial authority and legitimacy. In the Mongolian world view, as Nekliudov has forcefully argued, gold (*altan*) possessed a multitude of attributes and conveyed a multitude of meanings. Among other things, it represented value, the primordial, the sun and the heavens – in opposition to silver which represented the earth and moon – and the male principle – in opposition to silver, the female principle. In summarizing his findings, Nekliudov says that gold, "besides the meaning of shining, directly connected with the solar theme," had an even more profound significance. "At its base lay first of all, two mythological ideas: eternity (indestructibility,

69 Agathangelos, *History of the Armenians*, trans. by Robert W. Thomson (Albany: State University of New York Press, 1976), p. 41; Ełishē, *History of Vardan and the Armenian War*, trans. by Robert W. Thomson (Cambridge, Mass.: Harvard University Press, 1982), p. 66; Talāt Tekin, *Irk Bitig: The Book of Omens* (Wiesbaden: Otto Harrassowitz, 1993), pp. 9, 13, and 19; and Elisabetta Chiodo, "The Horse White-as-Egg (*öndegen čaγan*): A Study of the Custom of Consecrating Animals to Deities," *Ural-Altaische Jahrbücher* n.s. 11 (1992), 125–51.

70 Liu Ts'un-yan, "Traces of Zoroastrian and Manichaean Activities in pre-T'ang China," in his *Selected Papers from the Hall of Harmonious Wind* (Leiden: E. J. Brill, 1976), pp. 40–44; Albert von Le Coq, *Buried Treasures of Chinese Turkestan* (Hong Kong: Oxford University Press, 1985), p. 58 and plate 9, between pp. 56–57; and Hans-Joachim Klimkeit, *Manichaean Art and Calligraphy* (Leiden: E. J. Brill, 1982), pp. 29, 39, 40, 44, 45, 47 and plates 10a, 11, 28, 29, 41a, 43, and 47a.

71 Juvaynī/Qazvīnī, vol. I, pp. 42–43, and Juvaynī/Boyle, vol. I, p. 58.

72 Geo Widengren, *Mani and Manichaeism* (London: Weidenfeld and Nicolson, 1961), p. 25.

agelessness) and value (initiating principle, essence), which form four semantic categories (or fields): the golden source, golden principles, golden center, and golden essence (the very highest degree of quality)" On the foundation of the symbolism, he concludes, the Mongols constructed such mythological concepts as "the golden embryo," "the golden era," and "the golden lineage."[73] Whether or not we accept Nekliudov's comprehensive formulation exactly as it stands, the essential point is that this precious metal was not simply a glittering bauble to attract the eye of the avaricious barbarian, who, as Ammianus Marcellinus says of the Huns, "burn with an infinite thirst for gold," but a substance and a *color* with deep and specific cosmological meaning for the Mongols.[74] In some social contexts gold even partook of the sacred. Thus, when Ghazan formed a coalition in 1295 to contest Baidu's claim to the throne, his adherents among the "Muslims swore an oath on the *Qur'ān* and the Mongols on gold."[75]

The reference above to the "golden lineage," is, of course, the Chinggisid line and one of the many ways in which this precious metal is linked with their imperial enterprise. Henry Serruys, who first studied this issue, has convincingly demonstrated that the Mongolian custom of equating the color gold with Chinggis Qan was a widespread phenomenon with a history that predates the founding of the empire. The data he assembled from Mongolian and Chinese texts reveal that Chinggis Qan had a golden doorsill, a golden tether (i.e., a government), a golden face, body, corpse, throne, and family/posterity. Even the historical records relating to the early Mongols were contained in a "Golden Book [*Altan Debter*]."[76]

To Serruys' textual data we can now add a recently published Uighur inscription of the Yuan era that provides further examples of this literary convention. In this source, the Uighurs, originally a nomadic people, title their own ruler *altun iduq-qut*, literally, "golden sacred good fortune"; refer to the Chinggisids, their current sovereigns, as the *altun uruq*, the "golden lineage"; and to the *altun aghiz*, the "golden tongue" of Sechen (Qubilai) Qaghan.[77]

This association of gold and imperial power was known as well to peoples quite distant, geographically and culturally, from the Mongols. According to a tradition on the origin of the *ǰasagh*, the Chinggisid law code, recounted in the Armenian chronicle of Grigor of Akanc', "an angel appeared" to the

[73] Sergei Iu. Nekliudov, "Zametki o mifologicheskoi i fol'klorno-epicheskoi simvolike y mongol'skikh narodov: simvolike zolota," *Etnografia Polska* 24/1 (1980), 65–94. Quotes from p. 86. See also Zhukovskaia, *Kategorii*, pp. 162–64, who also views gold as "the universal cosmological symbol" of the Mongols.

[74] *Ammianus Marcellinus*, trans. by John C. Rolfe (Loeb Classical Library; Cambridge, Mass.: Harvard University Press, 1958), XXXI.ii.11.

[75] Rashīd/Karīmī, vol. II, p. 902.

[76] Henry Serruys, "Mongol *Altan* 'Gold' = 'Imperial'," *Monumenta Serica* 21 (1962), 355–78.

[77] Geng Shimin and James Hamilton, "L'inscription ouigoure de la stèle commemorative des Iduq Qut de Qočo," *Turcica* 13 (1981), 17 and 19, Uighur text, and 26 and 28, French translation.

Mongols "in the guise of an eagle with golden feathers" who spoke to Chinggis Qan, revealing to him the laws by which to guide his heavenly mandated state.[78] The bird motif is, of course, widespread in shamanism. Golden birds often appear as messengers or as epiphanies of gods in the mythology of state formation in central and northern Asia.[79] The same chronicle, moreover, contains a further passage relevant to our theme. Shiramun (Shiremün), one of the officers stationed in West Asia during the 1230s, Grigor relates, was "called the 'golden pillar' by the khans because of his many victories and battles."[80] In light of Serruys' conclusions we should understand his epithet as "Imperial Pillar," or "Pillar of the Empire," a Mongolian calque of the Arabic and Persian "Pillar of the State [*rukn al-daulat*]."

Mongolian usage in this regard was manifestly inspired by older Turkic and Iranian conventions that can be traced back to the ninth century at least, since the Khotanese Saka documents employ the term "gold" for "imperial" and designate the Khotanese sovereign as the *alattuna hana*, an obvious transcription of the Turkic *altun qan*, "golden ruler."[81]

In addition to the numerous mythical and literary expressions of this formula, there were more visible manifestations as well. Most notably, the effigies of Chinggis Qan kept at the early Mongolian courts. Benedict the Pole, when he encountered Batu (r. 1237–56), the founder of the Golden Horde, on the lower Volga in 1245 saw purifying fires at the qan's camp and "beyond the fires there stood a chariot bearing a gold statue of the Emperor, which also it is their custom to worship." And further east, Carpini came across another such object of veneration placed before Güyüg's court in Mongolia.[82]

Much more gold, however, was expended to decorate the immediate environment of emperors and princes. Although Chinggis Qan, for unexplained reasons, gave away the golden tent (*altan terme*) and golden flagons (*altan gürü'e*) captured from Ong Qan to several of his favorites, Ögödei had a "golden tent," so called, P'eng Ta-ya states, because it had "posts made of gold." More accurately, Hsü Ting adds that the "threshhold and the posts are completely overlaid with gold."[83] Thrones, naturally, were finished in the same fashion. When Chinggis Qan returned to Mongolia

78 Grigor of Akancʿ, "Nation of Archers," 289 and 291.

79 On this theme, see Jan Gonda, *The Functions and Significance of Gold in the Veda* (Leiden: E. J. Brill, 1991), pp. 184–90; A. P. Okladnikov, "Notes on the Beliefs and Religion of the Ancient Mongols: The Golden-Winged Eagle in Mongolian History," *Acta Ethnographica Academiae Scientiarum Hungaricae* 13 (1964), 411–14; and Manabu Waida, "Birds in the Mythology of Sacred Kingship," *East and West* n.s. 28 (1978), 283–89.

80 Grigor of Akancʿ, "Nation of Archers," 319. See also 377.

81 Harold W. Bailey, "Altun Khan," *Bulletin of the School of Oriental and African Studies* 30/1 (1967), 95, 96, and 99.

82 See *Mongol Mission*, p. 80 for quote and p. 9 for Carpini's account, and *Sinica Franciscana*, pp. 37–38 and 137.

83 *SH*/Cleaves, sect. 187, p. 114; *SH*/de Rachewiltz, sect. 187, p. 95; P'eng and Hsü, *Hei-ta*

from western Turkestan in 1224 "he ordered that they were to build a great camp [*ūrdū-ī buzurg*] and make a golden throne [*takhtī-i zarīn*]."[84] His descendents followed this precedent. Carpini saw Güyüg on a "dais richly ornamented with gold and silver," and Abagha, Rashīd al-Dīn records, expired on a "throne of gold [*kursī-i zarīn*]."[85] Finally, in the northwestern precincts of the Mongolian domains, Özbek also used gold and gold imagery to proclaim his lineage and majesty. According to Ibn Baṭṭūṭah, this ruler had a "Gold Pavilion" held up with "wooden rods covered with plaques of gold"; later on in his journeys, the Arab traveler visited a palace in New Sarai on the Volga called *Altūn Tāsh*, "the Golden Rock."[86] The combined effect of the sumptuous clothing and surroundings, as when Ghazan "placed a jewel-studded crown upon his head, the likes of which no one had seen, fastened on a matching belt, and clothed himself in extremely precious gold brocade robes [*jāmah-hāi zar-baft*]"[87] in the aforementioned golden pavilion at Ūjān, must have been dazzling in the extreme, and an unfailing means of projecting majesty and provoking awe. Clearly, Mongolian rulers, from the frontiers of Russia to North China, took special care to associate their person and their surroundings with this precious metal.

Gold, of course, is a widely recognized symbol of wealth, majesty, and power but it was not explicitly equated with imperial authority by other peoples of Eurasia in the Middle Ages.[88] This is true of the Chinese, who used yellow as the imperial color. And even the Jürchens, whose dynastic name Chin means "gold" in Chinese, understood its symbolic meaning in a different cosmological context. The Jürchens adopted the name "gold," according to their own traditions, because in their pre-dynastic phase one of their sacred early settlements was along the An-ch'un River, a tributary of the Sungari, the native form of which, *ancūn* or *alcūn*, meant "gold."[89] Moreover, it must be remembered that the Jürchens were not nomads, but forest peoples whose political tutors were the Chinese who quickly fitted the Jürchens dynastic name *chin*, also signifying metal in general, into the ancient Chinese Five Agents theory – the cycle of water, fire, metal, earth, and wood – for their own ideological ends.[90] Nor did the Mongols borrow the equation from the imperial traditions of the western end of Eurasia. The ʿAbbāsid Caliphate, which the Mongols brought down in 1258, used black,

shih-lüeh, pp. 473 and 474; and Haenisch and Yao, *Chinesischen Gesandtenberichte*, pp. 104 and 105.

84 Rashīd/Karīmī, vol. I, p. 383.

85 *Mongol Mission*, p. 82; *Sinica Franciscana*, p. 139; and Rashīd/Karīmī, vol. II, p. 779.

86 Ibn Baṭṭūṭah/Gibb, vol. II, pp. 483 and 503.

87 Rashīd/Karīmī, vol. II, p. 949.

88 See the comments of Clark, *Symbols of Excellence*, pp. 10 and 50–57.

89 The modern name is the A-she, a right affluent of the Sungari. See Lucien Gibert, *Dictionnaire historique et géographique de la Mandchourie* (Hong Kong: Imprimerie de la societé Missions-Estrangéres, 1934), pp. 72 and 94.

90 Hok-lam Chan, *Legitimation in Imperial China: Discussions under the Jürchen-Chin Dynasty (1115–1234)* (Seattle: University of Washington Press, 1984), pp. 55, 75–78, 80, and 144.

and very briefly green.[91] The Byzantines, it is true, used much gold for imperial display but in most cases it was combined with purple, particularly in royal vestments and decrees (chrysobulls).[92] Precedent for such pairing can be traced back to the Iranian and Hellenistic monarchies.[93] This partnership, however, was hardly equal. Purple, whose symbolic power rested in an extremely expensive dye derived from a Mediterranean marine snail, originated as a prestige color as early as the fourteenth century BC.[94] Its use grew under the Assyrians and was institutionalized as the imperial color by the Achaemenids, a practice that subsequently was widely diffused by Alexander the Great.[95] By the Byzantine era, both native and foreign sources clearly affirm that purple was systematically and explicitly equated with sovereignty and imperial majesty. After all, Byzantine emperors were to the purple born.[96]

Purple, as a political color, did circulate among the nomads as Manichaeanism spread to the East. When the Uighur qaghan Bögü converted in the eighth century he mounted his throne in a robe an early Turkic text describes as *al*, "crimson" or "scarlet."[97] In evaluating these data it must be remembered that to the ancients purple was not the modern color, a hue midway between red and blue, but any deep shade of red. In this context, then, *al* was certainly intended to convey the color purple in its political sense. There is a later echo of this tradition in the Mongolian era: at the time of the Uighur ruler's submission in 1209 he requested, according to the *Secret History*, a "shred" of Chinggis Qan's "crimson robe [*al de'el*]."[98] In the Chinese interlinear translation of this text the Mongolian *al* is defined

[91] See Hilāl al-Ṣābi', *Rusūm Dār al-Khilāfah: The Rules and Regulations of the 'Abbāsid Court*, trans. by Elie A. Salem (Beirut: American University of Beirut, 1977), pp. 73–74, and Bar Hebreaus, p. 212.

[92] Anna Comnena, *The Alexiad*, trans. by E. R. A. Sewter (New York: Penguin Books, 1985), pp. 42, 93, and 434, and John Kinnamos, *Deeds of John and Manuel Comnenus*, trans. by Charles M. Brand (New York: Columbia University Press, 1976), pp. 37, 156, and 187.

[93] Quintus Curtius, *History of Alexander*, III.iii.17, IV.i.21–23, VIII.ix.24, and IX.vii.10–16.

[94] See J. H. Munro, "The Medieval Scarlet and the Economics of Sartorial Splendor," in N. B. Harte and K. G. Panting, eds., *Cloth and Clothing in Medieval Europe: Essays in Memory of Professor E. M. Carus-Wilson* (London: Heineman, 1983), pp. 14–15. On the manufacture of purple dye see Lloyd B. Jensen, "Royal Purple of Tyre," *Journal of Near Eastern Studies* 22 (1963), 104–18.

[95] Meyer Reinhold, *History of Purple as a Status Symbol in Antiquity* (Brussels: Latomus, 1970), pp. 8, 17–19, 29–33, and 62–73; Xenophon, *Cyropaedia*, trans. by Walter Miller (Loeb Classical Library; Cambridge, Mass.: Harvard University Press, 1914), VIII.iii.13; and Xenophon, *Anabasis*, trans. by Carleton L. Bronson (Loeb Classical Library; Cambridge, Mass.: Harvard University Press, 1918), I.ii.20.

[96] Anna Comnena, *The Alexiad*, pp. 17, 20, 47, 92, 101, 103, and 113; Bar Hebreaus, pp. 25, 66, 69–70, 76, and 83; and Moses Khorenats'i, *History of the Armenians*, trans. by Robert W. Thomson (Cambridge, Mass.: Harvard University Press, 1978), p. 258.

[97] W. Bang and A. von Gabain, "Türkische Turfan-Texte, II, Manichaica," *Sitzungsberichte der Preussischen Akademie der Wissenchaften, Phil.-Hist. klasse* 22 (1929), 416, Turkic text and 417, German translation.

[98] *SH*/de Rachewiltz, sect. 238, p. 136, and *SH*/Cleaves, sect. 238, p. 172.

by the Chinese *ta-hung*, "crimson" or "vermillion."[99] The same color term was also used to designate one of the imperial seals, *al tamgha*, in possession of Chinggis Qan and his successors. Interestingly, this vermillion seal is often paired with the golden plaque (*altan gerege*), or badge of authority.[100] Thus, while "purple" penetrated the steppe, its influence was always marginal and it never seriously rivaled gold as the imperial color.

Gold, although a frequent means of displaying majesty, was not then a primary political color of any sedentary state, east or west, that was contemporary or nearly contemporary to the Mongols. There is a precedent in the ancient Near East where the Assyrian kings used clothing bedecked with gold ornaments as *vestis regia*, but their usage was far too remote in time to have served as a model for the Mongols.[101]

The roots of the Mongols' political preoccupation with gold are rather to be sought in the political traditions of the steppe, where both the metal and the color have long been equated with political authority. As Serruys points out, the immediate predecessors of the Mongols in the Eastern Steppe all used gold to signal their political aspirations and pretensions.[102] The qaghan of the nomadic Uighurs, for example, lived in a tent of gold and "sat upon a golden throne [*altunlugh örgin*]."[103] Such a practice, however, can be found much further afield and much further back in time. Mas'ūd, the sultan (r. 1030–41) of the Ghaznavids, a slave dynasty of Turkic origin, had a golden throne, with gold brocade cushions, that was set upon a dais draped with Rumī gold brocade. And Oghuz Qan, the legendary progenitor of Oghuz Turks, ruled, purportedly, from "a large pavilion, all the wooden parts of which were covered with gold."[104] Earlier, Zemarchus, the Byzantine envoy to the first Türk Qaghanate in 569–71 met the nomadic ruler in a valley of the "Golden Mountain." On the first day the qaghan was in a tent lined with multicolored silk and sat on a golden throne. On the second day he was in another pavilion, also lined with multicolored silk and sat on "a couch made completely of gold" around which there were golden urns,

99 *Yuan-chao pi-shih*, ed. by B. I. Pankratov (Moscow: Izdatel'stvo vostochnoi literatury, 1962), sect. 218, p. 467.

100 Juvaynī/Qazvīnī, vol. I, pp. 114, 116, etc.; Juvaynī/Boyle, vol. I, pp. 145, 148, etc.; and Francis W. Cleaves, "The Mongolian Documents in the Musée de Téhéran," *HJAS* 16 (1957), 26–27, 32–33, and 50, note 23. On Mongolian seals, see Paul Pelliot, "Notes sur le 'Turkestan' de M. W. Bartold," *T'oung-pao* 27 (1930), 35–38.

101 A. Leo Oppenheim, "The Golden Garments of the Gods," *Journal of Near Eastern Studies* 8/3 (1949), 172–93.

102 Serruys, "Mongol *Altan*," p. 377 and notes 59 and 60.

103 Vladimir M. Minorsky, "Tamīn ibn Barh's Journey to the Uighurs," *Bulletin of the School of Oriental and African Studies* 12/2 (1948), 283; Bang and von Gabain, "Türkische Turfan-Texte, II, Manichaica," 416, Turkic text and 417, German translation. See also Tekin, *Irk Bitig*, p. 9.

104 Clifford E. Bosworth, *The Ghaznavids: Their Empire in Afghanistan and Eastern Iran, 994–1040* (Edinburgh University Press, 1963), pp. 135–36, and Abu-l-Ghazi, *Rodoslovnaia Turkmen: Sochinenie Abu-l-Ghazi Khana Khivinskogo*, trans. by A. A. Kononov (Moscow-Leningrad: Izdatel'stvo akademii nauk SSSR, 1958), p. 48.

water-sprinklers, and pitchers. On the third day the audience was held in yet another tent "in which there were gilded wooden pillars and a couch of beaten gold which was supported by four golden peacocks."[105] At the very same time Zemarchus was in the qaghan's camp, the Chinese Buddhist pilgrim Sung Yün passed through the territory of the Hephthalites in southern Turkestan. He records that their ruler "sat on a golden chair supported by four phoenixes as legs" and that his wife, when she "went out . . . was seated in a golden, bejewelled sedan, carried on the back of a 'six-tusked' white elephant."[106] Finally, it should be noted that there is archeological, literary, and linguistic evidence that the "golden bow" was the principal symbol of political authority among the European Huns.[107]

The ethnic and linguistic affiliations of the Hephthalites and Huns remain clouded but some scholars hold that the former were Tokharians and therefore Indo-European in origin. There is no doubt, however, that the equation of gold with political authority long predates the emergence of the Turkic and Mongolian nomads, since it is in evidence among the Scythians, an Iranian-speaking people, and the earliest steppe society on which we have extended and reliable literary documentation.

According to the Scythians' own traditions, recorded by Herodotus, their progenitor, Targitaus, produced three sons. When they reached maturity four gold implements, a plough, yoke, battle axe, and drinking cup fell suddenly from the sky. When first the eldest, and then the second brother approached this treasure it burst into flames. When, however, the youngest reached toward these objects, the fire died and he carried the four implements home. In light of this demonstration, the two elder brothers took counsel and gave the kingdom over to the younger. Thereafter the golden treasure from on high became the center of an elaborate cult. The Royal Scythians, the inner core of the state, guarded this gold assiduously and offered sacrifices in its honor.[108]

This famous passage has often been mined for insights into the social structure and ideological life of the early nomads and their Indo-Iranian kin.[109] Most recently, B. A. Litvinskii has outlined the literary and archeological evidence to show that the equation – gold, the sun, fire, and sovereign authority – explicit in the Scythian myth, was a pervasive and central idea in early Indo-Iranian cultures.[110] And it is important to recall

[105] Menander, *The History of Menander the Guardsman*, trans. by R. B. Blockley (Liverpool: Francis Cairns Publications Ltd., 1985), pp. 119 and 121.

[106] Yang Hsüan-chih, *A Record of Buddhist Monasteries*, pp. 225–26.

[107] J. Harmatta, "The Golden Bow of the Huns," *Acta Archaeologica Academiae Scientiarum Hungaricae* 1 (1951), 107–49.

[108] Herodotus, *The Persian Wars*, IV.5–7.

[109] G. Dumézil, "La société scythique avait-elle des classes fonctionnelles?" *Indo-Iranian Journal* 5/3 (1962), 187–202, and A. M. Khazanov, "Legenda o proiskhozhdenii Skifov (Gerodot, IV. 5–7)," in *Skifskii mir* (Kiev: Naukova dumka, 1975), pp. 74–93.

[110] B. A. Litvinskii, "'Zolotye liudi' v drevnikh pogrebeniiakh Tsentral'noi Azii (opyt istolk-

in this regard that while Tengri in time assumed a dominant position in the religious and ideological life of the empire, the young Temüjin, as we have already seen, also made obeisance and sacrificed to the sun (*naran*), to whose favor he attributed his improving personal and political fortunes.[111]

The intimate linkage between the sun, imperial authority, and the color gold has, therefore, a continuous history that can be traced back to deep antiquity, a history that all of the nomads, Iranian, Turkic, and Mongolian, have in their turn shared. In the latter case, this linkage is perhaps most strikingly exemplified in the regulations on royal burial found in the *Yuan shih*. Here it is specified that when an emperor dies, his body is placed in a coffin of fragrant wood secured with "four golden bands." The imperial casket is then placed on a carriage "draped with blue-green *nasīj*" and the coffin itself is covered in "*nasīj*." The funeral procession was led by a "mounted Mongolian shamaness leading a horse with saddle and bridle of embellished gold and caparisoned in *nasīj*." The animal so led was called "the golden spirit horse" and presumably accompanied his deceased master to the beyond.[112] The question of how far these prescriptions were followed in practice in the Yuan realm cannot be verified but it is noteworthy that Marco Polo speaks generally of mounts sacrificed and buried with deceased qans and that Carpini heard rumors that the graves of the emperors and princes were full of precious metals. The latter practice is confirmed by the Persian historian Ḥāfiẓ-i Abrū, who reports that when Öljeitü (r. 1304–16) died, he was buried with "so much gold, ornaments, hats, belts and gilded bejewelled pieces [*muraṣṣaʿāt*]" that his tomb was "said to be a veritable treasure house."[113]

This set of customs, too, has antecedents among the Iranian and Indo-European peoples, both nomadic and settled. The burial of horses with their noble masters was of course quite common in Eurasian cultural history. More specifically, the "Golden Spirit Horse" has an analogue in the ancient Indic tradition by which a horse properly sacrificed in gold-bedecked cloth knows the way to heaven and can serve as a guide to gods or souls.[114] Interment with gold was equally widespread and well-documented in literary and archaeological sources. Qipchaqs buried their chieftans in clothing decorated with gold thread and plaques, while the Türk and

ovaniia v svete istorii religii)," *Sovetskaia etnografiia*, no. 4 (1982), 34–43. See also the comments of Gonda, *Functions and Significance of Gold*, pp. 8–10, 21–24, 54–63, and 216.

111 *SH*/de Rachewiltz, sect. 103, p. 40, and *SH*/Cleaves, sect. 103, p. 37. See also Marie-Lise Beffa, "Le concept de *Tänggärii*, 'ciel,' dans l'*Histoire Secréte des Mongols*," *Études mongoles et sibériennes* 24 (1993), 215–36.

112 *YS*, ch. 77, pp. 1925–26.

113 Marco Polo, p. 168; *Mongol Mission*, p. 13; *Sinica Franciscana*, p. 43; and Ḥāfiẓ-i Abrū, *Ẕayl jāmiʿ al-tavārīkh-i Rashīdī*, p. 120.

114 Stuart Piggot, *Wagon, Chariot and Carriage: Symbols and Status in the History of Transportation* (New York: Thames and Hudson, 1992), pp. 108–22, and Gonda, *Functions and Significance of Gold*, pp. 114 and 129–31.

Hsiung-nu placed gold objects in the graves of their nobles.[115] The Kushan royal line interred its own in glittering fashion: The six royal tombs uncovered at Tillya-tepe in northern Afghanistan, which date to the beginning of the Christian era, contained in total some 20,000 gold pieces as well as textiles of cotton and silk embroidered with gold thread and pearls.[116] Earlier, in the fifth or fourth century B.C., the Saka occupying the area near modern-day Alma Ata buried one of their princes in a splendid suit, belt, and headdress of gold.[117] And about a century before this, the Achaemenids, according to Strabo and Arrian, laid Cyrus the Great (r. 559–30) to rest in a golden coffin in a chamber containing a golden couch.[118] Interestingly, the Mongols' use of these ancient funerary customs was probably strengthened, though certainly not initiated, by familiarity with elements of the "Alexander Romance" which had circulated in the steppe from early times.[119] In the Mongolian version of his life, which mirrors earlier Greek and Armenian traditions, Alexander the Great requests, when death nears, that he be buried with large amounts of gold.[120]

The underlying reason for this practice was the incorruptability of gold, which was viewed as a means of preventing decay in the grave. For the nomads, gold possessed, therefore, some of the cosmological significance and ritual functions of jade in Chinese society. In the Chou period jade amulets were placed in the graves of notables to slow decomposition and later on royalty was entombed in elaborate burial suits composed of

[115] Ingeborg Petraschech-Heim, "Die Mittelalterlichen Textilfunde von Kordlar Tepe," *Archaeologische Mitteilungen aus Iran* 15 (1982), 287; Thomas S. Noonan, "Rus, Pechenegs and Polovtsy: Economic Interaction along the Steppe Frontier in the Pre-Mongol Era," *Russian History* 19 (1992), 319; S. Klyashtorny, D. Savinov and V. Shkoda, "The Golden Bracteatus from Mongolia: A Byzantine Motif in the Central Asian Toreutics," *Information Bulletin, International Association for the Study of Cultures of Central Asia* 16 (1984), 5–19; and Ssu-ma Ch'ien, *Records of the Grand Historian of China*, trans. by Burton Watson (New York: Columbia University Press, 1961), vol. II, p. 164.

[116] Victor Sarianidi, "The Treasure of the Golden Mound," *Archaeology* 33/3 (May–June 1980), 31–41.

[117] K. A. Akishev, *Kurgan Issyk: Iskusstvo sakov Kazakhstana* (Moscow: Iskusstvo, 1978), pp. 43–47, and L. A. Lelekov, "O simvolizme pogrebal'nykh oblachenii (zolotye liudi skifosakskogo mira)," in A. I. Martynov and V. I. Molodin, eds., *Skifo-Sibirskii mir: Iskusstvo i ideologiia* (Novosibirsk: Izdatel'stvo Nauka, Sibirskoe otdelenie, 1987), pp. 25–30. More accessible is Larisa R. Pavlinskaya, "The Scythians and Sakians, Eighth to Third Centuries B.C.," in Basilov, *Nomads of Eurasia*, pp. 24–33.

[118] Strabo, *The Geography of Strabo*, trans. by H. L. Jones (The Loeb Classical Library; Cambridge, Mass.: Harvard University Press, 1954), XV.iii.7; and Arrian, *History of Alexander and Indica*, trans. by E. Iliff Robson (Loeb Classical Library; Cambridge, Mass.: Harvard University Press, 1958), VI.29. Both authors' data go back to the lost history of Aristoboulus, who served at Alexander's court and was charged with investigating Cyrus' desecrated tomb at Pasargadae.

[119] John A. Boyle, "The Alexander Legend in Central Asia," *Folklore* 85 (1974), 217–28.

[120] Francis W. Cleaves, "An Early Mongolian Version of the Alexander Romance," *HJAS* 22 (1959), 45, Mongolian text and 61, English translation. Cf. Pseudo-Callisthenes, *The Romance of Alexander the Great*, trans. by Albert Mugrdich Wolohojian (New York: Columbia University Press, 1969), pp. 101 and 105.

thousands of wafer thin jade plaques.[121] Gold did gain a measure of popularity in China, particularly after intensified contact with the western regions in the Han and T'ang, when precious metals became more common in Chinese decorative arts. Nonetheless, gold, while it found a place in Chinese culture, never managed to supplant jade (or bronze) as a symbol of wealth and status.[122] This, of course, stands in sharp contrast to preferences of the nomads, for whom gold played a pivotal role in their political, artistic, and mythological life. In the realm of color symbolism, as in matters of clothing and cloth, the Mongols, as we shall see in the next chapter, had greater affinities with the Iranian than with the Chinese cultural world.

While gold was obviously the imperial color and *nasīj*, consequently, the imperial cloth, there remains the intriguing question of how the Mongols came to know and apply this very ancient political equation: was it taught to them anew by their more literate and politically sophisticated neighbors such as the Uighurs, or was knowledge of this venerable tradition already within the public domain, part of their own folk culture? The larger issue of how the imperial traditions of the steppe were conveyed over time has yet to be investigated, but in this particular instance there is reason to believe that folklore and mythology played a prominent role in the complex process of *translatio imperii*. The main evidence supporting this assertion comes from Rashīd al-Dīn's account of the history of the Onggirad, the consort clan of the Chinggisids, in which he relates and comments upon the following tradition:

They recount that their origin is such: Three sons were born of a golden vessel. These words ought certainly to be [seen as] portents and allusions. The meaning of this was that the person who had brought these sons into the world was inherently intelligent, accomplished, very refined and well-bred. They likened him [or her][123] to a golden vessel primarily because this usage is current among the Mongols, for they have a custom upon seeing the emperor to exclaim, "we saw the golden face of the emperor," [by which] is understood [his] heart of gold. And this very same metaphor and phraseology is in use among the other tribes, for gold is a noble and much needed substance and extremely pure and immaculate.[124]

Rashīd al-Dīn's interpolations aside, the Onggirad tradition he records derives from a Mongolian informant, most probably Bolad Aqa (d. 1313),

[121] Bertold Laufer, *Jade: A Study in Chinese Archaeology and Religion*, repr. (New York: Dover Publications, 1974), pp. 294–305; Robert L. Thorp, *Son of Heaven: Imperial Arts of China* (Seattle: Son of Heaven Press, 1988), pp. 178–81; and S. P. M. H., "Jade Shroud Found," *Archaeology* 49/3 (1996) 28.

[122] Bo Gyllensvärd, "T'ang Gold and Silver," *Bulletin of the Museum of Far Eastern Antiquities* 29 (1957), 3–9, and Emma C. Bunker, "Gold in the Ancient Chinese world: A Cultural Puzzle," *Artibus Asiae* 53 (1993), 27–50.

[123] Or possibly "her," since gender is not indicated by the Persian pronoun *ū*.

[124] Rashīd al-Dīn, *Jāmiʿ al-tavārīkh*, ed. by Alizade, vol. I, pt. 1, pp. 389–90.

famed among his own people as an expert on the tribes and their genealogies, and therefore tells us much about the imagery and associations of gold in Mongolian folk culture in the thirteenth century. First, there are elements here – the three brothers and the golden implement – that echo, albeit in a much distorted fashion, the ethnogenetic myth of the Scythians. Second, as Nekliudov has argued on the basis of other data, gold is equated with the most elevated qualities, purity, etc. Third, the Mongolian people project such qualities on to the person of their emperor and address him accordingly. Last, Rashīd al-Dīn asserts that the equation gold = imperial is widespread among the nomadic tribes.

While his data do not definitively prove the case, they strongly suggest that the connection between gold and political authority was an idea rooted in and transmitted by the nomads' folk culture, an idea, therefore, that the Chinggisids did not need to learn from outsiders, or even reinvent and revivify for the benefit of their nomadic adherents when they launched their quest for empire.

CHAPTER 5

Cultural transmission

The Mongols' well-documented preference for *nasīj* is hardly surprising for a culture that attributed great symbolic weight to cloth, particularly in the form of clothing, and to color, most specifically gold. This, however, was only one of the components of the West Asian textile tradition they adopted and transported to East Asia. As we shall see, other kinds of cloth together with tents, clothing conventions, personnel, technologies, and perhaps even dyes reach China under Mongolian auspices.

In approaching the issue of transfer it should be borne in mind that Islamic culture possessed, in the words of Lisa Golombek, "a textile mentality" which made extensive use of cloth not only in clothing but in the home, where carpets, curtains, and cushions to a large extent replaced furniture, doors, and walls.[1] This, of course, was quite compatible with nomadic usage, in which housing, mobile and not fixed, was largely constructed and festooned with textiles and carpets. On this level, at least, the two societies had much in common, and the Mongols, understandably borrowed heavily from their Muslim subjects, who, of course, were themselves the heirs to the rich clothing culture of Iran and the ancient Near East.

In addition to the very visible *nasīj*, several other types of Muslim fabric are found in the East. Some, such as *zandanīchī*, a textile originally produced in Zandanah, a village near Bukhara, are only mentioned by Islamic authors.[2] In the *Rasūlid Hexaglot*, a fourteenth-century Yemeni vocabulary, the Persian *zandanījī* is equated with the Mongolian **bürme*, an unattested form; unexpectedly, these terms, together with the Turkic *zandi*, are defined by the control language, Arabic, as a "kind of cotton garment (*nauʿ min thiyāb al-qutn*)." This, of course, contradicts the accepted view

[1] Lisa Golombek, "The Draped Universe of Islam," in Priscilla Soucek, ed., *Content and Context of Visual Arts in the Islamic World: Papers from a Colloquium in Memory of Richard Ettinghausen* (University Park and London: The Pennsylvania State University Press, 1988), pp. 25–50 and especially p. 30.

[2] Juvaynī/Qazvīnī, vol. I, p. 59; Juvaynī/Boyle, vol. I, p. 77, and Smirnova, *ʿAjāʾib al-dunyā*, p. 493, Persian text and p. 185, Russian translation.

that *zandanīchī* was made of silk.[3] Other West Asian textiles are attested, sometimes in their native nomenclature, in the Chinese sources. The chapter on official dress in the *Yuan shih* records "garments of *ch'ing*-colored[4] *su-fu* with gold brocade trimmings." "*Su-fu*," the text adds, "is a pure type of Muslim woolen cloth."[5] Here we have the Chinese transcription of the Arabic *ṣūf*, "wool."

There are also references to *mao-tuan*, literally, "hair satin," which is the Chinese name for the textile known to the Europeans as camlet. This, too, is a West Asian cloth, one which the Chinese knew as a foreign product before the coming of the Mongols. Chao Ju-kua, Sung Inspector of Foreign Trade in Fukien, who wrote in the early thirteenth century but whose sources date from an earlier period, states that "camel-hair satin of all colors [*wu-se t'o-mao tuan*]" is produced in Chi-tz'u-ni, a probable reference to Ghazna in Afghanistan, and later that "colored hair satin" is found in Lu-mei, clearly Rūm or Asia Minor.[6] Once the Mongols occupied China, hair satin, heretofore an occasional overseas import, became a domestically made product. The *Yuan shih* notes the existence of two "Gold Brocade Hair Satin Offices [*Na-shih-shih mao-tuan chü*]" but gives no information as to their founding or location.[7] Marco Polo, fortunately, has some helpful comments on this cloth. In describing Calacian, the capital of Tangut, that is, Ninghsia in Kansu, he says that the city was inhabited by idolators, Muslims and Christians and that in this locale there

> are made many cloths which are called camlets of camels hair, the most beautiful that are to be found in the world and the best; and again of white wool, for they have white camels; they make of it white camlet very beautiful and good, and they make very great quantity of it and thence many of the said camlets are sent for sale to other parts, or merchants carry them to sell through many places and especially to Catai [Cathay] and to other places through the midst of the world.[8]

Marco Polo's passage is the earliest European description of this stuff, and as Pelliot rightly remarks, the Venetian's account of its manufacture casts doubt on the derivation of the word camlet from the Arabic *khamlah*, "nap" or "pile," and strongly suggests that the term is to be associated with

[3] Peter B. Golden, ed., *The Rasūlid Hexaglot*, forthcoming, f. 11r, col. B, and Dorothy G. Shepard and W. B. Henning, "Zandanījī Identified?" in Richard Ettinghausen, ed., *Aus der Welt der islamischen Kunst: Festschrift für Ernst Kühnel zum 75 Geburtstag* (Berlin: Gebr. Mann Verlag, 1959), pp. 15–40.

[4] *ch'ing* is variously translated as "blue," "green," or "the color of nature."

[5] *YS*, ch. 78, p. 1938.

[6] Chau Ju-kua, *His Work on Chinese and Arab Trade in the Twelfth and Thirteenth Centuries, entitled Chu-fan-chi*, trans. by Friedrich Hirth and W. W. Rockhill, repr. (Taipei: Literature House, 1965), pp. 138 and 141. In this text the editors translate "colored hair satin [*se mao-tuan*]" as "colored woolen stuffs." See further, Paul Wheatley, "Geographical Notes on Some Commodities Involved in Sung Maritime Trade," *Journal of the Malayan Branch of the Royal Asiatic Society* 32/2 (1961), 121.

[7] *YS*, ch. 85, p. 2150.

[8] Marco Polo, p. 181. He also notes, p. 272, that in Tibet there "is camlet enough."

the camel, the supplier of the raw material from which it was made.[9] In any event, the production site was well chosen since down to this century Kansu was arguably the major center of Bactrian camel breeding in all of Asia.[10]

Another textile of foreign origin produced in Yuan China was made by the Sa-ta-la-ch'i Superintendency which was under the general direction of the Ministry of Works, a branch of the central government. In the somewhat cryptic phrasing of the *Yuan shih* this body came into being in 1287 when the Ministry "used Cha-ma-la-ting to lead civil artisans to make *sa-ta-la-ch'i*, which was produced together with silk in the same office. Consequently they changed the Silk Civil Artisans Superintendency to the *Sa-ta-la-ch'i* Superintendency."[11] As I understand this passage, a certain Jamāl al-Dīn, obviously a Muslim, brought in weavers to make the material in question and they were initially attached to another Superintendency for rations and quarters; and then, sometime after 1287, that Superintendency was converted over to the production of *sa-ta-la-ch'i* and appropriately redesignated. While this Superintendency and its officials are mentioned several times in the Chinese sources, the term *sa-ta-la-ch'i*, clearly of non-Chinese origin, is never defined.[12] Happily, a convincing explanation is now at hand; according to Francis W. Cleaves, *sa-ta-la-ch'i* transcribes an unattested Mongolian form, **sadragh*, which goes back to a Turkic original, *sädräk*.[13] The latter, found in Kāshghārī, the eleventh-century lexicographer, in the couplet *sädräk böz*, is there defined as "loosely woven [*muhalhal al-nasīj*] cloth."[14]

The *Yuan shih* further records the occasional presentation of something called "western brocade [*hsi-chin*]." These bestowals, which went to both military and civilian officials, began in Ögödei's reign and continued into Qubilai's.[15] Again, no formal definition of the term is offered but some light, albeit oblique, is cast on its character and manufacture by the following passage, *sub anno* 1287, from the *Yuan shih*: "The Hung-chou artisan officials used dog and rabbit hair to make garments similar to those of western brocade [*hsi-chin*] for presentation [to the court]. The receiving artisan officials acknowledged Hung-chou ['s gift]."[16] It appears, then, that

9 Pelliot, *Notes on Marco Polo*, vol. I, pp. 143–45. Later on camlet was known as watered cloth or mohair, and was made of diverse materials such as silk and wool, especially angora. See David French, "A Sixteenth Century English Merchant in Ankara?," *Anatolian Studies* 22 (1972), 242–43.

10 E. I. Kychanov, *Ocherki istorii Tangutskogo gosudarstva* (Moscow: Nauka, 1968), p. 80.

11 *YS*, ch. 85, p. 2149, and Farquhar, *Government*, p. 208.

12 *Yuan tien-chang*, ch. 7, pp. 12a, 16b, and 21b, and T'ao Tsung-i, *Nan-ts'un cho keng-lu* (Ssu-pu ts'ung-k'an ed.), ch. 21, p. 12b.

13 Francis W. Cleaves, "The Vocable *Sa-ta-la-ch'i* in the *Yuan shih* and the *Yuan tien-chang*," *Ural-Altaische Jahrbücher*, n.s. 10 (1991), 128–35.

14 Maḥmūd al-Kāšγarī, *Compendium of the Turkic Dialects* (*Dīwān Luγāt at-Turk*), trans. by Robert Dankoff (Sources of Oriental Languages and Literatures, vol. VII; Cambridge, Mass.: Printed at the Harvard University Printing Office, 1982), pt. I, p. 356.

15 *YS*, ch. 5, p. 97, ch. 8, p. 159, ch. 10, p. 215, and ch. 149, p. 3517.

16 *YS*, ch. 14, p. 199.

at least part of the "western brocade" granted by the court was, like *nasīj* and camlet, domestically produced.

Western-style tentage was also part of this package. Tents, as the famed Arab historian Ibn Khaldūn noted, are "one of the emblems of royal authority," which, he continues, are "used for display on journies."[17] The use of sumptuous pavilions for such purposes can be traced back to the Achaemenids, who established a tradition subsequently followed by both Muslim and Christian polities in West Asia.[18]

For the nomads, tents had great practical and symbolic importance. They were their main domicile, which efficiently protected them from the harsh climatic conditions of the steppe; at the same time, the directional orientation and internal spaces of tents had specific cosmological meanings.[19] When nomadic peoples formed states, elaborate tents were extensively used to display the grandeur and wealth of the ruler and his court. Marco Polo relates a revealing, if somewhat fanciful, incident relating to this theme. When Ulau (Hülegü) marched north beyond Darband to meet his rival Berca (Berke), he established a camp in which "there were many rich pavilions and many rich tents." Not to be outdone, Berke in his turn made camp some miles from Hülegü, which Marco Polo asserts

> was quite as beautiful as that of Ulau and as rich; for I tell you truly that whoever should have seen the pavilions of cloth of gold and of silk and the rich tents and precious stones and pearls which were in that camp could well say that scarcely ever was seen a more beautiful camp and more rich.[20]

The Venetian was not an eyewitness to this encounter, which took place several years before he arrived in the East, but it is not difficult to believe that princely rivals among the Chinggisids deployed, as Marco Polo claims, sumptuous tents as well as armed force in their confrontations.

The tentage used by the nomads falls into two very distinct typological categories: the native yurt (Mongolian *ger*), whose integrity rested on an internal trellis-work supporting the walls, and the pavilions of West Asian provenance, whose stability depended on external guy ropes. In the literary descriptions of such tentage, it is not always easy to distinguish the two, since they often shared common characteristics: great size and elaborate ornamentation. But as A. P. Andrews rightly remarks, it is clear that under conditions of empire the scaled-up trellis-walled tents as well as the guyed

17 Ibn Khaldūn, *The Muqaddimah: An Introduction to History*, trans. by Franz Rosenthal (New York: Pantheon Books, 1958), vol. II, pp. 67 and 69.
18 Quintus Curtius, *History of Alexander*, III.xi.23 and XIII.ii.; Vivian, *The Georgian Chronicle*, p. 2; and Serjeant, *Islamic Textiles*, pp. 159–60.
19 Nurila Zh. Shakhanova, "The Yurt in the Traditional Worldview of the Central Asian Nomads," in Gary Seaman, ed., *Foundations of Empire: Archaeology and Art of the Eurasian Steppe* (Los Angeles: Ethnographics Press, 1992), pp. 157–83.
20 Marco Polo, pp. 478 and 479.

pavilions were products, in both construction and decoration, of sedentary, non-nomadic artisanship.[21]

The chronology of the Mongols' acquisition of West Asian tentage can be reconstructed in broad terms. In the *Secret History* the tents of rulers such as Ong Qan of the Kereyid or Asha Gambu the Tangut, are regularly styled *terme ger*, "trellis-walled tent," or *altan terme*, "golden trellis-walled [tent]."[22] Only after their expansion westward, where they encountered and captured the tents of local rulers, for example, those of the Sultan of the Seljuqs of Rum, is there a change in terminology.[23] Batu, the *Secret History* informs us, made use of a *yeke chachir*, "great tent," while campaigning against the Qipchaqs in the late 1230s.[24] This word, attested in Turkic in the pre-Mongolian era, goes back in all likelihood to a Persian or Sanscrit form.[25] This type of tent, presumably the guyed pavilion, gained popularity among the Mongolian elite in the 1240s, so that by the reign of Möngke Qaghan there was a Tent Office (*Ch'a-t'ieh-erh chü*) charged with their management. Later on, in 1279, this Office was upgraded to a Directorate General which oversaw the preparation of tents.[26]

That this organization dealt mainly with West Asian-style tenting is supported by a passage in the *Yuan shih*. Under the year 1353 this source reports that Jani Beg, the ruler of the Golden Horde (r. 1342–57), sent the Yuan court a "great tent [*ta ch'a-ch'ih-erh*]," terminology which echoes the *yeke chachir* of the *Secret History*. To further underscore its western provenance, this tent, we are told, was made of *sa-ha-la*.[27] The foreign word underlying this Chinese transcription is the Byzantine Greek *sigillatos*, "seal," from which the Arabic *siqlāt* and the Persian *saqalāt*/*saqirlāt* are derived. These terms usually designated a cloth of wool or linen covered with decorative circles or seals. The background color varied but as Europeans preferred those of a deep red, *saqirlāt* gave rise to the European words for scarlet, while the variant form *saqalāt* produced the Chinese *sa-ha-la*.[28] So far as I know, there was no domestic production of *saqalāt* in

21 P. A. Andrews, "The Tents of Timur: An Examination of Reports on the Quriltay at Samarqand, 1404," in Philip Denwood, ed., *Arts of the Eurasian Steppe Lands* (Colloquies in Art and Archaeology in Asia, No. 7; London: Percival David Foundation of Chinese Art and The School of Oriental and African Studies, 1970), pp. 143–81, especially p. 144.

22 *SH*/de Rachewiltz, sect. 185, p. 94 and sect. 265, p. 206; and *SH*/Cleaves, sect. 185, p. 112, and sect. 265, p. 206. On these terms, see András Róna-Tas, "Preliminary Report on a Study of the Dwellings of the Altaic People," in Denis Sinor, ed., *Aspects of Altaic Civilization* (Bloomington: Indiana University Press, 1963), pp. 49–50.

23 Grigor of Akanc', "Nation of Archers," 311.

24 *SH*/de Rachewiltz, sect. 275, p. 165, and *SH*/Cleaves, sect. 275, p. 215.

25 Nadeliaev, *Drevnetiurkskii slovar*, pp. 135, 141 and 142; and Gerhard Doerfer, *Türkische und Mongolische Elemente im Neupersischen*, vol. III, *Türkische Elemente im Neupersischen* (Wiesbaden: Franz Steiner, 1967), pp. 16–22.

26 *YS*, ch. 85, p. 2147, and Farquhar, *Government*, p. 205.

27 *YS*, ch. 43, p. 911, and Pelliot, *Notes on Marco Polo*, vol. II, p. 640.

28 Munro, "The Medieval Scarlet and the Economics of Sartorial Splendor," pp. 18–29; Lombard, *Les textiles dans le monde musulman*, pp. 242–44; and E. Denison Ross, "Fresh

China; it did, however, gain a certain popularity during the Yuan and is frequently noticed in the Ming era as an imported textile from West and South Asia.[29]

Together with the other West Asian fabrics that went east on the coattails of *nasīj*, there is circumstantial evidence that dyes may have traveled as well. Various sources mention the red (*hung*) belts worked with gold thread and various garments of crimson (*ta-hung*) found at the Yuan court.[30] These may well have been colored with the famous *qirmiz* of West Asia, a dye derived from several insects of the coccid family, more specifically from the dried bodies of the females. One of its centers of manufacture was Armenia, which produced, among other items, crimson trouser bands and cords, and which the Mongols brought under their control in 1236.[31] While there is no direct testimony that this dye was actually sent to China, it is at least suggestive that following the population registration of 1254, Armenian dyers, according to a contemporary observer, were among the artisans the Mongols identified and upon whom they imposed endless demands.[32] The likelihood of such a transfer is further enhanced by the fact that, when properly prepared and packaged, this dye could be stored for long periods and shipped by land or by sea over great distances without loss of quality.[33]

Beyond the textiles themselves, West Asian clothing terminology and styles also exercised a certain influence on the Mongols. This is exemplified by the fact that the Persian word *jāmah*, "robe," "garment," entered Mongolian, perhaps through Turkic mediation, in the form of *chama* which, revealingly, the Mongols understood as "brocade."[34] More concretely, Chao Hung, who visited the Mongols in 1221, offers clear evidence of their eager receptivity to styles coming from the West. Chao describes Bo'ol, son of Muqali, as a handsome lad who does not wear his hair in the Mongolian fashion "but wraps it with a turban [*chin-mao*] and wears tight-fitting

Light on the Word 'Scarlet'," *Journal and Proceedings of the Asiatic Society of Bengal* 4 (1908), 403–04.

29 Henry Serruys, *Sino-Mongol Relations in the Ming*, II, *The Tribute System and Diplomatic Missions (1400–1600)* (Mélanges chinois et bouddhiques, vol. IV; Brussels: Institut belge des hautes Études chinoises, 1967), pp. 170, 204, and 220; and Ma Huan, *Ying-yai sheng-lan*: *The Overall Survey of the Oceans Shore (1433)*, ed. and trans. by J. V. G. Mills (Cambridge University Press for the Hakluyt Society, 1970), pp. 156 and 171.

30 Marco Polo, p. 225, and *YS*, ch. 78, pp. 1935 and 1938.

31 On the history and manufacture of *qirmiz*, consult Lombard, *Les textiles dans le monde musulman*, pp. 119–23; H. Kurdian, "Kirmiz," *JAOS* 61 (1941), 105–07; and G. Levi Della Vida, "On Kirmiz," *JAOS* 61, 287–88, which corrects Kurdian on a number of important points. See also Marco Polo, p. 95.

32 Kirakos, *Istoriia Armenii*, p. 221.

33 William F. Legget, *Ancient and Medieval Dyes* (Brooklyn: Chemical Publishing Company, 1944), pp. 69–82, especially p. 79, and Alexander Burnes, *Travels into Bokhara, being an Account of a Journey from India to Cabool, Tartary and Persia*, repr. (New Delhi: Asian Educational Services, 1992), vol. II, p. 434.

34 Mostaert, *Le matérial Mongol*, p. 45. The Turkic form is *zhamä*. See Nadeliaev, *Drevnetiurkskii slovar*, p. 640.

[literally, 'narrow'] garments."[35] Later on, when he reached Muqali's headquarters he found that the latter's Jürchen and Mongolian wives and concubines "all [wear] *hu* garments and *hu* hats and nothing else."[36] The term *hu* is somewhat ambiguous; originally associated with Sogdians and West Turkestanis, it later came to designate northern barbarians in general.[37] In this case, however, the word should be understood as referring to the eastern Islamic lands which the Mongols had recently invaded. This, of course, means that the ruling elite, especially the "younger set" were appropriating selected Muslim modes and styles immediately following initial contact.

The origin of the *jisün* robes, so prominent in the court life of the Mongolian Empire, has, to the best of my knowledge, yet to be investigated. In principle, of course, this usage may have been a nomadic or even a Mongolian innovation. It is more likely, however, that the inspiration for court clothing of one color was taken from subject peoples and adapted to Mongolian needs. There are various possibilities. The Chinese, as is well known, divide most phenomena into subclasses of five, all of which are correlated to one another. For example, the "five elements" or "agents," earth, metal, water, wood, and fire, have a corresponding color.[38] The difficulty of connecting this with Mongolian practice is that clothing, so far as I am aware, is not in any way associated with the "five colors" or the number five.

A West Asian precedent, mediated through the Uighurs is, for a variety of reasons, a more promising possibility. First, it will be recalled that the earliest reference to *jisün* garments comes in the wake of the Uighur submission to Chinggis Qan, around 1209.[39] Given the Mongols' indebtedness to the Uighurs in political and administrative matters, and the latter's extensive commercial, religious, and cultural ties with West Asia, such a line of transmission is neither unprecedented or unexpected. Second, Marco Polo and the Chinese sources, which provide the most extensive accounts of *jisün*, connect it, in one case, with "nine," the lucky number of the Mongols, but more generally with the thirteen lunar months, "the four seasons" or the "four seasonal feasts."[40] This division of the year into four official

35 Chao Hung, *Meng-ta pei-lu*, p. 441, and Haenisch and Yao, *Chinesische Gesandtenberichte*, p. 35. On Bo'ol and Muqali, see Igor de Rachewiltz, "Muqali, Bōl, Tas and An-t'ung," *Papers on Far Eastern History* 15 (1977), 45–55.

36 Chao Hung, *Meng-ta pei-lu*, p. 455, and Haenisch and Yao, *Chinesische Gesandtenberichte*, p. 79.

37 See Bertold Laufer, *Sino-Iranica: Chinese Contributions to the History of Civilization in Ancient Iran*, repr. (Taipei: Ch'eng-wen, 1967), pp. 194–95; and Edwin G. Pulleyblank, *The Background of the Rebellion of An Lu-shan* (London: Oxford University Press, 1965), p. 10.

38 Joseph Needham, *Science and Civilization in China* (Cambridge University Press, 1969), vol. II, pp. 232–65, especially the charts of symbolic correlations, pp. 262–63.

39 *YS*, ch. 124, p. 3050.

40 *Ming shih*, ch. 65, pp. 1597–98, and *YS*, ch. 122, pp. 3022–12 and ch. 143, p. 3414.

seasons, very old in Turkic, was later incorporated into the Sino-Uighur calendar based upon the duodecimal animal cycle, a system of chronology that was utilized throughout the Mongolian domains.[41] Such a method of dating – "first month of winter," "second month of spring," and so on – had, besides its administrative uses, important ceremonial functions as well. It appears, therefore, that, as we have already seen with regard to the "white festival," there was a close association of clothing of one color with annual cycles and good fortune, that is, with astrological and numerological ideas and the signs of the zodiac. And, indeed, there was a clear West Asian precedent for this: both Muslims and Nestorian Christians in the pre-Mongolian period identified planets with specific colors. Such schemes are found in the writings of the great scholar al-Bīrūnī, who died in 1050, and in the *Syriac Book of Medicines*, compiled sometime before the ninth century.[42] Even more compelling, royal clothing of a single color, inspired by the zodiac, was attributed to the Sasanian court, the ultimate model of statecraft in West Asia, by later Muslim authors. Niẓāmī of Ganja (ca. 1140–46 to ca. 1203–09), a widely admired and read Persian poet, develops this theme at length in his *Haft Paykar* ("Seven Portraits"), also called the *Bahrām nāmah* ("Book of Bahrām"), which describes in verse the adventures of Bahrām V Gor, the storied Sasanian emperor (r. 420–39).[43] In the principal tale, Bahrām acquires seven brides from the rulers of the seven habitable climes of the earth, whom he houses separately in monochrome palaces. He then visits each wife on successive days for wine and dalliance, and he does so attired in clothing of one color corresponding to that of the chosen one's palace.[44] In later portraiture inspired by this poem, it is interesting to note that the hero, his brides, and attendants all wear clothing of one color, which they changed in unison each day.[45] Whether pre-Islamic Persian rulers actually wore clothing of one color is, of course, less important than the fact that a literary tradition, ascribing such practice to

41 On the four seasons among the early Turks, see Louis Bazin, *Les systèmes chronologiques dans le monde Turk ancién* (Budapest and Paris: Akadémia Kiadó and Editions du CNRS, 1991), pp. 49–55, 319–20, 378–79, and 387–91. For its use in Mongolian chancelleries, see Antoine Mostaert and Francis W. Cleaves, *Les lettres de 1289 et 1305 des ilkhan Aryun et Öljeitü à Philippe le Bel* (Cambridge, Mass.: Harvard University Press, 1962), pp. 52–54, and Charles Melville, "The Chinese Uighur Animal Calendar in Persian Historiography of the Mongol Period," *Iran* 32 (1994), 93–95.

42 Al-Bīrūnī, *The Book of Introduction in the Elements of the Arts of Astrology*, trans. by R. Ramsay Wright (London: Luzac, 1924), pp. 240, 241, and 253, and Ernest A. Wallis Budge, trans., *The Syriac Book of Medicines: Syrian Anatomy, Pathology and Therapeutics in the Early Middle Ages*, repr. (Amsterdam: APA-Philo Press, 1976), vol. II, pp. 573–74.

43 On Niẓāmī, see Edward G. Browne, *A Literary History of Persia*, vol. II, *From Firdawsī to Sa'di* (Cambridge University Press, 1969), pp. 399–411.

44 Niẓāmī of Ganja, *The Haft Paikar* (*The Seven Beauties*), trans. by C. E. Wilson (London: Arthur Probsthain, 1924), vol. I, pp. 106–250, and especially pp. 111, 113, 114, 115, 157, 171, 213, and 234, where the color-coordinated clothing is noted.

45 Fazila Suleimanova, *Miniatury k 'khamse' Nizami* (Tashkent: Fan, 1985), plates 158 and 159, and Kerim Kerimov, *Nizami Giandzhevi khamse miniatiury* (Baku: Iazychy, 1983), plates 93–99.

the Sasanians, was very much alive in the eastern Islamic world on the eve of the Mongolian invasions.

For the Mongolian ruling strata, this convention, whatever its ultimate origin, had several attractive features. Viewed in a strictly sociological perspective, one desirable effect of clothing of one color was, naturally, to encourage the elite's sense of separateness, superiority, and corporate solidarity in relation to the rest of the qaghan's subjects and, indeed, to the rest of the known world. Their special status is unequivocally expressed in Chinggis Qan's order that the rank and file guardsmen were "higher than the outward captains of thousands," an edict that Ögödei reaffirmed upon his accession.[46] The use of distinctive dress, usually associated with sumptuary laws, is, of course, one of the most common mechanisms of boundary maintenance.[47] In ancient West Asia "the Immortals," the 10,000–strong imperial guard of the Achaemenid kings, wore "garments adorned with cloth of gold" and in the subsequent Hellenistic courts of the East the guards, boon companions and household officials were so often clothed in purple that Latin writers collectively called these "friends" of the emperor the *purpurati*.[48]

But while *jisün* robes created a strong sense of separateness and special privilege in relation to outsiders, within the elite itself such attire surely had the opposite and equally welcome effect of temporarily blurring or minimizing social distinctions and thereby enhancing feelings of comraderie on those clearly defined occasions, mainly court-sponsored feasts and celebrations, when their use was authorized. The means utilized in achieving these brief, and carefully orchestrated periods of equality was social elevation, not leveling. The technique is nicely expressed in Marco Polo's observation that courtiers in their *jisün* robes are so "richly adorned they all seem to be kings."[49]

The Mongolian qans' practice of personally investing their soldiers, officials and dependent rulers is also a convention of West Asian origin, one which they readily embraced and widely employed. Ibn Baṭṭūṭah, among many others, bears witness to the currency of this practice among the Mongols. He himself received robes of honor from Abū Sa'id and from Qutlugh Temür, the governor-general of Khwārazm, and was present when Özbek robed his military commanders.[50] In these instances, of course, the Mongolian rulers in question were converts to Islam, so that such behavior could be expected, but in fact, non-Muslim qans were equally concerned

[46] *SH*/Cleaves, sect. 228, p. 166 and sect. 278, p. 223, and *SH*/de Rachewiltz, sect. 228, p. 131 and sect. 278, pp. 170–71.
[47] See Robert T. Anderson, *Traditional Europe: A Study in Anthroplogy and History* (Belmont, Calif.: Wadsworth Publishing Co., 1971), pp. 29–34.
[48] Quintus Curtius, *History of Alexander*, III.iii.13; "I Maccabbees" 21.18–20; and Reinhold, *History of Purple*, pp. 34–35.
[49] Marco Polo, p. 221.
[50] Ibn Baṭṭūṭah/Gibbs, vol. II, pp. 345 and 493–94, and vol. III, p. 549.

with and regularly used investiture ceremonies to confirm subordinates in office. Arghun (r. 1284–91), who patronized Buddhism, personally invested Step'annos, the Armenian metropolitan of Siwnik', following a purely ecclesiastical installation at which the Catholicos presided: "As for the Monarch, he clothed him, in imitation of the Catholicos himself, with royal vestments, and placed upon his head, for the second time, the sovereign crown of pure gold."[51] This personal participation is also mentioned in connection with Qubilai's robing of a Qitan secretary who had inherited his father's position in the imperial guard: "The Emperor held a feast at Lo-lin and ordered Lü-ma to occupy his father's place and bestowed upon [him] a *jisün* garment."[52] Similarly, in 1289, Taqai, a Qarluq, had an audience with Qubilai, who enrolled him as a cook in the imperial household and "conferred upon [him] a *jisün* hat and garment."[53] Even more informative on the clothing involved is the report of the robing of Shams al-Dīn, the Kart ruler of Herat, who received his regalia of office from Möngke, a firm adherent of the Mongols' native religion, the Tengri cult: "The Emperor Möngke qan," in the words of Sayf, "invested [*būshānīd*] Malik Shams al-Dīn with royal robes of honor [*khil'at-i khaṣṣ*] and gave him two precious bejeweled gilded[54] belts [*kamar*] and nine garments of gold brocade [*jāmah-i zar-baft*]. . ."[55] From other sources it is known that Möngke made a similar bestowal of robes on the ruler of Kirmān.[56]

In the foregoing cases, the recipients were individuals; we know, however, that Mongolian princes frequently gave out large numbers of robes to their followers to mark special events. In 1253, it will be remembered, Möngke granted robes of honor (*tashrīf*) to Hülegü and all his officers, and three years later, after the defeat of the Isma'īlīs, Hülegü himself rewarded his commanders with a further bestowal of robes.[57] What procedures were used for these mass robings? Fortunately, one such occasion, Ghazan's dispensation of clothing to his officers, is described in some detail by Rashīd al-Dīn, a contemporary and very likely an eyewitness. Ghazan, he says, first laid out various types of robes and purses filled with gold and silver, each of which was carefully labeled and weighed, and then "one by one he called out [the commanders' names] and ordered them to take their shares personally; for the course of ten or eleven days he granted riches in this fashion."[58] This, to be sure, was a cumbersome, time-consuming duty but in the context of Mongolian political culture an extremely crucial one.

Given the importance the Mongols attached to the act of investiture,

[51] Stephannos Orbelian, *Histoire de la Siounie*, p. 239. [52] *YS*, ch. 150, p. 3550.
[53] *YS*, ch. 122, p. 3005. [54] The text has *razīn* in place of *zarīn*.
[55] Sayf, *Ta'rīkh-i nāmah-i Harāt*, p. 171.
[56] Mu'īn al-Dīn Naṭanzī, *Muntakhab al-tavārīkh-i Mu'īnī*, ed. by Jean Aubin (Tehran: Librairie Khayyam, 1957), p. 23.
[57] Rashīd/Karm, vol. II, pp. 687 and 696.
[58] Rashīd/Karm, vol. II, p. 981, and Martinez, "The Third Portion of the Story of Gāzān Xān," 64.

there were various offices and officers charged with the administration of the royal wardrobe and the disbursement of ceremonial garments and cloths. In West Asia a Georgian source records that Hülegü was so pleased with the military assistance provided by the Georgians that he appointed many young nobles to his guard, one of whom became a "*qubchʿachʿi* . . . charged with the care of garments and footwear," a title which answers to the Mongolian *qubchachi*, "valet."[59] Another office concerned with cloth and clothing was the *sügürchi*, the "parasol-holder." In Iran, it is interesting to note, one *shūkurchī*, upon his father's death "became the senior [among] all the *yūrtchīān*," the royal "tenters" responsible for the qan's brocade-lined pavilions.[60] At the Yuan court the *sügürchi*s (*su-ku-erh-ch'ih*), also officers in the guard, were "in charge of garments for imperial use within the palace."[61] The bestowal of clothing outside the court was apparently in the hands of two organizations formed in 1282, both under the Imperial Treasuries Directorate, the Palace Treasury (*Nei ts'ang-ku*) which oversaw the receipt and disbursement of *nasīj*, and the Treasury of the Right (*Yu-ts'ang*) which received and distributed the robes of one color (*jīsün*).[62]

The model for the Mongolian practice of investiture, as well as some of the machinery that supported it, can be traced back to West Asian practices. It is true, of course, that the Chinese also viewed cloth and clothing as an important element of cultural and political life: The state carefully regulated and prescribed ceremonial wear and official dress, promulgated sumptuary laws (which were difficult to enforce), and in general ascribed great symbolic significance to textiles.[63] While they bestowed vast amounts of silk on their own officials and on foreign rulers, this was typically in the form of uncut cloth clearly intended as salary or as tribute.[64] In the pre-Han period, of course, rulers frequently invested subordinates with various articles of clothing but this practice never assumed a central place in the political life of imperial China.[65]

In West Asia and the Mediterranean, by contrast, investiture, especially by the hand of the sovereign, was an integral and in some regards a central

59 Brosset, *Histoire de la Géorgie*, p. 540. Brosset's French translation has "*qaptchak*." I wish to thank Peter B. Golden for pointing out that the most common Georgian form is *qubchʿachʿi*. On the Mongolian form, see Gerhard Doerfer, *Türkische und Mongolische Elemente im Neupersischen*, vol. I, *Mongolische Elemente im Neupersischen* (Wiesbaden: Franz Steiner, 1963), pp. 385–86.

60 Rashīd al-Dīn, *Jāmiʿ al-tavārīkh*, ed. by Alizade, vol. I, pt. 1, p. 219. On the term *sügürchi*, see Doerfer, *Türkische und Mongolische Elemente*, vol. I, pp. 357–58.

61 *YS*, ch. 99, p. 2524.

62 *YS*, ch. 90, p. 2292, and Farquhar, *Government*, p. 91.

63 On Sung sumptuary laws and their gradual erosion, see Jacques Gernet, *Daily Life in China on the Eve of the Mongol Invasion* (Stanford University Press, 1962), pp. 127–29.

64 On grants of silk as salary and tribute, see Fang Hao, *Chung-hsi chiao-t'ung shih*, vol. I (Taipei: Chung-hua wen-hua ch'u-pien shih-yeh wei-yuan-hui, 1953), p. 134.

65 See Cho-yun Hsu and Katheryn M. Linduff, *Western Chou Civilization* (New Haven: Yale University Press, 1988), pp. 177–78; Zhou Xun and Gao Chunming, *5000 Years of Chinese Costumes* (San Francisco: China Books and Periodicals, 1987), p. 32; and Schuyler Cammann, "The Making of Dragon Robes," *T'oung-pao* 40 (1951), 297–301.

part of the region's shared political culture from ancient times. Both the Old and New Testaments record instances of the bestowal of raiment which strongly imply the subordination of the recipient.[66] But it was Iran, one of the early centers of textile development and diffusion, that played the pivotal role in the fashioning of a political culture of cloth that had profound effect throughout the greater part of Eurasia.[67] Cyrus (r. 559–30), according to Xenophon's fictionalized biography of the Achaemenid king, "called to him those of the Persians and of the Allies who held office, and distributed Median robes among them."[68] Such robes were accounted as the most valuable and honorable gifts in ancient Iran, the granting of which was considered a prerogative of the court.[69] So important was the Achaemenid precedent that Greek writers routinely attributed the invention of the practice of investiture to Cyrus.[70] Even more telling is the equation of Persian attire with imperial authority found in Quintus Curtius' account of the "conspiracy of the pages." When Hermolaüs, a member of the imperial court, is accused of joining the plot against Alexander the Great, he justifies this act by saying "it is the Persian garb and habits [*vestis et disciplina*] that delight you; you have come to loathe the customs of your native land. Therefore," he continues, "it was the king of the Persians, not of the Macedonians, that we wished to kill, and by the law of war we justly pursue you as a deserter."[71] Alexander, at least in the eyes of his alienated pages, had become the original "turncoat."

While some railed against Persian clothing and custom, many others sought to emulate their practice. This is particularly true in client states such as Armenia. Tigran II the Great (r. 95–55), in later Armenian tradition amassed great wealth in precious metals, gems and textiles, which he bestowed upon his court.[72] More importantly, the Sasanians continued these conventions and their great prestige did much to further diffuse and popularize this usage throughout Eastern Christendom, western and central Asia. Ardashir (r. 226–40), the founder of the dynasty, was famed for his liberality, and one extant Middle Persian work, the "Book of Deeds of Ardashir, Son of Papak," relates his presentation of garments (*jamag*) to servitors over a three-day period.[73] Yazdagird III (r. 632–51), the last

[66] F. W. Buckler, "Two Instances of *Khil'at* in the Bible," *Journal of Theological Studies* 23 (1922) 197–99.

[67] Trudy S. Kawami, "Archaeological Evidence for Textiles in Pre-Islamic Iran," *Iranian Studies* 25 (1992), 7–18; Bernard Goldman, "Origin of the Persian Robe," *Iranica Antiqua* 4 (1964), 133–52; and Geo Widengren, "Some Remarks on the Riding Costume and Articles of Dress among Iranian Peoples in Antiquity," *Studia Ethnographica Upsaliensia* 11 (1956), 228–76.

[68] Xenophon, *Cyropaedia*, VII.iii.1.

[69] Herodotus, *The Persian Wars*, III.84 and VII.540; and Xenophon, *Anabasis*, I.ii.27.

[70] Xenophon, *Cyropaedea*, VIII.i.40–41 and ii.7–9.

[71] Quintus Curtius, *History of Alexander*, VII.vii.12–13.

[72] Moses Khorenats'i, *History of the Armenians*, p. 113.

[73] O. M. Chunakova, ed. and trans., *Kniga deianii Ardashira syna Papaka* (Moscow: Nauka, 1987), p. 76 Russian translation and p. 53 transcribed Middle Persian text.

Sasanian emperor, solidified his relations with vassal rulers through such bestowals. Sometime in the late 630s, according to the Armenian chronicler Movsēs Dasxuranci, he invested J̌uansher, a prince of Ałuankʿ (Caucasian Albania), with "silken Persian coats with fringes of spun gold" and with an item that appears again in the Mongolian era, "a belt of gold studded with pearls." Interestingly, the same author relates a few pages later that when the Sasanians fell to the Arabs, J̌uansher sought the protection of Byzantium and Constans II (r. 641–68) conferred upon him "robes of spun gold."[74]

Byzantine investiture practices, firmly rooted in the ancient Near Eastern/Iranian tradition, were complex and well-regulated.[75] The procedures used on these occasions provide a clear precedent for Ghazan's elaborate dispensations of monies and robes noted above. Liutprand, on his first embassy to Constantinople in 949, witnessed Constantine's "payment" of his court officials. By his account, bags of money "according to each man's due," all carefully labeled, were placed on a large table. The intended recipients were then called forward in order of rank and given, by the hand of the emperor, the coins and "cloaks of honor." And, as was the case in Ghazan's day, this procedure was extremely time consuming, taking, according to Liutprand, the better part of three days.[76]

Such practices, well known through Arabic epitomes of Middle Persian historial materials, were in time taken over by the Muslims. While the Caliph ʿUmar (r. 634–44), unlike Alexander, reputedly rejected Persian finery and "never changed his attire," Persian political norms were nonetheless assimilated and fully institutionalized in ʿAbbāsid times.[77] The caliphs systematically granted robes of honor, Arabic *khilʿat*, to their generals, governors, *wazīrs* and boon companions. They gave clothing as a reward for well received entertainments, to provide protection and security to favored subjects, and to celebrate important military victories.[78]

[74] Movsēs Dasxuranci, *The History of the Caucasian Albanians*, trans. by C. J. F. Dowsett (London: Oxford University Press, 1961), pp. 111–12 and 116.

[75] On the Byzantine practice of robing high court officals, see Averil Cameron, "The Construction of Court Ritual: The Byzantine *Book of Ceremonies*," in David Cannadine and Simon Price, eds., *Rituals of Royalty: Power and Ceremonial in Traditional Societies* (Cambridge University Press, 1987), p. 117; and Pamela G. Sayre, "The Mistress of the Robes – Who Was She?," *Byzantine Studies/Études Byzantines* 13 (1986), 229–39.

[76] Liutprand of Cremona, *The Embassy to Constantinople and Other Writings*, trans. by F. A. Wright and ed. by John Julius Norwich, repr. (London and Rutland, Vermont: Everyman's Library, 1993), pp. 155–56.

[77] Bar Hebreaus, p. 96. For the Sasanian imprint on Islamic political culture, see Shaul Shaked, "From Iran to Islam: On Some Symbols of Royalty," *Jerusalem Studies in Arabic* 7 (1986), 75–91. For an example of the Arabs' knowledge of Sasanian investiture practices, see al-Thaʿālibī, *Histoire des rois perses*, ed. and trans. by H. Zotenberg (Paris: Imprimerie nationale, 1900), pp. 555 and 565.

[78] N. A. Stillman, "*Khilʿa*," *Encyclopedia of Islam*, 2nd edn. (Leiden: E. J. Brill, 1979), vol. V, pp. 6–7; Hilāl al-Ṣābiʾ, *Rusūm Dār al-khilāfah*, pp. 75–78, and Bar Hebreaus, pp. 143, 182, and 305.

When the caliphate weakened after the ninth century, the emerging sultanates continued the custom. In the West, the Ayyubid ruler Saladin (r. 1119–93) granted robes of honor to the Norman Crusader Bohemund and to Count Henry of Champagne (*al-kund* Hirī), the Frankish ruler of Palestine.[79] In the eastern Islamic world, the Sāmānids dressed their newly purchased slave soldiers, *mamlūks*, who formed their personal guard, in *zandanīchī* robes.[80] Their successors, the Ghaznavids, invested vassals with robes, hats and golden belts, while the retinue of Masʿūd (r. 1030–41) wore a great variety of expensive brocade robes with bejewelled and gilded sashes. Pictorial representation of the Sultan's guard has been found in murals unearthed in a palace near the town of Bust.[81] The Qarakhanid rulers of Kashgar also invested officials and granted robes of honor.[82] Finally, the Khwārazmshāhs, with whom the Mongols had direct contact, regularly conferred robes of honor on their military officers and invested vassal princes. Their treasury, according to contemporary documentation, was well supplied with robes, inscribed tunics (*qalāʿ-i muṭarraz*), headgear, and belts.[83]

In the West Asian tradition, as in later Mongolian practice, recipients of royal clothing who dissatisfied their sovereign were "divested" of their attire as a show of disfavor and as a prelude to more severe punishment. Under the Seleucid emperor Antiochus IV (175–64 BC), one such disloyal official, Andronikos, was stripped of his purple robes and then paraded around the city prior to his execution ("II Maccabees" 4.38).

The function and form of belts so widely utilized in investiture ceremonies further underscore the importance of West Asian models for the Mongolian political culture. Among the early Iranians belts were associated with martial virtues and warriors, for whom "girding the loins" meant preparing for combat. Indeed, like modern medals, belts were awarded as emblems of valor.[84] This relationship is borne out by another of the Scythians' ethnogenetic myths, in which a father, Heracles, to test the abilities of his three sons, has them string a bow and fasten a girdle around their waists. The youngest, Scythes, succeeded and he established the Scythian royal

[79] Bar Hebreaus, pp. 340–41, and Ibn al-Athīr, *Al-Kāmil fī al-taʾrīkh*, vol. XII, p. 79.

[80] Niẓām al-Mulk, *The Book of Government or Rules for Kings*, trans. by Hubert Darke (London: Routledge & Kegan Paul, 1960), pp. 106–07. Liutprand, *Embassy to Constantinople*, p. 198 records that forty Hungarian soldiers taken prisoner during a raid were subsequently released and dressed "in the most costly garments" and became the emperor's "bodyguard and defenders."

[81] Bosworth, *The Ghaznavids*, pp. 136 and 242, and D. Schlumberger, "Le palais ghaznévide de Lashkari Bazar," *Syria* 29 (1952), 251–70.

[82] Yūsuf Khāṣṣ Ḥajib, *Wisdom of Royal Glory*, p. 259.

[83] Juvaynī/Qazvīnī, vol. II, pp. 85 and 170; Juvaynī/Boyle, vol. I, p. 353 and vol. II, p. 438; and Heribert Horst, *Die Staatsverwaltung der Grosselǧūgen und Hōrazmšahs (1038–1231): Eine Untersuchung nach Urkundenformularen der Zeit* (Wiesbaden: Franz Steiner, 1964), pp. 23 and 100.

[84] P. R. S. Moorey, "Some Ancient Metal Belts: Their Antecedents and Relatives," *Iran* 5 (1967), 98.

line.[85] At the same time, the girdle was a symbol of the personal dependency of the servitors (*bandaka* in old Persian and *bandah* in New Persian, literally, "the bound ones") on their sovereign. This symbolism is made explicit by Ibn al-Balkhī, who in the early twelfth century wrote of Kaī Kūvās, one of the heroic kings of the Persian national tradition, that whoever "went before the pādshāh the custom was this, that each of them fastened a girdle over their robe and this," he continues, "they call the girdle of servitude [*kamar-i bandagī*]."[86] Thus, investiture ceremonies typically included belts and conversely, dependents charged with disloyalty or treason were seized by the belt and so "bound over" for punishment.[87]

Any guardsman of Qubilai's, magically transported back to an early Iranian court, would have easily understood the symbolism and meaning of belts in those court's robing ceremonies. And he most certainly would have been familiar with the belt's actual appearance as well. Gold, most certainly, was the preferred color: such girdles are mentioned in the *Avesta*, were worn by Achaemenid monarchs, and granted by Sasanian shahs. In the latter case, Yazdagird II (r. 439–57) invested high court officials with robes of honor and a "girdle of pure hammered gold set with pearls and precious stones."[88] While the political use of belts, closely linked to the symbolism of tying and binding, was of particular importance in the religious, cosmological, and magical beliefs of Indo-Europeans and Iranians, it was by no means restricted to them.[89] In later centuries it was found among the Armenians, Arabs, Abkhaz, Byzantines, as well as nomadic Oghuz Turks.[90]

Between ancient Iran and Yuan China there was an impressive continuity of clothing culture, one that was mediated through eastern Islamic courts – the Abbasids, Samānids, Ghaznavids, and Khwārazmshāhs. As a model of political behavior, the complex of practices associated with belting, robing, and investiture was remarkably stable and long-lived. It was a well-established tradition by the sixth century BC and survived in recognizable form down to the twentieth century. Further, it was the common property of many peoples and cultures, an "international" institution that readily

[85] Herodotus, *The Persian Wars*, V.9–10.

[86] Ibn al-Balkhī, *Fārsnāmah*, ed. by Guy Le Strange and R. A. Nicholson (London: Luzac, 1968), p. 43.

[87] P. Jamzadeh, "The Function of the Girdle on Achaemenid Costume in Combat," *Iranica Antiqua* 32 (1987), 267–73; and G. Widengren, "Le symbolisme de la ceinture," *Iranica Antiqua* 8 (1968), 133–55 and especially 140–46.

[88] Georgina Thompson, "Iranian Dress in the Achaemenid Period: Problems Concerning the *kanys* and Other Garments," *Iran* 3 (1965), 123; Quintas Curtius, *History of Alexander*, III.iii.17; and Ełishē, *History of Vardan*, p. 187.

[89] Mircea Eliade, *Images and Symbols: Studies in Religious Symbolism* (Princeton University Press, 1991), pp. 92–124.

[90] Iovannes Draskhanakerttsi, *Istoriia Armenii*, trans. by M. O. Dardinian-Melikan (Erevan: Izdatel'stvo "Sovetakan Grokh," 1986), pp. 128, 148, 151, 153, 179, and 197; and A. M. Shcherbak, trans., *Oguz-nāme. Mukhabbat-nāme* (Moscow: Izdatel'stvo vostochnoi literatury, 1959), p. 25.

crossed political, religious, social, and ethnic boundaries. Muslims robed Jews and Christians, Byzantines robed Armenians, Armenians robed Abkhaz, and the Mongols, it seems, robed everyone else.[91]

Early Iranian traditions of kingly headgear, diadems or crowns, also exercised a certain influence on Mongolian practice, albeit in a considerably modified fashion.

Among the Iranian nomads, Scythians and Sakas, political leadership was closely associated with the ritual functions of the ruler as mediator between heaven and earth, gods and humans. This role was symbolized by their formal headdress, which was decorated with the tree of life and birds, well-known shamanistic symbols. Not unexpectedly, the nomads were receptive to the practice of crowning rulers that developed in the settled areas of West Asia.[92] Consequently, when the Iranians formed states in central and western Asia ca. 500 BC–700 AD, crowns were a central element in a monarch's investiture ceremony. This is well reflected in the coinage of the Kushans, Khwārazmshāhs, and most particularly the Sasanians, which regularly depicts the sitting monarch in such headgear.[93] This convention was passed on to the early Turkic peoples: In 762, when Bögü Qaghan of the Uighurs converted to Manichaeanism, a religion that of course originated in an Iranian political milieu, he marked this important transition by placing a diadem (*didim*) upon his own head.[94]

In the Mongolian era, however, there is no evidence that crowns *per se* were used. The literary sources make no mention of them and, more persuasively, the official portraiture of the Yuan emperors shows them wearing a cloth or felt double-brimmed hat with a rounded crown. These are exactly like the hats found on the numerous stone figurines, dating to the period of the twelfth–fourteenth centuries, frequently unearthed in Mongolia.[95] So far as one can tell, the emperor's headgear was simply a more elegant version of traditional, native styles.

91 Draskhanakerttsi, *Istoriia Armenii*, pp. 99, 128, 148, 150, 151, 153, 157–58, 179, and 197; Benjamin of Tudela, *Itinerary*, pp. 101 and 118; and Bar Hebreaus, p. 175.

92 E. E. Kuz'mina, "Dionis u usunei (o semantike Kargalinskoi diademy)," in B. B. Piotrovskii and G. M. Bongard-Levin, eds., *Tsentral'naia Aziia, novye pamiatniki, pis'mennosti i iskusstva: Sbornik statei* (Moscow: Nauka, 1987), p. 173.

93 For data on the use of crowns among the people of western and central Asia in this period, see E. E. Kuz'mina and V. I Sarianidi, "Dva golovnykh ubora iz pogrebenii Tilliatepe i ikh semantika," *Kratkie soobshcheniia Instituta arkheologii* 170 (1982), 19–27; B. I. Vainberg, *Monety drevnego Khorezma* (Moscow: Nauka, 1977), pp. 18–32; and Robert Göbl, "Investitur im sasanidischen Iran und ihr numismatische Bezeugung," *Weiner Zeitschrift für die Kunde des Morgenlandes* 56 (1960), 38–51.

94 Bang and Gabain, "Türkische Turfan-Texte, II, Manichaica," 416, Turkic text and 417, German translation. For the historical background, see Peter B. Golden, *An Introduction to the History of the Turkic Peoples: Ethnogenesis and State Formation in Medieval and Early Modern Eurasia and the Middle East* (Wiesbaden: Otto Harrassowitz, 1992), pp. 174–76.

95 Baiar, "Kamennye izvaianiia iz Sukhe-Batorskogo Aimaka," pp. 149–50; and Mostaert, "A propos de quelques portraits d'empereurs Mongols," 149.

Despite the absence of crowns, there is nonetheless good reason to believe that the association of headgear with rulership continued into the Mongolian period. This is borne out by the discussions ca. 1218, concerning a suitable heir to Chinggis Qan recorded in the *Secret History*. Here Chaghadai, his second son, recommends his third son, saying: "Ögödei being at the side of father Qan, if [the latter] make [him] to recognize the precept of the hat [*maqalai-yin bauliya*] of which the appearance [is] great, it will do."[96] What this somewhat cryptic passage says is that Chinggis Qan will pass on the special, perhaps even sacred, principles of rulership to Ögödei and that this is sufficient to prepare him for the succession. Thus, while the crown, as a physical object was no longer in vogue, the West Asian/Iranian equation of hats, esoteric knowledge, and sovereign power was still alive among the Chinggisids.

The Mongols not only adopted the formalized investiture ceremonies from West Asia but the more irregular practice of granting favorites garments worn by the monarch as well. Precedent for this can be found among the early Persians. Cyrus, in Xenophon's biography, once took off a "Median robe" he was wearing and gave it directly to a favorite in his retinue.[97] And according to the "Book of Esther," 6.6–8, when the Achaemenid ruler Ahasuerus (Xerxes I, r. 486–65) asked his chamberlain, Haman, "what shall be done unto a man whom the king delighteth to honor?," the chamberlain, wrongly thinking that the reward was to be his, answered: "Let the royal apparel be brought which the king *useth to wear*, and a horse that the king rideth upon and the crown royal which is set upon his head." The reasons behind this particular request are at least partially revealed by another episode from Xerxes' reign. According to Herodotus, while the emperor was still anguishing over a full-scale invasion of Greece, he began receiving portents in his dreams that seemed to indicate success for such a venture. To confirm that the gods indeed willed an invasion, he called before him Artabanus, a kinsman and adviser, saying "put on the dress which I wear, and then after taking your seat upon my throne, lie down to sleep in my bed." In consequence of this direct physical contact with the king's possessions, Artabanus had the very same dream and was able to affirm that the gods promised victory.[98] In this instance, clearly, some of the persona of the king, his psychic and spiritual properties, was transfered to his adviser through the medium of the royal attire and bedclothes.

Under the later Achaemenids we find an interesting variation on this theme. When Artaxerxes II (r. 404–359) assumed the throne he went to Pasargadae for a royal initiation which involved, according to Plutarch, "laying aside his own proper robe" and donning in its stead "that which

[96] *SH*/Cleaves, sect. 255, p. 59; and *SH*/de Rachewiltz, sect. 255, p. 151–52.
[97] Xenophon, *Cyropaedia*, I.iv.26 and V.i.2.
[98] Herodotus, *The Persian Wars*, VII.15–18.

Cyrus the Elder used to wear before he became king."[99] Similarly, when the Sasanian emperor Khusro II (r. 591–628) made the Armenian prince Smbat Bagratuni (595–616) one of his march wardens, he granted him, among other bestowals, "the belt and sword of his very own father Hormizd [II, r. 579–90]."[100] In another example of capturing the spiritual force of a deceased person through his clothing, the Byzantine emperor Theodosius (r. 408–50) took the tunic of a dead ascete, the Bishop of Hebrōn and "filthy though it was . . . put it on so that he might be blessed thereby."[101] In Western Christendom such transfers of sanctity were regularly effected by placing cloth next to the remains of saints, cloth which over time absorbed holiness from the deceased. These "secondary" or "contact relics" were considered even more potent when stained with bodily effluvia, especially blood.[102]

More commonly, however, rulers gave their own garments to retainers and subjects as dramatic gestures of special favor. In Iceland, a Viking king, moved by the recitation of a poet, rewarded him with "his own cloak of new scarlet."[103] Further east, but in the same vein, the Umayyad Caliph Walīd II (r. 743–44) removed his own robe and presented it to a court singer whose perfomance greatly pleased him.[104]

Even the Isma'īlīs (Assassins), the main domestic foe of orthodox Islam, adhered to this custom. Around 1250, 'Alā' al-Dīn Muḥammad II (r. 1221–55), the ruler of the Assassins, famed as the "Old Man of the Mountain" among the Crusaders, sent an embassy to the French king, Louis IX (r. 1226–70), then in the Holy Lands, in hopes of securing allies against the growing Mongolian menace. This embassy, Joinville informs us, first presented to

> the king [Louis] the Old Man's shirt; they told him from their master that it was a symbol that, as the shirt is closer to the body than any other garment, so the Old Man wished to hold the king closer in love than any other king.[105]

Finally, this practice was continued down to more recent times in India, where the Mughal emperors gave their own clothes to favored servitors. On the occasion of the birth of a grandson Babur sent presents to all of his

[99] *Plutarch's Lives*, trans. by Bernadotte Perrin (The Loeb Classical Library; New York: Putnams, 1926), "Life of Artaxerxes" 3.

[100] Sebēos, *Histoire d'Heraclius*, trans. by Fréderic Macler (Paris: Imprimerie nationale, 1904), p. 42.

[101] Bar Hebreaus, pp. 66–67.

[102] John M. McCulloh, "The Cult of Relics in the Letters and 'Dialogues' of Pope Gregory the Great: A Lexicographical Study," *Traditio* 32 (1976), 147, 155, 165–69, and 175–80.

[103] M. H. Scargill and Margaret Schlanch, trans., *Three Icelandic Sagas* (Princeton University Press for the American Scandinavian Foundation, 1950), pp. 24–25.

[104] Alfred von Kremer, *Culturgeschichte des Orients unter den Chalifen* (Vienna: Wilhelm Braumüller, 1875), vol. I, pp. 153–54.

[105] John of Joinville, *The Life of St. Louis*, trans. by René Hague (New York: Sheed and Ward, 1955), p. 140.

commanders; for each, Babur writes in his memoirs, there was "a coat I had worn."[106] Whatever its symbolic significance in northern Europe, West and South Asia, the Mongols' adoption of this practice is most probably linked to the nomads' particular attitudes toward water, washing, and the scent of the human body.

As is well known, there was a widespread and long-lasting water taboo, a sanctification of water conservation, among the steppe peoples that can be traced from the time of the Scythians down to the medieval Turks.[107] In the Mongolian era, there are numerous references from travelers and chroniclers to a ban on the cleaning of one's person or clothing. Even the *Secret History*, the Mongols' own account of their rise to power, takes notice of the opinion of the Naiman, Chinggis' last major rival in the eastern steppe, that the Mongols scent was strong and their clothing dark, that is, grimy.[108] In most of these instances it is reported that violation of the prohibition against washing brought down heaven's wrath in the form of thunder and lightning storms.[109] The rationale for this firmly held belief was that water was deemed to be one of the four basic constituents of the universe and had, consequently, cosmological significance for Turks and Mongols. Moreover, in large accumulations, such as lakes, water reflected the sky and in the form of rain it descended from the heavens and therefore partook of Tengri, the sky deity and chief god of the nomads. To use water in washing the body or the clothing was to pollute a cosmological element.[110]

It seems likely, too, that this taboo was further reinforced by the belief that the aroma of the body is somehow associated with an individual's essence or soul, an essence which should be preserved, not removed. Like shadows, reflections, and breath, body odor is insubstantial yet detectable and is therefore identified with the soul or spirit in some cultures.[111]

In the Mongolian case, two episodes in the *Secret History* express something of the important associations of the body's aroma for the medieval nomads and help to explain why the emperor's clothes were so precious. The first is connected with the abduction of Chinggis Qan's mother, Hö'elün. Sometime in the mid twelfth century, according to the chronicle,

[106] Ẓahir al-Dīn, *The Bābur-Nāma in English*, trans. by Annette Susannah Beveridge (London: Luzac, 1969), p. 642; and Bernard S. Cohn, "Cloth, Clothing and Colonialism: India in the Nineteenth Century," in Weiner and Schneider, *Cloth and Human Experience*, pp. 313–14.

[107] Herodotus, *The Persian Wars*, IV.75, and Ibn Faḍlān, *Ibn Faḍlān's Reisebericht*, trans. and ed. by A. Zeki Validi Togan (Abhandlungen für die Kunde des Morgenlandes, Bd. 24, Nr. 3; Leipzig: Deutsche Morgenländische Gesellschaft, 1939), pp. 20–21.

[108] *SH*/Cleaves, sect. 189, p. 117; and *SH*/de Rachewiltz, sect. 189, p. 98.

[109] *Mongol Mission*, pp. 17 and 103; Rubruck/Jackson, p. 90; *Sinica Franciscana*, pp. 48–49 and 184; Juvaynī/Qazvīnī, vol. I, pp. 161–63; Juvaynī/Boyle, vol. I, pp. 204–06; Rashīd/Karmīnī, vol. I, pp. 487–88; Rashīd/Boyle, pp. 137–41; Chao Hung, *Meng-ta pei-lu*, p. 451; and Haenisch and Yao, *Chinesische Gesandtenberichte*, p. 69.

[110] Jean-Paul Roux, *La religion des Turcs et les Mongols* (Paris: Payot, 1984), pp. 137–41.

[111] D. Michael Stoddart, *The Scented Ape*: *The Biology and Culture of Human Odour* (Cambridge University Press, 1990), p. 123.

Hö'elün was traveling along the Onan River with her fiancé, Chiledü, when they chanced upon Yesügei, who took an instant fancy to her. With the help of his brothers, Yesügei pursued the pair and Hö'elün, sensing their intent, persuaded her betrothed to flee for his life. As a parting gesture she pulled off her chemise (*chamcha*) so that the departing Chiledü could at least call her to mind by her scent (*hünür*) which inhered in the garment. Yesügei then seized the noble Hö'elün and shortly thereafter she gave birth to Temüǰin, the future Chinggis Qan.[112]

The next episode, dating to about 1207, recounts the break between Chinggis Qan and his chief shaman, Teb Tenggeri. When it came to the attention of the Mongolian leader that his shaman was trying to divide him from his brothers, he arranged a "wrestling match" to rid himself of this meddlesome priest. Münglig, Teb Tenggeri's father, realizing that this was in reality an execution, and that his son's back was about to be broken, took up the latter's hat, which had come off at the start of the struggle, clutched it to his bosom and breathed in its scent.[113]

In these contexts, obviously, body aroma provided a means of recognition and remembrance. But as Annick Le Guérer has argued, the matter does not end there: the act of smelling is also an act of incorporation because in smelling we "breathe in" the substance of another, and thus partake, in some degree, of their individual nature.[114] For the medieval Mongols, then, the transfer of clothing, an unwashed receptacle of residual bodily odor, also transmitted some of the vital essence of the original wearer. In other words, a sovereign's bestowal of his personal garments on a subject was a particular honor which transferred, in the physical and political sense, some of the monarch's aura, his charisma, to the recipient. Indeed, such transference was a common feature of North Asian religious belief, in which the various spiritual forces inhering in a shaman's costume could be imparted to another when properly acquired and consecrated.[115]

The West Asian convention of investiture was closely tied to the institution of the *ṭirāz*. This term, of Persian derivation, originally meant embroidery, especially an inscription on a band encircling the sleeve of a garment. Subsequently the word was extended to the clothing bearing the inscription and then, finally, to the court workshops, *dar al-ṭirāz*, producing such

[112] *SH*/Cleaves, sect. 55, p. 12, and *SH*/de Rachewiltz, sect. 55, pp. 22–23. For further comment, see Leonardo Olschki, "Ölün's Chemise: An Episode from the *Secret History of the Mongols*," *JAOS* 67 (1947), 54–56, who draws attention to the similarity between the Mongolian form (*chamcha*) and its Greek (*kamison*) and Arabo-Persian (*qamīṣ*) equivalents. *The Rasūlid Hexaglot*, ed. by Golden, f. 11r, col. B defines the Mongolian *jamjā* (*chamcha*) as a *qamīṣ*.

[113] *SH*/Cleaves, sect. 245, p. 181, and *SH*/de Rachewiltz, sect. 245, p. 142.

[114] Annick L. Guérer, *Scent: The Mysterious and Essential Powers of Smell* (New York: Kodansha International, 1994), pp. 23–26.

[115] Mircea Eliade, *Shamanism: Archaic Techniques of Ecstasy* (Princeton University Press, 1964), p. 147.

garments. Typically, the embroidery was done in gold thread against a dark cloth background so that the inscription would stand out.[116] Ibn Khaldūn held that the *ṭıraz*, as a workshop, originated in the pre-Islamic era and modern scholarship sustains his argument. While the exact origin of the *ṭirāz* system is unsettled, Serjeant inclines to the view that robes and palace factories began in Iran even if the custom of inscriptions started elsewhere, quite probably in Egypt.[117]

The honorific armbands found on Uighur court attendants depicted in the Bezeklig Murals, which date from T'ang times, reveal that the use of *ṭirāz* robes spread eastward in the Middle Ages and raises the question of organizational transfer.[118] By the thirteenth century, as we have seen, workshops and artisan colonies making textiles and inscribed garments for the court were found throughout the Mongolian Empire and are particularly well documented in Yuan China. Unfortunately, there is insufficient evidence on the internal operations of these production centers to determine if organizational characteristics of the *dar al-ṭirāz* were transferred to China under Mongolian auspices. Certainly it is likely that the numerous Muslim weavers transported to China organized themselves along traditional lines, but the issue is complicated by the fact that court-sponsored production of textiles and clothing was hardly new to China. All of the Mongols' immediate predecessors in China, the Liao, Chin and Sung, had such workshops, including those specializing in silk brocade (*ling-chin yuan*).[119]

The possibility of Chinese influence on the royal workshops of West Asia has also been discussed. However, the argument, first broached by A. M. Belenitskii, that the institution of the *dar al-ṭirāz* died out in the eastern Islamic world prior to the Mongolian invasion and was then reintroduced under the name *kar-khānah* by the conquerors on the basis of Far Eastern models is simply not in accord with the known facts.[120] There is explicit and contemporary documentation that clearly demonstrates the existence of court workshops and "manufactories for royal robes" under the later

116 A. Grohman, "*Ṭirāz*," *Encyclopedia of Islam* (London: Luzac and Leiden: E. J. Brill, 1934), vol. IV, pp. 785–93. For an overview of extant *ṭirāz* textiles, see Nancy Micklewright, "*Ṭirāz* Fragments: Unanswered Questions about Medieval Islamic Textiles," in Carol Barrett Fisher, ed., *Brocade of the Pen: The Art of Islamic Writing* (East Lansing: Kresage Art Museum, Michigan State University, 1991), pp. 31–45.

117 Ibn Khaldūn, *The Muqaddimah*, vol. II, pp. 65–67, and Serjeant, *Textiles*, pp. 7–31.

118 On *ṭirāz* garments among the Uighurs, see Emil Esin, "The Court Attendants in Turkish Iconography," *Central Asiatic Journal*, 14/1–3 (1970), 93 and plate 10 between pp. 96 and 97.

119 *Liao shih* (Peking: Chung-hua shu-chü, 1974), ch. 37, pp. 441 and 442; Wittfogel and Feng, *History of Chinese Society*, pp. 143, 144, 157, and 369; *Chin shih* (Peking: Chung-hua shu-chü, 1975), ch. 57, p. 1322; *Sung shih* (Peking: Chung-hua shu-chü, 1977), ch. 175, p. 4231; and Werner Eichorn, "Zur Vorgeschichte des Aufstandes von Wang Hsiao-po and Li Shun in Szuchuan (993–995)," *Zeitschrift der Deutschen Morgenländischen Gesellschaft* 105/1 (1955), 192–209.

120 A. M. Belenitskii, "K voprosu o sotsial'nykh otnosheniiakh v Irane v Khulaguidskuiu epokhu," *Sovetskoe vostokovedenie* 5 (1948), 123.

Ghaznavids and Khwārazmshāhs, that is, in the century immediately preceding the rise of the Mongols.[121] This, of course, does not preclude some kind of East Asian imprint on the *kar-khānahs* of thirteenth-century Iran but again no such evidence is presently at hand.

While the question of institutional transfer remains obscure, there is ample evidence for the transfer of personnel. Large numbers of artisans, as we have seen, came to China from the "Western Region" and so, too, did many of the *sügürchis*, the officers in charge of the imperial wardrobe. Rashīd al-Dīn informs us that during Qubilai's reign the commanders of the *sūkūrchī* were Isma'īl, Muḥammad Shāh, Akhtāchī, Mubārak, Tūrmīsh, and his brother Yīghmīsh.[122] Of the six enumerated, three, Isma'īl, Muḥammad Shāh, and Mubārak, bear Muslim names; two, Tūrmīsh and Yīghmīsh, are Uighurs; and one has the Mongolian name or title, Aqtachi, "the equerry." The latter cannot be identified with certainty, but the most prominent Aqtachi in Qubilai's reign was an Alan, the latter an Iranian-speaking people from North Caucasia, the ancestors of the modern-day Ossetians.[123] Thus, five, or more likely six, of the officials who managed the imperial wardrobe in the formative stages of the Yuan dynasty came from central Asia and the Islamic world. It is hardly surprising that the Yuan court's use of and attitude toward textiles and dress had such a pronounced West Asian flavor.

Clothing practices inspired by West Asian conventions had a great symbolic and practical importance to Mongolian rulers. The messages and meanings actually conveyed by a given bestowal were of course complex and contingent, that is, dependent on the context of the ceremony, the intent of the principals, and the cultural perception of the participants and observers, and, consequently, open to differing interpretations, emphases, and levels of understanding.[124] What follows, then, is only a preliminary attempt to identify the more obvious and important messages conveyed by investiture in the Mongolian Empire.

On the most general level, robing was a form of conspicuous consumption, a dazzling demonstration of the ruler's control over energy, which as Bruce Trigger so forcefully argues, "constitutes the most fundamental and universally recognized measure of political power." In sedentary societies this was most often expressed by means of monumental architecture, in which the scale of buildings far exceed their functional requirements.[125]

121 I. M. Safi, "Fresh Light on the Ghaznavids," *Islamic Culture* 12 (1938), 199 and 201, and Horst, *Die Staatsverwaltung der Grosselǧūqen und Hōrazmšāhs*, pp. 26, 27, 105, 106, and 108.

122 Rashīd/Karīmī, vol. I, p. 657, and Rashīd/Boyle, p. 297.

123 On Aqtachi, see the *YS*, ch. 132, pp. 3205–06.

124 To use Eliade's terminology, successful symbolic systems, whether religious or political, are "multivalent," that is, every image contains a "bundle of meanings," all of which are "true." See *Images and Symbols*, p. 15.

125 Bruce G. Trigger, "Monumental Architecture: A Thermodynamic Explanation of Symbolic Behavior," *World Archaeology* 22 (1990), 119–32, quote on 128.

Among the nomads, however, this expenditure of energy was more often manifested, for obvious cultural reasons, in clothing rather than in building. Myriads of servitors swathed in cloth of gold was both eye-catching and telling evidence of the qaghan's enormous power, of his unlimited access to natural resources and to other people's talent and labor. At the same time, of course, the emperor's bestowal of *nasīj*, given the associations of gold in the nomads' world view, advertised and promoted the ruler's connectedness to the cosmos, the universe at large.[126] On a more mundane level, a grant from the qaghan's wardrobe can be read, correctly, as a reward or salary, a tangible share in the profits of empire. Such a grant was also a political act, establishing a reciprocal bond between subject and ruler, the essential purpose of formalized investiture ceremonies everywhere. While reciprocity was thereby created, so was hierarchy, for such grants also asserted and confirmed claims of sovereignty on the part of the giver and the acknowledgment of subordinate status on the part of the receiver. In the apt phrase of Robert Lopez, this was a "hierarchy through clothing," maintained in both the Old and New Worlds by means of a complex system of imperial monopolies on textile production, sumptuary laws, and investiture ceremonies.[127] Subordination, manifestly, is the message intended when Mongolian qaghans invested dependent rulers. And it deserves emphasis that in the highly personalized political system of the Mongols the act of subordination was typically repeated whenever a new ruler came to the throne; the previously established hierarchy, rendered void by the death of the principal, had to be formally and publicly reconstituted. This is the reason why Het'um, the king of Armenia sought investiture from Baidu and then from his rival and successor Ghazan, and why K'urd, an Armenian prince and garrison commander, was granted "respect and honor and *xilay* [*khil'at*]" by at least three Mongolian rulers of Iran in the course of the late thirteenth and early fourteenth centuries.[128] Equally important, robing communicated the delegation of royal authority to the inner circle. The frequent robing of household/government officials advertised their right to act on behalf of their sovereign. Such authority, in Buckler's fomulation, "was exercised in virtue of this incorporation into the royal person by means of a succession established by physical contact through royal clothing."[129] Finally, robing can also be understood as a rite of passage into a Chinggisid's extended political family which conferred upon those so initiated a new social identity

126 See Clark, *Symbols of Excellence*, p. 42.

127 Robert S. Lopez, "Silk Industry in the Byzantine Empire," *Speculum* 20 (1945), 10, 12, and 20–22. For the New World, see Patricia Anawalt, "Costume and Control: Aztec Sumptuary Laws," *Archaeology* 33/1 (1980), 33–43.

128 Bar Hebreaus, p. 506; and Avedis K. Sanjian, trans. and ed., *Colophons of Armenian Manuscripts: A Source for Middle Eastern History* (Cambridge, Mass.: Harvard University Press, 1969), p. 74.

129 F. W. Buckler, "The Oriental Despot," *Anglican Theological Review* 10/3 (1928), 242–43.

as a member of a prince's patrimonial household, the locus of power in all the Mongolian regimes.[130]

This connection between gifts of clothing and the act of incorporation was well understood by Rubruck. As a churchman sensitive to the implications of investiture, and as an individual deeply concerned about Mongolian designs on western Europe, he was most hesitant to accept such a gift. When Möngke offered him costly raiment he politely refused until he was ready to depart Mongolia for home, at which time he was persuaded to take, as a show of respect to the emperor, "a simple tunic."[131] Similarly, when Hülegü offered to honor Vardan, an Armenian monk, "with a garment of gold," the cleric declined, requesting instead "mercy for the world."[132] These two medieval men of the cloth, like Thomas Roe, the English ambassador to the Mughal court in 1615–19, studiously avoided these offers because they were already members of good standing of other equally exclusive corporations and they had, consequently, no desire to switch loyalties and join a new firm.[133]

For the Mongols, clothing was always a key and mandatory element in the establishment of new relationships. Yen Fu, eulogizing Bayan the Barin, says that the great general extended the realm to the far north and south and that "all [peoples] accepted our calendar and [all] adopted our [mode of] dress."[134] The first criterion for submission is, of course, Chinese, while the second graphically expresses the Mongolian idea that political incorporation required acceptance of their style of clothing.

The Yuan court's adoption of West Asian textiles and the practice of investiture raises the further question of the Chinese response to these imports. Were any of the clothing traditions or manufacturing techniques passed on to the Chinese?

The imprint of the Mongols on Chinese culture of the Ming was extensive and is found in such diverse areas as governmental institutions, language, personal names, hairstyles, greetings, and even in marriage customs.[135] The Mongolian impact on China is also evident in military organization, particularly the Ming guard system. Interestingly, the elite unit, which served as the political police of the early Ming, was the Brocade Uniform

130 On clothing and incorporation, see Arnold van Gennep, *The Rite of Passage* (University of Chicago Press, 1990), pp. 65–115 and 166; and Meyer Fortes, "Ritual and Office in Tribal Society," in M. Gluckmann, ed., *Essays on the Ritual of Social Relations* (Manchester University Press, 1962), pp. 53–88, especially pp. 56–57 and 66–67.

131 *Mongol Mission*, pp. 196 and 205; Rubruck/Jackson, pp. 228 and 251; and *Sinica Franciscana*, pp. 299 and 310.

132 Thompson, "Historical Compilation," 221.

133 On Roe's experiences, see Cohn, "Cloth, Clothing, and Colonialism," p. 31.

134 Su T'ien-chüeh, *Yuan wen-lei*, ch. 24, p. 19a, and Cleaves, "Biography of Bayan," 290.

135 See the pioneering work of Henry Serruys, "Remains of Mongol Customs in China during the Early Ming," *Monumenta Serica* 16 (1957), 137–90 and especially pp. 151–67 for a discussion of clothing.

Guard (*Chin-i wei*). This is certainly a direct inheritance of the Yuan, which, as Marco Polo testifies, dressed its *kesig* in sumptuous clothes.[136] And, on a small scale at least, *jisün* robes were still in vogue in the early Ming. In 1373, during the reign of Hung-wu, orders were issued that Commandants (*hsiao-wei*), a prestige title for junior officers, were "to wear *chih-sun* garments, belts, headgear and boots." By way of explanation, the text then adds that according to Yuan regulations *chih-sun* "is clothing of one color."[137] The introduction and wording of the definition probably indicates that the practice had died out by the end of the Ming and that the Ch'ing editors therefore felt the need to explain this by now obscure term.

As for technological transfer, it is well to stress from the outset that the Chinese produced their own gold brocade long before the Mongols. According to the findings of E. I. Lubo-Lesnichenko, the earliest meaning of the character *chin* was a patterned textile woven from dyed silk thread. Chinese familiarity with gold thread occurred initially at the end of the Han in consequence of closer contact with the Western Region. Sources of this era describe true gold brocade as a product of Syria and Northern India. Domestic production began in China in the fifth century but only in the T'ang era does *chin* take on its modern meaning of gold brocade.[138] In the following centuries, Chinese brocade became known in West Asia.[139] Obviously, then, the Mongols did not introduce gold brocade into China, but their preoccupation with *nasīj* left behind a detectable artistic and technological legacy.

First of all, the Ming, like its predecessor, continued to produce and dispense for political purposes a considerable quantity of gold brocade, variously called *chin-chin* or *chin-chih*, some of which found its way to the Mongols as tributary goods. During the 1440s and 1450s when the Oyirads, the Western Mongols under Esen were on the rise, and again in the 1570s when the Southern Mongols under Altan Qan formed a powerful state, the Ming court regularly sent gold brocade to these rulers and their retinues.[140] Whether this cloth was still woven in the West Asian manner is unknown but this is certainly a possiblity since we have explicit textual evidence that the Chinese were taught to make *nasīj*. According to the *Yuan shih*, when

[136] On the Mongolian roots of the Ming guard, see Romeyn Taylor, "Yuan Origins of the *Wei-so* System," in Charles M. Hucker, ed., *Chinese Government in Ming Times: Seven Studies* (New York: Columbia University Press, 1969), pp. 23–40. On the early history of the Brocade Uniform Guard, see Peter Greiner, *Die Brokatuniform-Brigade* (*Chin-i wei*) *der Ming-Zeit von den Anfängen bis zum Ende der T'ien-shun Periode (1368–1464)* (Wiesbaden: Otto Harrassowitz, 1975), pp. 13–18.

[137] *Ming shih*, ch. 67, p. 1648. On the title *hsiao-wei*, see Charles O. Hucker, *Dictionary of Official Titles in Imperial China* (Stanford University Press, 1988), pp. 238–39.

[138] E. I. Lubo-Lesnichenko, "Nekotorye terminy dlia shelkovykh tkanei v drevnem Kitae," *Trudy gosudarstvennogo Ermatizha* 5 (1961), 254–55.

[139] Oliver Wardrop, trans., *Visramiani: The Story of the Loves of Vis and Ramin* (London: Royal Asiatic Society, 1914), pp. 220 and 282.

[140] Serruys, *Sino-Mongol Relations during the Ming*, II, pp. 213–14, 141, 144–57 and 273–74.

the Hung-chou and Hsün-ma-lin Gold Brocade Offices were established in 1278 they "gathered together displaced persons, freed slaves, and other households to train them as civil artisans to weave and prepare *na-shih-shih*."[141] Hung-chou, which, it will be recalled, was initially composed of people from the Western Region and Chinese from K'ai-feng, now received a fresh complement of recruits from the local, floating population. Thus, two of the three colonies of West Asian weavers producing *nasīj* in the Yuan realm also functioned as training centers for Chinese apprentices.

And by implication at least, one of the Gold Thread Offices also had educational responsibilities. These offices have a complex history that must be untangled before the question of technological transfer can be assessed. In 1261 two Gold Thread Offices were founded under the Bureau for Imperial Manufactures and then in 1287 merged into one Office. Yet another Gold Thread Office was established in 1275 "to manage the affairs of the gold thread artisans' production."[142] The latter office, which apparently retained its separate identity, was subordinated to the Directorate-General for the Management of Sons of the Yurt (*ch'ieh-lien-k'ou*),[143] established in 1264 with orders to "assemble displaced persons, freed slaves, laicized Buddhists and Taoists and other households to teach them various categories of crafts and skills."[144] Given the function of its parent body, it seems quite probable that this Gold Thread Office taught as well as manufactured. But even if this was an instructional facility, the question of who did the teaching remains. Unlike the Gold Brocade Offices, whose personnel we can trace back to the eastern Islamic world, there is no indication of the ethnic background of the staff of this, or any other, Gold Thread Office. All that can be said with confidence is that the Mongols did in fact collect many Muslim and Christian goldsmiths, including the well-known Parisian artisan, Guillaume Boucher, and that they brought them east to serve the imperial court.[145] There is, then, circumstantial evidence that the Gold Thread Office formed in 1275 may have had personnel relocated from the Western Region and that they taught their highly specialized craft to Chinese.

The type of metallic thread most valued in West Asia and the Mediterranean world was either drawn or beaten from gold of high purity, *auro puro*, which provided the needed flexibility for the weaving operation. Such gold

141 *YS*, ch. 89, p. 2263, and Farquhar, *Government*, p. 319.

142 *YS*, ch. 88, pp. 2226–27, and ch. 89, p. 2256, and Farquhar, *Government*, pp. 83–84 and 313.

143 This phrase transcribes the colloquial Mongolian *ger-in k'e'ü*, the literary form of which is *ger-ün köbegüd*. See Cleaves, "Sino-Mongolian Inscription of 1335 in Memory of Chung Ying-jui," 51–52, note 170.

144 *YS*, ch. 89, p. 2254, and Farquhar, *Government*, p. 310.

145 *Mongol Mission*, pp. 43, 66, and 157; Rubruck/Jackson, p. 183; and *Sinica Franciscana*, pp. 92, 122, and 253. See also Leonardo Olschki, *Guillaume Boucher, a French Artist at the Court of the Khans* (Baltimore: Johns Hopkins Press, 1946), pp. 28–44.

thread was then usually twisted around a textile thread. Another technique used in the West was "membrane" gold which was applied to a substrate of animal gut or leather and then wrapped around textile thread. In China, gold thread was made of gilded strips of mulberry paper.[146] Of the various types, the Mongols, by all available evidence, were most attracted to the beaten or drawn gold threads of the West, which are famed for holding their luster for long periods. Presumably, this is why Ögödei publicly proclaimed *nasīj* superior to the fabrics of China.

The Mongolian courts, obviously, had ready access to the western and Chinese varieties of gold thread and recent technical analysis of two brocades dating from the thirteenth century demonstrates that both were used. The textiles in question, now in the Cleveland Museum of Art, have much in common: both were preserved in Tibet before coming on the market and their designs, while differing in theme, are predominantly Persian in inspiration with secondary motifs of Chinese origin. In one textile, however, gold has been applied to an animal (membrane or leather) substrate wrapped around a silk core and is clearly of the West Asian type. In the other, gilt has been applied to a paper substrate in the Chinese fashion. In the latter case, it seems most likely that West Asian weavers, sent east by the Mongols, were experimenting with local Chinese materials and techniques.[147] Moreover, since large numbers of West Asian and Chinese weavers were most certainly working side-by-side in the Yuan, it is easy to believe that technical information and design features of this kind were frequently exchanged. Indeed, the use of animal substrate in the manufacture of gold thread during the Ming, noted in the *Exploitation of the Work of Nature*, the famous seventeenth-century Chinese manual of technology, may be the result of such contact in the Yuan.[148] This may explain as well one of the technical features of an imperial robe of the early Ch'ing which was decorated, in Western fashion, with flat gold wire wrapped around a thread core.[149] Naturally, the proofs for this assumption can only be established by minute investigations of historical textiles themselves, their weave structures, dyes, and thread types. While the literary sources, such as those assembled here, cannot alone and unaided bring in a

[146] Braun Ronsdorf, "Gold and Silver Fabrics from Medieval to Modern Times," *CIBA Review* (1961–63), 2–8; Hans Wulff, *The Traditional Crafts of Persia: Their Development, Technology, and Influence on Eastern and Western Civilizations* (Cambridge, Mass.: The MIT Press, 1966), pp. 40–47 and 175–77; Petrascheck-Heim, "Mittelalterlichen Textilfunde," 302–33; and Ernst Hoke, "Mikroanalytische Untersuchungen von Edelmetellfäden an Textilien in Gräbern vom Kordlar Tepe (Westaserbaidschan)," *Archaeologische Mitteilungen aus Iran* 15 (1982), 307–10.

[147] Anne E. Wardwell, "Two Silk and Gold Textiles of the Early Mongol Period," *The Bulletin of the Cleveland Museum of Art*, 79/10 (December 1992), 354–78 and especially 362–64 on thread types.

[148] Sung Ying-hsing, *T'ien-kung k'ai-wu*, pp. 338–39.

[149] Schuyler Cammann, "A Robe of the Ch'ien-lung Emperor," *Journal of the Walters Art Gallery* 10 (1947), 119.

final verdict on the extent of West Asian influence on Chinese textile traditions in the thirteenth and fourteenth centuries, they can document the concrete opportunities the Mongols created for such exchanges which suggest new possibilities for the specialist to consider.

Lastly, in exploring these possibilities it is well to remember Arnold Pacey's stricture that the transfer of technology always involves a dialogue in which the receiving culture "interrogates" the introduced technique "on the basis of their own experience and knowledge of local conditions."[150] Thus, the evidence for such transfers, in weaving or any other craft, is usually to be found in a series of adaptations and modifications resulting in a new synthesis, not in the direct transfer and acceptance of entire technological (or artistic) packages.

[150] Arnold Pacey, *Technology in World Civilization: A Thousand Year History* (Cambridge, Mass.: MIT Press, 1991), p. viii.

CHAPTER 6

Conclusion

While West Asian textiles, most notably *nasīj*, were found in great abundance in Yuan China, this did not constitute a new departure in Eurasian cultural history. Long before the rise of the Mongolian Empire, China and the peoples of the West exchanged textiles and textile technology. Indeed, fabrics were so central to this relationship that the shorthand term "Silk Road," first coined by the German geographer Ferdinand von Richthofen, has been used in the West since the late nineteenth century to designate this complex web of commercial and cultural interaction.[1] These contacts, anchored by China in the east, by Iran in the west, and mediated by the nomads and oasis dwellers of central Asia, constitute the longest and best documented example of sustained, intercultural communication in Eurasian and, indeed, in world history.

In more recent times this Western usage has been adopted in China, where in the last few years several conferences on "Silk Road Studies" have been held. The term has gained such wide acceptance, of course, because the demand for Chinese silk in the Mediterranean world is generally believed to have initiated and sustained contact between East and West thoughout antiquity and the Middle Ages. Moreover, the story of the passage of Chinese silk manufacturing techniques to the West is perhaps the most celebrated, if not the most consequential, instance of cultural diffusion in world history.[2]

The origins and character of this exchange are, however, somewhat more complex than was once thought. While it is true that intensive and regular commerce only began in the late first millennium B.C. with the rise of

[1] Ferdinand von Richthofen, "Ueber die Zentralasiatischen Seidenstrassen bis zum 2. Jahrhundert n. Chr.," *Verhandlungen der Gesellschaft für Erdkunde zu Berlin* 4 (1877), 96–122.

[2] For recent treatments of this transfer, see E. I. Lubo-Lesnichenko, *Kitai na shelkovom puti: Shelk i vneshnie sviazi drevnego i rannesrednevekogo Kitaia* (Moscow: Vostochnaia literatury, 1994), pp. 217–69; Kuhn, *Textile Technology: Spinning and Reeling*, pp. 418–33; and Xinru Liu, *Ancient India and Ancient China: Trade and Religious Exchanges, AD 1–600* (Delhi: Oxford University Press, 1988), pp. 64–75. The linguistic evidence for its diffusion is analyzed by Penglin Wang, "On the Etymology of English Silk: A Case Study of IE and Altaic Contact," *Central Asiatic Journal* 37 (1993), 225–48.

Alexander the Great's empire and the subsequent emergence of the Parthian and Kushan states between Han China and the Roman Empire, such economic exchange was by no means unprecedented.[3] Earlier, in the fourth and third millennia, there was long-distance trade in semi-precious stones, lapis lazuli, and nephrite, which maintained its dominance until the centuries immediately preceding the Christian era when it was displaced by cloth, mainly silk, as the principal commodity.[4] Whether this circulation of prestige goods between Afghanistan and the ancient Near East constituted a Bronze Age "world system," an extended zone of integrated economic exchange, is now being debated.[5] Further complicating this picture is the recent discovery of a strand of silk in the hair of an Egyptian mummy, which a combination of infrared and chemical analysis strongly suggests came from China. If correct, this means that Chinese silk reached the eastern Mediterranean around 1000 B.C., centuries before the traditional date.[6]

The movement of silk westward, whatever its precise chronology, certainly gave rise to our current nomenclature for East–West exchange at large, but it should not be forgotten that other goods – Chinese bronze mirrors and Syrian glass – contributed substantially to the overall volume of trade.[7] Nor should we lose sight of the fact that textiles of diverse types moved eastward as well: cotton cloth, for example, initially reached China as gifts from Türk qaghans and in later centuries the techniques of cotton cultivation spread to the Middle Kingdom through the oases of central Asia, that is, along the old Silk Road.[8] There is also ample evidence that

[3] On the intensification of exchange between China and the West and its chronology, see A.-P. Frankfor (H.-P. Francfort), "Sushchestvoval li velikii shelkovyi put vo II–I tys. do N.E.," in V. M. Masson, ed., *Vzaimodeistvie kochevykh kul'tur i drevnikh tsivilizatsii* (Alma Ata: Nauka Kazakhskoi SSR, 1989), pp. 203–17; Osamu Sudzuki, "Silk Road and Alexander's Eastern Campaign," *Orient: Report of the Society for Near Eastern Studies in Japan* 11 (1975), 67–92; and Michael Loewe, "Spices and Silk: Aspects of World Trade in the First Seven Centuries of the Christian Era," *Journal of the Royal Asiatic Society*, no. 2 (1971), 166–79.

[4] T. W. Beale, "Early Trade in Highland Iran: A View from the Source Area," *World Archaeology* 5 (1973), 133–48; V. I. Sarianidi, "O velikom lazuritovom puti na Drevnem Vostoke," *Kratkie soobshcheniia Instituta arkheologii* 114 (1968), 3–9; V. I. Sarianidi, "The Lapis Lazuli Route in the Ancient East," *Archaeology* 24/1 (1971), 12–15; Georgina Herrman, "Lapis Lazuli: The Early Phases of its Trade," *Iraq* 30 (1968), 21–57, especially 52–54; and Joan Crowfoot Payne, "Lapis Lazuli in Early Egypt," *Iraq* 30 (1968), 58–61.

[5] See Andre Gunder Frank, "Bronze Age World System Cycles," *Current Anthropology* 34 (1993), 383–429 with commentary.

[6] G. Lubec, *et al.*, "Use of Silk in Ancient Egypt," *Nature* 362 (March 4, 1993), 25. Previous to this discovery Chinese silk was thought to have reached the West in the middle of the first millennium BC. See Barber, *Prehistoric Textiles*, pp. 30–32 and 203–05.

[7] See E. I. Lubo-Lesnichenko, "Velikii shelkovyi put," *Voprosy istorii* 9 (September 1985), 100 and J. Thorley, "The Silk Trade between China and the Roman Empire at its Height, *circa* A.D. 90–130," *Greece and Rome*, 2nd series, 18 (1971), 71–80.

[8] On the diffusion of cotton across Eurasia, see Hilda Ecsedy, "Böz – An Exotic Cloth in the Chinese Imperial Court," *Altorientalische Forschungen* 3 (1975), 145–53; András Róna-Tas, "Böz in the Altaic World," *Altorientalische Forschungen* 3 (1975), 155–63; Kung Chao, *The Development of Cotton Textile Production in China* (Cambridge, Mass.: Harvard University

Western felts, woolens, asbestos, carpets, and gold brocades traveled to China and did so well before the Yuan period.[9]

In many respects the Mongolian era should be viewed as a culmination of this history of textile exchange and as a prelude, or even an incubator of a new phase, one heralded by the emergence of European seaborne empires.[10] Yet, while the Yuan was not an aberration, it was unique in one important respect: under Mongolian auspices large numbers of West Asian weavers and textile workers, not just the products of their looms, were sent east and became permanent residents in China. This may not be entirely unprecedented but surely the scale on which these forced resettlements were undertaken was extraordinary, and, as argued previously, created unparalleled opportunities for technical and artistic interchange.

The specifics underlying the Mongols' attraction for elements of the textile traditions of West Asia have already been treated and here this phenomenon will be analyzed in broader terms, as an example of the general process of cultural borrowing and the centrality of nomadic peoples to East–West exchange.

Pastoral nomads do not and cannot supply all their needs from domestic resources. They are, to use Anatoly Khazanov's phrase, "non-autarchic" in either the economic, political, or cultural sense.[11] They regularly acquire necessary economic resources from the sedentary world and appropriate various aspects of sedentary culture, e.g., alphabets, religions, etc., when deemed advantageous. Borrowing is typically most frequent during phases of state formation, very much a cyclical phenomenon in nomadic history, when their contact with sedentaries is intensified through conquest and their need for specialists is greatest.

However, nomads, like all other peoples do not borrow randomly, but selectively by filtering new, external elements through their own cultural norms and aspirations. This process, known as reidentification to psychologists and anthropologists, is one of the principal mechanisms by which

Press, 1977), pp. 4–24; and Andrew M. Watson, *Agricultural Innovation in the Early Islamic World: The Diffusion of Crops and Farming Techniques* (Cambridge University Press, 1983), pp. 31–41.

9 Laufer, *Sino-Iranica*, pp. 488–502; Edward H. Schafer, *The Golden Peaches of Samarkand: A Study of T'ang Exotics* (Berkeley: University of California Press, 1963), pp. 195–207; Dorothy G. Shepard, "Iran between East and West," in Theodore Bowie, ed., *East–West in Art: Patterns of Cultural and Aesthetic Relationships* (Bloomington: Indiana University Press, 1966), pp. 99–104; and Chau Ju-kua, *Chinese and Arab Trade*, pp. 116 and 138.

10 On this connection see J. R. S. Phillips, *The Medieval Expansion of Europe* (Oxford University Press, 1988), pp. 245–53, and Abbas Hamdani, "Columbus and the Recovery of Jerusalem," *JAOS* 99 (1979), 41 ff.

11 This discussion relies on Anatoly M. Khazanov's "Ecological Limitations of Nomadism in the Eurasian Steppes and Their Social and Cultural Implications," *Asian and African Studies: Journal of the Israel Oriental Society* 24 (1990), 1–15.

culture is transmitted, modified, and rejected.[12] Whenever individuals or cultures encounter a new phenomenon, there is a pronounced tendency to place it into an established category, that is, to identify the new with something already familiar from previous experience. This is continuously reflected in language. The Amerindians, for example, confronted with steam locomotives categorized them as "iron horses," and we still say in English "ready, aim, fire," not "ready, aim, explode," because our predecessors originally reidentified guns, or "fire arms" with napalm or "Greek fire." If the new element can be comfortably inserted, often following substantial modification, into a pre-existing category and is deemed somehow useful, borrowing and cultural change occur. On the other hand, if the new item is so alien that no category can be found to accommodate it, or if perceived as a danger to a society's basic system of cultural categorization, it will be rejected or at best only grudgingly accepted in the presence of external pressure.

The great advantage of this approach to the study of cultural exchange is that it shifts the emphasis from the fact of transfer, the preoccupation of the earlier generation of diffusionists, to the act of borrowing, the domain of the acculturationists.[13] Although pioneered by ethnographers working with contemporary documentation, theories of acculturation, which provide a theoretical framework for analyzing the cultural dynamics of contact, borrowing, and rejection, can profitably be applied to historical materials, a point repeatedly made by the anthropologist Margaret Hodgen.[14]

In the Mongolian case, they were receptive to West Asian textiles and investiture ceremonies because they were culturally preadapted, already possessing well-established categories that favored such borrowings: most specifically the cosmological and political significance of gold and the messages imparted by the manipulation of clothing. The Mongols, in other words, drew on long-standing nomadic traditions for their ideology and political symbolism; what they borrowed from the sedentary world were the physical means of expressing and propagating these native notions on a vast, imperial scale. In a similar vein, Amerindians were preadapted to

[12] On this process, also called identification and substitution, see H. G. Barnett, "Culture Processes," *American Anthropologist* 42 (1940), 31–37, and Melville J. Herskovits, *Man and His Works: The Science of Cultural Anthropology* (New York: Alfred A. Knopf, 1951), pp. 553–58, especially p. 557.

[13] For examples of the different emphases of the two schools, see Wilhelm Koppers, "Diffusion: Transmission and Acceptance," in William L. Thomas, ed., *Yearbook of Anthropology, 1955* (New York: Wenner-Gren Foundation for Anthropological Research, 1955), pp. 169–81, and Leonard Broom, Bernard J. Siegel, Evan Z. Vogt, and James B. Watson, "Acculturation: An Explanatory Formulation," *American Anthropologist* 56 (1954), 973–1000, especially 982–87. On the importance of the shift from the question of "what" to that of "how," see Herskovits, *Man and His Works*, pp. 523–41.

[14] See Margaret Hodgen, "Glass and Paper: An Historical Study of Acculturation," *Southwestern Journal of Anthropology* 1 (1945), 466–97 and her major monograph, *Change and History: A Study of Dated Distributions of Technological Innovations in England* (New York: Wenner-Gren Foundation for Anthropological Research, 1952).

accept European trinkets of glass and copper because these substances had long-established "ideological value" for their religious and ceremonial life.[15]

The Mongols' use of gold cloth in their imperial ceremonies had clear antecedents in their own folk tradition and was therefore fashioned from recognizable cultural materials.[16] This is typical of much royal ritual, since to be effective in conveying images of authority and claims of legitimacy it must be comprehensible to the participants and observers, to the rank and file. Thus it is not splendor in and of itself that projects royal authority, but splendor of a particular kind.[17]

Luxury goods, as we have seen, were critical ingredients in the political system of the nomads. Consequently, Gibbon's description of such objects as "splendid and trifling" is extremely misleading.[18] As Jane Schneider has pointed out in another context, scholarship on premodern economic systems has generally and wrongly opposed "luxuries" to "necessities," an opposition which implies that the splendid and trifling can be eliminated without consequence. This, she argues, is patently untrue, since luxuries are necessary in fashioning loyal retinues and ramifying chains of clientage.[19] These strictures apply with particular force to nomadic society in which power is derived from the acquisition and retention of followers, not the acquisition of land. Thus "luxuries" were in fact "necessities" in their political culture, a point well understood by the Byzantine ruler Constantine Porphyrogenitus (r. 945–59), who in the very same passage of his mirror for princes warns his sons and heirs to avoid giving imperial cloths, crowns, and Greek fire to the northern barbarians.[20] To his mind, at least, luxury cloth and advanced weapons technology had an equal weight in maintaining the political and military integrity of the realm. The use of modern notions of utility, necessity, and extravagance can lead to considerable distortion of medieval societies' set of cultural and economic values.[21]

[15] Christopher L. Miller and George R. Hamell, "A New Perspective on Indian-White Contact: Cultural Symbols and Colonial Trade," *The Journal of American History* 73/2 (1986), 311–28.

[16] In many societies the imagery and uses of cloth at the highest political levels are firmly rooted in widely held notions about the place and power of cloth among the populace at large. See, for example, C. A. Bayly, "The Origins of Swadeshi (Home Industry): Cloth and Indian Society," in Arjun Appadurai, ed., *The Social Life of Things: Commodities in Cultural Perspective* (Cambridge University Press, 1988), pp. 286–93 and Elisha P. Renne, *Cloth That Does Not Die: The Meaning of Cloth in Bùnú Social Life* (Seattle: University of Washington Press, 1995), pp. 85–103.

[17] Maurice Bloch, "The Ritual of the Royal Bath in Madagascar: The Dissolution of Death, Birth and Fertility into Authority," in Cannadine and Price, *Rituals of Royalty*, pp. 271–97 and especially p. 295.

[18] Edward Gibbon, *The History of the Decline and Fall of the Roman Empire*, ed. by J. B. Bury (London: Methuen, 1909), vol. I, p. 60.

[19] Jane Schneider, "Was There a Pre-Capitalist World System?" *Peasant Studies* 6/1 (January 1977), 20–29.

[20] Porphyrogenitus, *De Administrando Imperio*, pp. 67 and 69.

[21] Cf. the comments of Lopez, "Silk Industry in the Byzantine Empire," 1.

Luxuries were then a form of political currency, an essential element in the formation and maintenance of premodern states of various types and levels of complexity.[22] For the Mongolian rulers, as for many others, the creation of a following required a sustained system of what might be called conspicuous redistribution. And once started, such presentations, like the Roman bread and circuses, essentially expenditures on legitimacy and loyalty, could not be halted or even significantly reduced, and typically became a permanent and heavy drain on the treasury.[23] Indeed, for the nomads at least, the imperial treasury was essentially a mechanism for the redistribution of luxuries, most especially cloth and clothing. And this in turn reveals something important about the actual nature of trans-Eurasian trade. We normally think of nomadic states as stimulating long-distance exchange through the creation of a pax that provides security and transportation facilities;[24] but in fact the process of state formation among the nomads in and of itself stimulates trade through an increased demand for precious metals, gems, and, most particularly, fine cloths. Politics, especially imperial politics, was impossible without such commodities.

Further, it must also be borne in mind that even the basic ecological and logistical requirements of nomadic life facilitated this process of borrowing and transmission. Since nomadism depends on mobility, material possessions had to be kept to a minimum and individual wares had to be light and transportable. From the Scythians down to this century nomads had no other option but to "wear the wealth" in the form of horse trappings, jewelry, garments, and elaborately decorated headgear.[25] And what, in their cultural world, could compete with a gold brocade robe and crimson, pearled belt?

Obviously, the transmission of cultural wares between East and West is a complex process and has to be approached from a number of directions. Some have concentrated on the economics of long-distance trade, focusing on the questions of markets, transportation costs, commercial agents, and routes.[26] Others have investigated the influences exerted by the great

[22] Rita Smith Kipp and Edward M. Schortman, "The Political Impact of Trade on Chiefdoms," *American Anthropologist* 91 (1989), 370–85, and Marshall D. Sahlins, "Poor Man, Rich Man, Big Man, Chief: Political Types in Melanesia and Polynesia," *Comparative Studies in Society and History* 5 (1962–63), 296–300.

[23] Joseph A. Tainter, *The Collapse of Complex Societies* (Cambridge University Press, 1990), pp. 116–17.

[24] Such views are expressed, among others, by David Christian, "Inner Eurasia as a Unit of World History," *Journal of World History* 5 (1994), 182–83; Andre Gunder Frank, *The Centrality of Central Asia* (Amsterdam: V. U. University Press, 1992), pp. 25–40; and William H. McNeil, *The Rise of the West* (University of Chicago Press, 1963), pp. 322–26.

[25] Herodotus, *The Persian Wars*, I.215 and IV.104 and Strabo, *The Geography*, XI.v.8. See also A. M. Khazanov, *Zoloto Skyfov* (Moscow: Sovetskii khudozhnik, 1975), pp. 6–7.

[26] See, for example, Robert S. Lopez, "China Silk in Europe in the Yuan Period," *JAOS* 72 (1952), 72–76, and M. V. Fekhner, "K istorii torgovykh sviazei Rusi so stranami Vostoka v

sedentary civilizations on one another, especially in the area of art and material culture.[27] Still others have focused on the expansion of religions, a process which typically provided both a motive and a matrix for the movement of numerous commodities, including silk, across Eurasia.[28] As has been recently argued, world religions constituted world systems without world empires and did so long before the advent of capitalism. The "Buddhist international," to use Adshead's term, was already an effective "world" institution at the beginning of the Christian era, and Islam, another "community of discourse," as Voll notes, survived and flourished following the disintegration of its imperial institutions. Such systems were essentially communications networks within which ideas, commodities, and peoples circulated throughout Eurasia.[29] These, of course, are perfectly valid concerns and all contribute to a better understanding of East–West exchange. What needs to be added to this discussion, however, are the nomads, their social and cultural priorities. And while the nomads' role in the mutual interaction of the sedentary civilizations is to some extent always acknowledged, they have remained secondary figures in the equation of exchange.[30]

To some extent, the limited role assigned the nomads is a byproduct of the long-held stereotypes in the sedentary world which viewed, with some consistency, the steppe peoples as barbarians, destroyers of civilizations, or

domongol'skoe vremia (Po materialam shelkovykh tkanei)," in *Kavkaz i Sredniaia Aziia v drevnosti i srednevekov'e*, ed. B. A. Litvinskii (Moscow: Nauka, 1981), pp. 139–45.

[27] For two excellent studies of the process of reidentification in artistic exchange, see Richard Ettinghausen, *From Byzantium to Sassanian Iran and the Islamic World: Three Modes of Artistic Influences* (The L. A. Mayer Memorial Studies in Islamic Art and Archaeology, vol. III; Leiden: E. J. Brill, 1972), pp. 1–2, and Marina D. Whitman, "The Scholar, the Drinker, and the Ceramic Pot-Painter," in Soucek, ed., *Content and Context of the Visual Arts in the Islamic World*, pp. 255–78. On the diffusion of material culture, see, for example, Ryōichi Hayashi, *The Silk Road and the Shoso-in* (New York: Weatherhill, 1975), pp. 85–103.

[28] See Liu Xinru, "Silks and Religions in Eurasia," *Journal of World History* 6 (1995), 25–48. These themes are now explored in greater detail in her excellent monograph, *Silk and Religion: An Exploration of Material Life and the Thought of People, 600–1200* (Delhi: Oxford University Press, 1996).

[29] S. A. M. Adshead, *China in World History* (London: Macmillan, 1988), pp. 52 and 102, and John Obert Voll, "Islam as a Special World System," *Journal of World History* 5 (1994), 213–26, especially 219.

[30] Among those who have noted the importance of nomadic culture in this exchange are Manfred G. Raschke, "New Studies in Roman Commerce with the East," in Hildegard Temporini, ed., *Aufstieg und Niedergang der Römische Welt* (Berlin and New York: Walter de Guyter, 1978), vol. II, pt. 9.2, pp. 606–10; Hero Granger-Taylor and John Peter Wild, "Some Ancient Silk from the Crimea in the British Museum," *Antiquaries Journal* 61 (1981), 305; and Victor H. Mair, "Dunhuang as a Funnel for Central Asian Nomads into China," in Gary Seaman, ed., *Ecology and Empire: Nomads in the Cultural Evolution of the Old World* (Los Angeles: Ethnographics Press, 1989), p. 158. For more traditional views, see Joseph Needham, *Clerks and Craftsmen in China and the West: Lectures and Addresses on the History of Science and Technology* (Cambridge University Press, 1970), pp. 30–39; and Olov Janse, "L'Empire des Steppes et les relations entre l'Europe et l'Extrême-Orient dans l'Antiquité," *Revue des Arts Asiatiques* 9 (1935), 9–26.

at best children of nature and noble savages.[31] This, however, should not blind contemporary investigators to the fact that the followers of Attila, Chinggis Qan, and Temür had complex cultures with their own cosmological precepts, aesthetic norms, and systems of moral and economic values. And it was these indigenous world views and tastes that provided their criteria for borrowing when they encountered and surveyed the cultural riches of the sedentary world. The peoples of the steppe were not a premodern equivalent of United Parcel Service, disinterestedly conveying wares hither and yon between the centers of civilization. Their history and their priorities must be brought more fully into the discussion if we are to understand these important contacts between East and West.

In summation, the process at work in the transference of Muslim textiles within the Mongolian Empire is by no means an isolated case: many of the commodities and ideas that successfully made the long journey across Eurasia from antiquity to early modern times did so because the intermediaries, "those who lived in felt-walled tents," and who in the best of times dressed in gold brocade, found them meaningful in the context of their own cultural traditions.

[31] On these widely held stereotypes, see Michel Cartier, "Barbarians through Chinese Eyes: The Emergence of an Anthropological Approach to Ethnic Differences," *The Comparative Civilizations Review* 6 (1981), 1–14; Ruth I. Merserve, "The Inhospitable Land of the Barbarian," *Journal of Asian History* 16 (1982), 51–89; and Denis Sinor, "The Greed of the Northern Barbarians," in Clark and Draghi, *Aspects of Altaic Civilization, II*, pp. 171–82.

APPENDIX

Designs on Mongolian Clothing

In the course of this investigation into *nasīj*, I have come across several references in contemporary sources to the types of decoration and symbols found on Mongolian clothing. These cast some further light on the role of clothing in Mongolian society and may, as well, prove of use to specialists attempting to identify historical textiles.

The earliest statement on the subject comes from P'eng Ta-ya, who visited the Mongols in the late 1230s: He reports that "as for designs [the Mongols] use the sun and moon and the dragon and phoenix. There is no difference," he adds, "between the elevated and the humble."[1] The continued use of the dragon and phoenix, long Chinese symbols for imperial power and auspicious good fortune, is confirmed by the chapter on official dress in the *Yuan shih* which notes that certain of the emperor's garments were decorated with gold dragons and his hats with gold phoenixes.[2] The Mongols carried these symbols with them when they turned west and conquered much of the Islamic world in the period 1220–60. Dragon and phoenix designs are found on the frieze tiles at Takht-i Sulaymān, a palace in Azerbaijan built for Abagha sometime between 1270 and 1275.[3]

The sun and moon played an important role in the religion and art of the early Iranian peoples, both settled and nomadic, a tradition which had its origins in the astrological cults of the ancient Near East. From the Iranians these notions spread to the Turks and Mongols, for whom the sun and moon were objects of worship and veneration.[4] According to Carpini, the Mongols, together with fire, water, and earth, "venerate and adore the sun

[1] P'eng and Hsü, *Hei-ta shih-lüeh*, p. 479, and Haenisch and Yao, *Chinesische Gesandtenberichte*, p. 121.

[2] *YS*, ch. 78, p. 1938.

[3] Oliver Watson, *Persian Lustre Ware* (London and Boston: Faber and Faber, 1985), p. 136 and color plate La.

[4] A. M. Belenitskii, "Novye pamiatniki iskusstva drevnego Piandzhikenta: Opyt ikonograficheskogo istolkovaniia," in A. M. Belenitskii and B. B. Piotrovskii, eds., *Skul'ptura i zhivopis drevnego Piandzhikenta* (Moscow: Izdatel'stvo akademii nauk SSSR, 1959), pp. 53–64, and Roux, *La religion des turcs et des Mongols*, pp. 127–32.

[and] the moon."[5] By the thirteenth century this was part of a very old tradition in Mongolia and southern Siberia which can be traced in the decorations on locally produced ceramic ware.[6]

Lastly, it should be noted that while in P'eng Ta-ya's day "there was no difference between elevated and humble" in matters of dress, this situation changes abruptly during Qubilai's reign. In 1270, according to the *Yuan shih*, the court "prohibited the weaving of the sun, moon, dragons and tigers on silk and satin fabric and the use of dragons and rhinoceros to decorate horse saddles."[7] The prohibition on the use of the sun and moon is in no way surprising, since these two symbols had become intimately associated with imperial power during the intervening decades. This transition is evidenced in Marco Polo's statement that Qubilai's "ensign royal" was decorated "with the figure of the sun and of the moon."[8] Sumptuary laws, following Sung and Liao precedent, henceforth tried to reserve the symbolic power and magical properties of the sun and moon, dragons, tigers, and rhinoceros for the exclusive use of the imperial court.[9]

[5] *Mongol Mission*, p. 10, see also p. 12, and *Sinica Franciscana*, pp. 39 and 41.

[6] See the discussion of E. V. Shavkunov, "O semantike tamgoobraznykh znakov i nekotorykh vidov ornamenta na keramike s Shaiginskogo gorodishcha," *Sovetskaia etnografiia* 3 (1972), 128–33.

[7] *YS*, ch. 7, p. 131.

[8] Marco Polo, p. 197.

[9] In 1078, by order of the Liao emperor, the common people were forbidden to wear "brocade and variegated silk with decorations of the sun, moon, mountains, or dragons." See Wittfogel and Feng, *History of Chinese Society, Liao*, p. 236.

Bibliography

Sources: Texts, translations and collections

Abu-l-Ghazi, *Rodoslovnaia Turkmen: Sochinenie Abu-l-Ghazi Khana Khivinskogo*, trans. by A. A. Kononov (Moscow-Leningrad: Izdatel'stvo akademii nauk SSSR, 1958).

Abū'l Fidā The Memoirs of a Syrian Prince, trans. by P. M. Holt (Wiesbaden: Franz Steiner, 1983).

Agathangelos, *History of the Armenians*, trans. by Robert W. Thomson (Albany, New York: State University of New York Press, 1976).

Ammianus Marcellinus, trans. by John C. Rolfe (Loeb Classical Library; Cambridge, Mass.: Harvard University Press, 1958).

The Analects of Confucius, trans. by Arthur Waley (London: George Allen and Unwin, 1938).

Arrian, *History of Alexander and Indica*, trans. by E. Iliff Robson (Loeb Classical Library; Cambridge, Mass.: Harvard University Press, 1958).

Bang, W. and A. von Gabain, "Türkische Turfan-Texte, II, Manichaica," *Sitzungsberichte der Preussischen Akademie der Wissenchaften, Phil.-Hist. klasse* 22 (1929), 411–30.

Bar Hebraeus, *The Chronography of Gregory Abūl-Faraj . . . commonly known as Bar Hebraeus*, trans. by Ernest A. Wallis Budge (London: Oxford University Press, 1932), vol. I.

Benjamin of Tudela, *The Itinerary*, trans. by M. N. Adler, repr. (Malibu, California: Pangloss Press, 1987).

Al-Bīrūnī, *The Book of Introduction in the Elements of the Arts of Astrology*, trans. by R. Ramsay Wright (London: Luzac, 1924).

Bodrogligeti, A., *The Persian Vocabulary of the Codex Cumanicus* (Budapest: Akadémia Kiadó, 1971).

Brosset, M., trans., *Histoire de la Géorgie*, 1re partie, *Histoire ancienne, jusqu'an en 1469 de J.C.* (St. Petersburg: Académie des sciences, 1850).

Budge, Ernest A. Wallis, trans., *The Syriac Book of Medicines: Syrian Anatomy, Pathology and Therapeutics in the Early Middle Ages* repr. (Amsterdam: APA-Philo Press, 1976), vol. II.

The Monks of Kūblāi Khān (London: The Religious Tract Society, 1928).

Chao Hung, *Meng-ta pei-lu*, in Wang, *Meng-ku shih-liao*.

Chardin, John, *Travels in Persia, 1673–1677*, repr. (New York: Dover Publications, 1988).
Chau Ju-kua, *His Work on Chinese and Arab Trade in the Twelfth and Thirteenth Centuries, entitled Chu-fan-chi*, trans. by Friedrich Hirth and W. W. Rockhill, repr. (Taipei: Literature House, 1965).
Chaucer, Geoffrey, *The Canterbury Tales*, trans. by Nevill Coghill (London: Penguin Books, 1977).
Chin shih (Peking: Chung-hua shu-chü, 1975).
Chunakova, O. M., trans., *Kniga deianii Ardashira syna Papaka* (Moscow: Nauka, 1987).
Clavijo, Ruy González de, *Embassy to Tamerlane, 1403–1406*, trans. by Guy Le Strange (New York and London: Harper Brothers, 1928).
Cleaves, Francis W., "The Sino-Mongolian Inscription of 1362 in Memory of Prince Hindu," *HJAS* 12 (1949), 1–133.
"The Sino-Mongolian Edict of 1453 in the Topkapi Sarayi Müzesi," *HJAS* 13 (1950), 431–46.
"The Sino-Mongolian Inscription of 1335 in Memory of Chang Ying-jui." *HJAS* 13 (1950), 1–131.
"The Biography of Bayan of the Barīn in the *Yuan shih*," *HJAS* 19 (1956), 185–303.
"The Fifteen 'Palace Poems' by K'o Chiu-ssu," *HJAS* 20 (1957), 391–479.
"The Mongolian Documents in the Musée de Téhéran," *HJAS* 16 (1957), 1–107.
"An Early Mongolian Version of the Alexander Romance," *HJAS* 22 (1959), 1–99.
Comnena, Anna, *The Alexiad*, trans. by E. R. A. Sewter (New York: Penguin Books, 1985).
Constantine Porphyrogenitus, *De Administrando Imperio*, rev. edn., ed. by Gy. Moravcsik and trans. by R. J. H. Jenkins (Dumbarton Oaks Texts, 1; Washington, DC: Dumbarton Oaks and Harvard University, 1967).
Dasxuranci, Movsēs, *The History of the Caucasian Albanians*, trans. by C. J. F. Dowsett (London: Oxford University Press, 1961).
Dawson, Christopher, ed., *The Mongol Mission: Narratives and Letters of the Franciscan Missionaries in Mongolia and China in the Thirteenth and Fourteenth Centuries* (New York: Sheed and Ward, 1955).
Draskhanakerttsi, Iovannes, *Istoriia Armenii*, trans. by M. O. Dardinian-Melikan (Erevan: Izdatel'stvo "Sovetakan Grokh," 1986).
Dzhuansheriani, Dzhuansher, *Zhizn Vakhtanga Gorgasala*, trans. by G. V. Tsulaia (Tbilisi: Izdatel'stvo "Metsnierba," 1986).
Ełishē, *History of Vardan and the Armenian War*, trans. by Robert W. Thomson (Cambridge, Mass.: Harvard University Press, 1982).
Geng Shimin and James Hamilton, "L'inscription ouigoure de la stèle commemorative des Iduq Qut de Qočo," *Turcica* 13 (1981), 10–54.
Golden, Peter B., ed., *The Rasūlid Hexaglot*, forthcoming.
Grigor of Akancʿ, "History of the Nation of Archers (The Mongols)," ed. and trans. by Robert P. Blake and Richard N. Frye, *HJAS* 12, (1949), 269–399.
Haenisch, Erich and Yao Ts'ung-wu, trans. and eds., *Meng-ta pei-lu und Hei-ta shih-lüeh: Chinesische Gesandtenberichte über die frühen Mongolen* (Wiesbaden: Otto Harrassowitz, 1980).

Haidar, Muhammad, *A History of the Moghuls of Central Asia*, trans. by E. D. Ross and ed. by N. Elias, repr. (New York: Praeger, 1970).

Ḥāfiẓ-i Abrū, *Ẕayl jāmiʿ al-tavārīkh-i Rashīdī*, ed. by Khānbābā Bayānī (Salsatat-i intishārāt-i anjuman-i aṣār millī, no. 88; Tehran, 1971).

Ḥājib, Yūsuf Khāṣṣ, *Wisdom of Royal Glory (Kutudgu Bilig): A Turko-Islamic Mirror for Princes*, ed. and trans. by Robert Dankoff (University of Chicago Press, 1983).

Herodotus, *The Persian Wars*, trans. by George Rawlinson (New York: Modern Library, 1942).

Hilāl al-Ṣābi', *Rusūm Dār al-Khilafāh: The Rules and Regulations of the ʿAbbāsid Court*, trans. by Elie A. Salem (American University of Beirut, 1977).

Hsü Yu-jen, *Kuei-t'ang hsiao-kao* (Ying-yin wen-yuan ko-ssu k'u-ch'uan-shu ed.).

Ibn al-Athīr, *Al-Kāmil fī al-ta'rīkh*, ed. by C. J. Tornberg, repr. (Beirut, 1966), vol. XII.

Ibn al-Balkhī, *Fārsnāmah*, ed. by Guy Le Strange and R. A. Nicholson (London: Luzac, 1968).

Ibn Baṭṭūṭah, *Travels in Asia and Africa*, trans. by H. A. R. Gibb (London: Routledge and Kegan Paul, 1929).

The Travels of Ibn Baṭṭūṭah, trans. by H. A. R. Gibb (Cambridge University Press for the Hakluyt Society, 1958–71), 3 vols.

Ibn Faḍlān, *Ibn Faḍlān's Reisebericht*, trans. and ed. by A. Zeki Validi Togan (Abhandlungen für die Kunde des Morgenlandes, Bd. 24, Nr. 3; Leipzig: Deutsche Morgenländische Gesellschaft, 1939).

Ibn Khaldūn, *The Muqaddimah: An Introduction to History*, trans. by Franz Rosenthal (New York: Pantheon Books, 1958), vol. II.

Jackson, Peter, trans. and David Morgan, ed., *The Mission of Friar William of Rubruck* (London: The Haklyut Society, 1990).

John of Joinville, *The Life of St. Louis*, trans. by René Hague (New York: Sheed and Ward, 1955).

Juvaynī, ʿAtā-Malik, *Ta'rīkh-i Jahāngushā*, ed. by Mīrzā Muḥammad Qazvīnī (E. J. W. Gibb Memorial Series, vol. XVI; London: Luzac, 1912–37), 3 vols.

The History of the World Conqueror, trans. by John Andrew Boyle (Cambridge, Mass.: Harvard University Press, 1958), 2 vols.

Jūzjānī, *Ṭabaqāt-i nāṣirī*, ed. by ʿAbd al-Ḥayy Habībī (Kābul: Anjuman-i tārīkh-i Afghānistān, 1963), vol. II.

Kent, Roland G., *Old Persian: Grammar, Texts, Lexicon*, 2nd edn. (New Haven: American Oriental Society, 1953).

Khorenatsʿi, Moses, *History of the Armenians*, trans. by Robert W. Thomson (Cambridge, Mass.: Harvard University Press, 1978).

Kinnamos, John, *Deeds of John and Manuel Comnenus*, trans. by Charles M. Brand (New York: Columbia University Press, 1976).

Kirakos Gandzaketsi, *Istoriia Armenii*, trans. by L. A. Khanlarian (Moscow: Nauka, 1976).

Klimkeit, Hans-Joachim, trans., *Gnosis on the Silk Road: Gnostic Parables, Hymns and Prayers from Central Asia* (San Francisco: Harper, 1993).

Li Chih-chang, *Hsi-yü chi*, in Wang, *Meng-ku shih-liao*.

The Travels of an Alchemist, trans. by Arthur Waley (London: Routledge and Kegan Paul, 1963).

Liao shih (Peking: Chung-hua shu-chü, 1974).

Liutprand of Cremona, *The Embassy to Constantinople and Other Writings*, trans. by F. A. Wright and ed. by John Julius Norwich, repr. (London and Rutland, Vermont: Everyman's Library, 1993).

Ma Huan, *Ying-yai sheng-lan: The Overall Survey of the Oceans Shore (1433)*, ed. and trans. by J. V. G. Mills (Cambridge University Press for the Hakluyt Society, 1970).

I Maccabees, trans. by Jonathan A. Goldstein (Garden City: Doubleday, 1976).

II Maccabees, trans. by Jonathan A. Goldstein (Garden City: Doubleday, 1983).

Mackerras, Colin, ed. and trans., *The Uighur Empire according to the T'ang Dynastic Histories: A Study in Sino-Uighur Relations* (Canberra: Australian National University Press, 1972).

Maḥmūd al-Kāšγarī, *Compendium of the Turkic Dialects* (*Dīwān Luγāt at-Turk*), trans. by Robert Dankoff (Sources of Oriental Languages and Literatures, vol. VII; Cambridge, Mass.: Printed at the Harvard University Printing Office, 1982), part I.

Malov, S. E., trans., *Pamiatniki drevnetiurkskoi pis'mennosti Mongoli i Kirgizii* (Moscow-Leningrad: Izdatel'stvo akademii nauk SSSR, 1959).

Marco Polo, *The Description of the World*, trans. by A. C. Moule and Paul Pelliot (London: Routledge, 1938), vol. I.

de Marignolli, John, "Recollections of Travel in the East," in Yule, *Cathay*, vol. III, pp. 177–269.

Martinez, A. P., "The Third Portion of the Story of Gāzān Xān in Rašīdu'd-Dīn's *Ta'rīx-e mobark-e Gāzānī*," *Archivum Eurasiae Medii Aevi* 6 (1986 [1988]), 41–127.

Menander, *The History of Menander the Guardsman*, trans. by R. B. Blockley (Liverpool: Francis Cairns Publications Ltd., 1985).

Ming shih (Peking: Chung-hua shu-chü, 1974).

Minorsky, Vladimir, "Tamīn ibn Barh's Journey to the Uighurs," *Bulletin of the School of Oriental and African Studies* 12/2 (1948), 275–305.

Minorsky, Vladimir, ed. and trans., *Hudūd al-'Ālam*, 2nd edn. (London: Luzac and Co., 1970).

Morgan, E. Delmar and C. H. Coote, eds., *Early Voyages and Travels to Russia and Persia by Anthony Jenkinson and Other Englishmen*, repr. (New York: Burt Franklin, n.d.), vol. I.

Mostaert, Antoine, *La matérial Mongol du Houa i i iu de Houng-ou (1398)*, ed. by Igor de Rachewiltz (Mélanges chinois et bouddhiques, 18; Brussels: Institut belge des hautes études chinoises, 1977), vol. I.

Mostaert, Antoine and Francis W. Cleaves, eds. and trans., *Les lettres de 1289 et 1305 des ilkhan Arγun et Öljeitü à Philippe le Bel* (Cambridge, Mass.: Harvard University Press, 1962).

Mu'īn al-Dīn Naṭanzī, *Muntakhab al-tavārīkh-i Mu'īnī*, ed. by Jean Aubin (Tehran: Librairie Khayyam, 1957).

Niẓām al-Mulk, *The Book of Government or Rules for Kings*, trans. by Hubert Darke (London: Routledge and Kegan Paul, 1960).

Niẓām of Ganja, *The Haft Paikar* (*The Seven Beauties*), trans. by C. E. Wilson (London: Arthur Probsthain, 1924), vol. I.

Odoric of Pordenone, "The Eastern Parts of the World Described," in Yule, *Cathay*, vol. II, pp. 3–367.

Orbelian, Stephannos, *Histoire de la Siounie*, trans. by M. Brosset (St. Petersburg: Academie impériale des sciences, 1864).
Pegolotti, Francesco Balducci, *La Practica della Mercatura*, ed. by Allan Evans (Cambridge, Mass.: Medieval Academy of America, 1936).
"La Practica della Mercatura," in Yule, *Cathay*, vol. III, pp. 137–73.
P'eng Ta-ya and Hsü T'ing, *Hei-ta shih-lüeh*, in Wang, *Meng-ku shih-liao*.
Plutarch's Lives, trans. by Bernadotte Perrin (The Loeb Classical Library; New York: Putnams, 1926).
Poppe, N. N., trans., *Mongol'skii slovar Mukaddimat al Adab* (Moscow-Leningrad: Akademii nauk SSSR, 1938).
Pseudo-Callisthenes, *The Romance of Alexander the Great*, trans. by Albert Mugrdich Wolohojian (New York: Columbia University Press, 1969).
Al-Qāshānī, Abū al-Qasīm, *Ta'rīkh-i Ūljaytū*, ed. by Mahin Hambly (Tehran: B.T.N.K., 1969).
Quintus Curtius, *History of Alexander*, trans. by John C. Rolfe (The Loeb Classical Library; Cambridge, Mass.: Harvard University Press, 1946).
de Rachewiltz, Igor, *Index to the Secret History of the Mongols* (Indiana University Publications, Uralic and Altaic Series, vol. CXXI; Bloomington, 1972).
Rashīd al-Dīn, *Mukātabāt-i Rashīdī*, ed. by Muḥammad Safīʿ (Lahore: The Punjab Educational Press, 1947).
Jāmiʿ al-tavārīkh, ed. by B. Karīmī (Tehran: Eqbal, 1959), 2 vols.
The Successors of Ghenghis Khan, trans. by John Andrew Boyle (New York: Columbia University Press, 1971).
Die Chinageschichte, ed. and trans. by Karl Jahn (Vienna: Hermann Böhlaus, 1971).
Jāmiʿ al-tavārkh, ed. by A. A. Alizade (Moscow: Nauka, 1980), vol. II, pt. 1.
Rust'haveli, Shot'ha, *The Man in the Panther's Skin*, trans. by Marjory Scott Wardrop (London: Luzac, 1966).
Sanjian, Avedis K., trans. and ed., *Colophons of Armenian Manuscripts: A Source for Middle Eastern History* (Cambridge, Mass.: Harvard University Press, 1969).
Sayf ibn Muḥammad ibn Yaʿqub al-Havarī, *Ta'rīkh nāmah-i Harāt*, ed. by M. Ṣiddīqī (Calcutta: Baptist Mission Press, 1944).
Scargill, M. H. and Margaret Schlanch, trans., *Three Icelandic Sagas* (Princeton University Press for the American Scandinavian Foundation, 1950).
Sebēos, *Histoire d'Heraclius*, trans. by Fréderic Macler (Paris: Imprimerie nationale, 1904).
The Secret History of the Mongols, trans. by Francis W. Cleaves (Cambridge, Mass.: Harvard University Press, 1982).
Shcherbak, A. M., trans., *Oguz-nāme. Mukhabbat-nāme* (Moscow: Izdatel'stvo vostochnoi literatury, 1959).
Sheng-wu ch'in-cheng lu, in Wang, *Meng-ku shih-liao*.
Smirnova, L. P., trans. and ed., *ʿAjā'ib al-dunyā* (Moscow: Nauka, 1993).
Ssu-ma Ch'ien, *Records of the Grand Historian of China*, trans. by Burton Watson (New York: Columbia University Press, 1961), vol. II.
Strabo, *The Geography of Strabo*, trans. by H. L. Jones (The Loeb Classical Library; Cambridge, Mass.: Harvard University Press, 1954).
Su T'ien-chüeh, *Yuan wen-lei* (Taipei: Shih-chiai shu-chü ying-hsing, 1967).
Sung shih (Peking: Chung-hua shu-chü, 1977).

Sung Ying-hsing, *T'ien-kung k'ai-wu: Exploitation of the Work of Nature* (Taipei: China Academy, 1980).

Al-Ṭabarī, *The History of al-Ṭabarī*, vol. XXVI, *The Waning of the Umayyad Caliphate*, trans. by Carole Hillenbrand (Albany: State University of New York Press, 1989).

T'ao Tsung-i, *Nan-ts'un cho keng-lu* (Ssu-pu ts'ung-k'an ed.).

Ta-yuan chan-chi kung-wu chi (Hsüeh-shu ts'ung-pien ed.; Taipei, 1971).

Ta-yuan sheng-cheng kuo-ch'ao tien-chang (Repr. of the Yuan ed.; Taipei: Kuo-li ku-kung po-wu yuan, 1976).

Tekin, Talât, *A Grammar of Orkhan Turkic* (Indiana University Publications, Uralic and Altaic Series, vol. LXIX; Bloomington, 1968).

Tekin, Talât, trans., *Irk Bitig: The Book of Omens* (Wiesbaden: Otto Harrassowitz, 1993).

Al-Tha'ālibī, *Histoire des rois perses*, ed. and trans. by H. Zotenberg (Paris: Imprimerie nationale, 1900).

Thomson, Robert W., "The Historical Compilation of Vardan Arewelc'i," *Dumbarton Oaks Papers*, no. 43 (1989), 125–226.

Al-'Umarī, Ibn Faḍl Allah, *Ibn Faḍlallah al-'Omarīs Bericht über Indien in seinem Werke Masālik al-abṣar fi mamālik al-amṣar*, ed. and trans. by Otto Spies (Sammlung orientalistischer Arbeiten, vol. XIV; Leipzig: Otto Harrassowitz, 1943).

Vivian, Katherine, trans., *The Georgian Chronicle: The Period Giorgi Lasha* (Amsterdam: Adolf M. Hakkert, 1991).

Wang Kuo-wei, ed., *Meng-ku shih-liao ssu-ching* (Taipei: Cheng-chung shu-chü, 1975).

Wardrop, Oliver, trans., *Visramiani: The Story of the Loves of Vis and Ramin* (London: Royal Asiatic Society, 1914).

Wyngaert, P. Anastasius van den, ed., *Sinica Franciscana*, vol. I, *Itinera et Relationes Fratrum Minorum Saeculi XIII et XIV* (Quaracchi-Firenze: Collegium S. Bonaventurae, 1929).

Xenophon, *Cyropaedia*, trans. by Walter Miller (Loeb Classical Library; Cambridge, Mass.: Harvard University Press, 1914).

Anabasis, trans. by Carleton L. Bronson (Loeb Classical Library; Cambridge, Mass.: Harvard University Press, 1918).

Yang Hsüan-chih, *A Record of Buddhist Monasteries in Lo Yang*, trans. by Yi-t'ung Wang (Princeton University Press, 1984).

Yuan shih (Peking: Chung-hua shu-chü, 1978).

Yuan-chao pi-shih, ed. by B. I. Pankratov (Moscow: Izdatel'stvo vostochnoi literatury, 1962).

Yule, Sir Henry, *Cathay and the Way Thither, being a Collection of Medieval Notices of China*, repr. (Taipei: Ch'eng-wen Publishing Company, 1966), 4 vols.

Ẓahir al-Dīn, *The Bābur-Nāma in English*, trans. by Annette Susannah Beveridge (London: Luzac, 1969).

Secondary works

Adshead, S. A. M., *China in World History* (London: Macmillan, 1988).

Akishev, K. A., *Kurgan Issyk: Iskusstvo sakov Kazakhstana* (Moscow: Iskusstvo, 1978).

Allsen, Thomas T., "The Yuan Dynasty and the Uighurs of Turfan in the 13th Century," in Morris Rossabi, ed., *China among Equals: The Middle Kingdom and its Neighbors, 10th–14th Centuries* (Berkeley: University of California Press, 1983), 243–80.

"Archeology and Mid-Imperial History: The Chin and Yuan," in Gilbert Rozman, ed., *Soviet Studies of Premodern China: Assessments of Recent Scholarship* (Ann Arbor: Center for Chinese Studies, The University of Michigan, 1984), 81–95.

"Guard and Government in the Reign of the Grand Qan Möngke, 1251–59," *HJAS* 46 (1986), 495–521.

"Mongolian Princes and Their Merchant Partners," *Asia Major*, 3rd series, 2 (1989), 83–126.

"Changing Forms of Legitimation in Mongol Iran," in Gary Seaman and Daniel Marks, eds., *Rulers from the Steppe: State Formation on the Eurasian Periphery* (Los Angeles: Ethnographics Press, 1991), 223–41.

Anawalt, Patricia, "Costume and Control: Aztec Sumptuary Laws," *Archaeology* 33/1 (1980), 33–43.

Anderson, Robert T., *Traditional Europe: A Study in Anthroplogy and History* (Belmont, Calif.: Wadsworth Publishing Co., 1971).

Andrews, P. A., "The Tents of Timur: An Examination of Reports on the Quriltay at Samarqand, 1404," in Philip Denwood, ed., *Arts of the Eurasian Steppe Lands* (Colloquies in Art and Archaeology in Asia, no. 7; London: Percival David Foundation of Chinese Art and The School of Oriental and African Studies, 1970), 143–81.

Baiar, D., "Kammennye izvaianiia iz Sukhe-Batorskogo Aimaka (Vostochnaia Mongoliia)," in R. S. Vasil'evskii, ed., *Drevnie kul'tury Mongolii* (Novosibirsk: Nauka, Sibirskoe otdelenie, 1985), 148–59.

Bailey, Harold W., "Altun Khan," *Bulletin of the School of Oriental and African Studies* 30/1 (1967), 95–104.

Barber, E. J. W., *Prehistoric Textiles: The Development of Cloth in the Neolithic and Bronze Ages* (Princeton University Press, 1991).

Barker, Juliet R. V., *The Tournament in England, 1100–1400* (Woodbridge, Sussex: Boydell Press, 1986).

Barnett, H. G., "Culture Processes," *American Anthropologist* 42 (1940), 21–48.

Basilov, Vladimir N., ed., *Nomads of Eurasia* (Seattle: University of Washington Press, 1989).

Bayly, C. A., "The Origin of Swadeshi (Home Industry): Cloth and Indian Society," in Arjun Appadurai, ed., *The Social Life of Things: Commodities in Cultural Perspective* (Cambridge University Press, 1988), 285–321.

Bazin, Louis, *Les systèmes chronologiques dans le monde Turk ancién* (Budapest and Paris: Akadémia Kiadó and Editions du CNRS, 1991).

Beale, T. W., "Early Trade in Highland Iran: A View from the Source Area," *World Archaeology* 5 (1973), 133–48.

Beckwith, C. I., "Aspects of the Early History of the Central Asian Guard Corps in Islam," *Archivum Eurasiae Medii Aevi* 4 (1984), 29–43.

Beffa, Marie-Lisa, "Le concept de *Tänggäri*, 'ciel', dans l'*Histoire Secréte des Mongols*," *Études mongoles et sibériennes* 24 (1993), 215–36.

Belenitskii, A. M., "K voprosu o sotsial'nykh otnosheniiakh v Irane v Khulaguidskuiu epokhu," *Sovetskoe vostokovedenie* 5 (1948), 111–28.

"Novye pamiatniki iskusstva drevnego Piandzhikenta: Opyt ikonograficheskogo istolkovaniia," in A. M. Belenitskii and B. B. Piotrovskii, eds., *Skul'ptura i zhivopis drevnego Piandzhikenta* (Moscow: Izdatel'stvo akademii nauk SSSR, 1959), 53–64.

Biblioteque Nationale, *Le Livres des Merveilles* (Paris: Berthand Frères, n.d.), vol. I.

Bloch, Maurice, "The Ritual of the Royal Bath in Madagascar: The Dissolution of Death, Birth and Fertility into Authority," in Cannadine and Price, *Rituals of Royalty*, 271–97.

Bombaci, Alessio, "Qutluγ Bolzun!," *Ural-Altaische Jahrbücher* 36 (1965), 284–91 and 38 (1966), 13–43.

Boodberg, Peter A., "Marginalia to the Histories of the Northern Dynasties," *HJAS* 4 (1939), 230–83; repr. in Alvin P. Cohn, comp., *Selected Works of Peter Boodberg* (Berkeley: University of California Press, 1979), 296–349.

Bosworth, Clifford E., *The Ghaznavids: Their Empire in Afghanistan and Eastern Iran, 994–1040* (Edinburgh University Press, 1963).

Boyle, John A., "The Seasonal Residences of the Great Khan Ögedei," *Central Asiatic Journal* 16 (1972), 125–31.

"The Alexander Legend in Central Asia," *Folklore* 85 (1974), 217–28.

Broom, Leonard, Bernard J. Siegel, Evan Z. Vogt, and James B. Watson, "Acculturation: An Explanatory Formulation," *American Anthropologist* 56 (1954), 973–1000.

Browne, Edward G., *A Literary History of Persia*, vol. II, *From Firdawsī to Sa'di* (Cambridge University Press, 1969).

Buckler, F. W., "Two Instances of *Khil'at* in the Bible," *Journal of Theological Studies* 23 (1922), 197–99.

"The Oriental Despot," *Anglican Theological Review* 10/3 (1928), 238–49.

Budagov, A. Z., *Sravnitel'nii slovar Turetsko-Tatarskikh narechii* (St. Petersburg: Imperatorskoi akademii nauka, 1869), vol. I.

Bunker, Emma C., "Gold in the Ancient Chinese World: A Cultural Puzzle," *Artibus Asiae* 53 (1993), 27–50.

Burnes, Alexander, *Travels into Bokhara, being an Account of a Journey from India to Cabool, Tartary and Persia*, repr. (New Delhi: Asian Educational Services, 1992), vol. II.

Cameron, Averil, "The Construction of Court Ritual: The Byzantine *Book of Ceremonies*," in Cannadine and Price, *Rituals of Royalty*, 106–36.

Cammann, Schuyler, "A Robe of the Ch'ien-lung Emperor," *Journal of the Walters Art Gallery* 10 (1947), 9–19.

"The Making of Dragon Robes." *T'oung-pao* 40 (1951), 297–321.

Cannadine, David and Simon Price, eds., *Rituals of Royalty: Power and Ceremonial in Traditional Societies* (Cambridge University Press, 1987).

Cartier, Michel, "Barbarians through Chinese Eyes: The Emergence of an Anthropological Approach to Ethnic Differences," *The Comparative Civilizations Review* 6 (1981), 1–14.

Chabros, Krystyna and L. Batčuluun, "Mongol Examples of Proto-Weaving," *Central Asiatic Journal* 37 (1993), 20–32.

Chan, Hok-lam, *Legitimation in Imperial China: Discussions under the Jürchen-Chin Dynasty (1115–1234)* (Seattle: University of Washington Press, 1984).

Chiodo, Elisabetta, "The Horse White-as-Egg (*öndegen čayan*): A Study of the

Custom of Consecrating Animals to Deities," *Ural-Altaische Jahrbücher* n.s. 11 (1992), 125–51.
Christian, David, "Inner Eurasia as a Unit of World History," *Journal of World History* 5 (1994), 173–211.
Chü, Ch'ing-yuan, "Government Artisans of the Yuan Dynasty," in E-tu Zen Sun and John De Francis, eds. and trans., *Chinese Social History: Translations of Selected Studies*, repr. (New York: Octogon Books, 1966), 234–46.
Clark, Grahame, *Symbols of Excellence: Precious Materials as Expressions of Status* (Cambridge University Press, 1986).
Clark, Larry V., "The Turkic and Mongol Words in William of Rubruck's Journey," *JAOS* 93, 2 (1973), 181–89.
Clark, Larry V. and Paul Alexander Draghi, eds., *Aspects of Altaic Civilization, II* (Indiana University Publications, Uralic and Altaic Series, CXXXIV; Bloomington, 1978).
Clausen, Sir Gerard, *An Etymological Dictionary of Pre-Thirteenth-Century Turkish* (Oxford: The Clarendon Press, 1972).
Cleaves, Francis W., "The Vocable *Sa-ta-la-ch'i* in the *Yuan shih* and the *Yuan tien-chang*," *Ural-Altaische Jahrbücher*, n.s. 10 (1991), 128–35.
Cohn, Bernard S., "Cloth, Clothing and Colonialism: India in the Nineteenth Century," in Weiner and Schneider, *Cloth and Human Experience*, 303–53.
Cort, Louise Allison, "The Changing Fortunes of Three Archaic Japanese Textiles," in Weiner and Schneider, *Cloth and Human Experience*, 377–415.
Della Vida, G. Levi, "On Kirmiz," *JAOS* 61 (1941), 287–88.
Doerfer, Gerhard, *Türkische und Mongolische Elemente im Neupersischen* (Wiesbaden: Franz Steiner, 1963–1975), 4 vols.
Dozy, R. P. A., *Dictionnaire détaillé des noms des vêtements chez les Arabes*, repr. (Beirut: Librairie du Liban, n. d.,).
Supplément aux dictionnaires arabes, 3rd edn. (Leiden: E. J. Brill, 1967), vol. II.
Dumézil, G., "La société scythique avait-elle des classes fonctionnelles?," *Indo-Iranian Journal* 5/3 (1962), 187–202.
Ecsedy, Hilda, "Böz – An Exotic Cloth in the Chinese Imperial Court," *Altorientalische Forschungen* 3 (1975), 155–63.
Eichorn, Werner, "Zur Vorgeschichte des Aufstandes von Wang Hsiao-po and Li Shun in Szuchuan (993–995)," *Zeitschrift der Deutschen Morgenländischen Gesellschaft* 105/1 (1955), 192–209.
Eliade, Mircea, *Shamanism: Archaic Techniques of Ecstasy* (Princeton University Press, 1964).
Images and Symbols: Studies in Religious Symbolism (Princeton University Press, 1991).
Endicott-West, Elizabeth, *Mongolian Rule in China: Local Administration under the Yuan* (Cambridge, Mass.: Harvard University Press, 1989).
Esin, Emil, "The Court Attendants in Turkish Iconography," *Central Asiatic Journal* 14/1–3 (1970), 78–117.
Ettinghausen, Richard, *From Byzantium to Sassanian Iran and the Islamic World: Three Modes of Artistic Influences* (The L. A. Mayer Memorial Studies in Islamic Art and Archaeology, vol. III; Leiden: E. J. Brill, 1972).
Evtiukhova, L. A., "Izdeliia razlichnykh remesel iz Kara Koruma," in S. V. Kiselev, *et al.*, eds., *Drevnemongol'skie goroda* (Moscow: Nauka, 1965), 274–96.

Fang Hao, *Chung-hsi chiao-t'ung shih* (Taipei: Chung-hua wen-hua ch'u-pien shih-yeh wei-yuan-hui, 1953), vol. I.

Farquhar, David M., *The Government of China under Mongolian Rule: A Reference Guide* (Stuttgart: Franz Steiner, 1990).

Fekhner, M. V., "K istorii torgovykh sviazei Rusi so stranami Vostoka v domongol'skoe vremia (Po materialam shelkovykh tkanei)," in B. A. Litvinskii, ed., *Kavkaz i Sredniaia Aziia v drevnosti i srednevekov'e* (Moscow: Nauka, 1981), 139–45.

Floor, Willem, "Economy and Society: Fibers, Fabrics, Factories," in Carol Bier, ed., *Woven from the Soul, Spun from the Heart: Textile Arts of Safavid and Qajar Iran, 16th–19th Centuries* (Washington, DC: Textile Museum, 1987), 20–32.

Fortes, Meyer, "Ritual and Office in Tribal Society," in M. Gluckmann, ed., *Essays on the Ritual of Social Relations* (Manchester University Press, 1962), 53–88.

Frank, Andre Gunder, *The Centrality of Central Asia* (Amsterdam: V. U. University Press, 1992).

"Bronze Age World System Cycles," *Current Anthropology* 34 (1993), 383–429.

Frankfor, A.-P. (H.-P. Francfort), "Sushchestvoval li velikii shelkovyi put vo II–I tys. do N.E.," in V. M. Masson, ed., *Vzaimodeistvie kochevykh kul'tur i drevnikh tsivilizatsii* (Alma Ata: Nauka Kazakhskoi SSR, 1989), 203–17.

French, David, "A Sixteenth Century English Merchant in Ankara?" *Anatolian Studies* 22 (1972), 242–43.

van Gennep, Arnold, *The Rite of Passage* (University of Chicago Press, 1990).

Gernet, Jacques, *Daily Life in China on the Eve of the Mongol Invasion* (Stanford University Press, 1962).

Gervers, Veronica, "Felt in Eurasia," in Anthony N. Landreau, ed., *Yörük: The Nomadic Weaving Traditions of the Middle East* (Pittsburgh: Museum of Art and Carnegie Institute, 1978), 16–22.

Gibbon, Edward, *The History of the Decline and Fall of the Roman Empire*, ed. by J. B. Bury (London: Methuen, 1909), vol. I.

Gibert, Lucien, *Dictionnaire historique et géographique de la Mandchourie* (Hong Kong: Imprimerie de la societé Missions-Estrangéres, 1934).

Göbl, Robert, "Investitur im sasanidischen Iran und ihr numismatische Bezeugung," *Weiner Zeitschrift für die Kunde des Morgenlandes* 56 (1960), 38–51.

Golden, Peter B., "Imperial Ideology and the Sources of Political Unity amongst the Pre-Činggisid Nomads of Western Eurasia," *Archivum Eurasiae Medii Aevi* 2 (1982), 37–76.

An Introduction to the History of the Turkic Peoples: Ethnogenesis and State Formation in Medieval and Early Modern Eurasia and the Middle East (Wiesbaden: Otto Harrassowitz, 1992).

"The Černii Klobouci," in Á. Berta, *et al.*, eds., *Symbolae Turcologicae* (Swedish Research Institute in Istanbul, Transactions, vol. VI; Uppsala, 1996), 97–107.

Goldman, Bernard, "Origin of the Persian Robe," *Iranica Antiqua* 4 (1964), 133–52.

Golombek, Lisa, "The Draped Universe of Islam," in Soucek, *Content and Context of Visual Arts in the Islamic World*, 25–50.

Gonda, Jan, *The Functions and Significance of Gold in the Veda* (Leiden: E. J. Brill, 1991).

Granger-Taylor, Hero, and John Peter Wild, "Some Ancient Silk from the Crimea in the British Museum," *Antiquaries Journal* 61 (1981), 302–06.

Greiner, Peter, *Die Brokatuniform-Brigade (Chin-i wei) der Ming-Zeit von den Anfängen bis zum Ende der T'ien-shun Periode (1368–1464)* (Wiesbaden: Otto Harrassowitz, 1975).
Grohman, A., "*Ṭirāz*," *Encyclopedia of Islam* (London: Luzac and Leiden: E. J. Brill, 1934), vol. IV, 785–93.
Guérer, Annick L., *Scent: The Mysterious and Essential Powers of Smell* (New York: Kodansha International, 1994).
Gyllensvärd, Bo, "T'ang Gold and Silver," *Bulletin of the Museum of Far Eastern Antiquities* 29 (1957), 1–230.
Hamdani, Abbas, "Columbus and the Recovery of Jerusalem," *JAOS* 99 (1979), 39–48.
Han Ju-lin, "Lun Ch'eng-chi-ssu," *Li-shih Yen-chiu* 3 (1962), 1–10.
Hansen, Henny Harald, *Mongolian Costumes* (London: Thames and Hudson, 1993).
Harmatta, J., "The Golden Bow of the Huns," *Acta Archaeologica Academiae Scientiarum Hungaricae* 1 (1951), 107–49.
Hayashi Ryōichi, *The Silk Road and the Shoso-in* (New York: Weatherhill, 1975).
Herrman, Georgina, "Lapis Lazuli: The Early Phases of its Trade," *Iraq* 30 (1968), 21–57.
Herskovits, Melville J., *Man and His Works: The Science of Cultural Anthropology* (New York: Alfred A. Knopf, 1951).
Hodgen, Margaret, "Glass and Paper: An Historical Study of Acculturation," *Southwestern Journal of Anthropology* 1 (1945), 466–97.
Change and History: A Study of Dated Distributions of Technological Innovations in England (New York: Wenner-Gren Foundation for Anthropological Research, 1952).
Hoke, Ernst, "Mikroanalytische Untersuchungen von Edelmetallfäden an Textilien in Gräbern vom Kordlar Tepe (Westaserbaidshcan), *Archaeologische Mitteilungen aus Iran* 15 (1982), 307–10.
Horst, Heribert, *Die Staatsverwaltung der Grosselğūqen und Hōrazmšāhs (1038–1231): Eine Untersuchung nach Urkundenformularen der Zeit* (Wiesbaden: Franz Steiner, 1964).
Hsiao Ch'i-ch'ing, *The Military Establishment of the Yuan Dynasty* (Cambridge, Mass.: Harvard University Press, 1978).
Hsu, Cho-yun and Katheryn M. Linduff, *Western Chou Civilization* (New Haven: Yale University Press, 1988).
Hucker, Charles O., *Dictionary of Official Titles in Imperial China* (Stanford University Press, 1988).
Hyer, Paul, "The Re-evaluation of Chinggis Khan: Its Role in the Sino-Soviet Dispute," *Asian Survey* 6 (1966), 696–705.
Isono, Fujiko, "A Few Reflections on the *Anda* Relationship," in Clark and Draghi, *Aspects of Altaic Civilization, II*, 81–87.
Ivanov, V. A. and V. A. Kriger, *Kurgany kypchakskogo vremeni na Iuzhnom Urale (XII–XIV vv)* (Moscow: Nauka, 1988).
Jagchid, Sechin and Paul Hyer, *Mongolia's Culture and Society* (Boulder, Colorado: Westview Press, 1979).
Jahn, Karl, "Wissenschaftliche Kontakte zwischen Iran und China in der Mongolenzeit," *Anzeiger der phil.-hist. Klasse der Österreichischen Akademie der Wissenschaften* 106 (1969), 199–211.

Jamzadeh, P., "The Function of the Girdle on Achaemenid Costume in Combat," *Iranica Antiqua* 32 (1987), 267–73.

Janse, Olov, "L'Empire des Steppes et les relations entre l'Europe et l'Extrême-Orient dans l'Antiquité," *Revue des Arts Asiatiques* 9 (1935), 9–26.

Jensen, Lloyd B., "Royal Purple of Tyre," *Journal of Near Eastern Studies* 22 (1963), 104–18.

Kawami, Trudy S., "Archaeological Evidence for Textiles in Pre-Islamic Iran," *Iranian Studies* 25 (1992), 7–18.

Kerimov, Kerim, *Nizami Giandzhevi khamse miniatiury* (Baku: Iazychy, 1983).

Kessler, Adam T., *Empires beyond the Great Wall: The Heritage of Genghis Khan* (Los Angeles: Natural History Museum of Los Angeles County, 1993).

Khazanov, A. M., "Legenda o proiskhozhdenii Skifov (Gerodot, IV. 5–7)," in *Skifskii mir* (Kiev: Naukova dumka, 1975), 74–93.

Zoloto Skyfov (Moscow: Sovetskii khudozhnik, 1975).

Khazanov, Anatoly M., *Nomads and the Outside World* (Cambridge University Press, 1984).

"Ecological Limitations of Nomadism in the Eurasian Steppes and Their Social and Cultural Implications," *Asian and African Studies: Journal of the Israel Oriental Society* 24 (1990), 1–15.

Khudiadov, Yu. S., "Pamiatniki uigurskoi kul'tury v Mongoli," in V. E. Larichev, ed., *Tsentral'naia Aziia i sosednie territorii v srednie veka* (Novosibirsk: Nauka, Sibirskoe otdelenie, 1990), 84–89.

Kiknadze, A. G., "Iz istorii remeslennogo proizvodstva (Karkhane) v Iran XIII–XIV vv," in A. I. Falina, ed., *Blizhnii i Srednii Vostok* (Moscow: Izdatel'stvo vostochnoi literatury, 1962), 47–55.

Kipp, Rita Smith and Edward M. Schortman, "The Political Impact of Trade on Chiefdoms," *American Anthropologist* 91 (1989), 370–85.

Klimkeit, Hans-Joachim, *Manichaean Art and Calligraphy* (Leiden: E. J. Brill, 1982).

Klyashtorny, S., D. Savinov, and V. Shkoda, "The Golden Bracteatus from Mongolia: A Byzantine Motif in the Central Asian Toreutics," *Information Bulletin, International Association for the Study of Cultures of Central Asia* 16 (1984), 5–19.

Kononov, A. N., "Semantika tsvetooboznachenii v Tiurkskikh iazykakh," *Tiurkologicheskii sbornik, 1975* (Moscow: Nauka, 1978), 159–79.

Koppers, Wilhelm, "Diffusion: Transmission and Acceptance," in William L. Thomas, ed., *Yearbook of Anthropology, 1955* (New York: Wenner-Gren Foundation for Anthropological Research, 1955), 169–81.

von Kremer, Alfred, *Culturgeschichte des Orients unter den Chalifen* (Vienna: Wilhelm Braumüller, 1875), vol. I.

Kuhn, Dieter, *Textile Technology: Spinning and Reeling*, part 9 of *Science and Civilization in China*, vol. V, *Chemistry and Chemical Technology*, ed. by Joseph Needham (Cambridge University Press, 1988).

Kung Chao, *The Development of Cotton Textile Production in China* (Cambridge, Mass.: Harvard University Press, 1977).

Kurdian, H., "Kirmiz," *JAOS* 61 (1941), 105–07.

Kuz'mina, E. E., "Dionis u usunei (o semantike Kargalinskoi diademy)," in B. B. Piotrovskii and G. M. Bongard-Levin, eds., *Tsentral'naia Aziia, novye pamiatniki, pis'mennosti i iskusstva: Sbornik statei* (Moscow: Nauka, 1987), 158–81.

Kuz'mina, E. E. and V. I Sarianidi, "Dva golovnykh ubora iz pogrebenii Tilliatepe i ikh semantika," *Kratkie soobshcheniia Instituta arkheologii* 170 (1982), 19–27.

Kychanov, E. I., *Ocherki istorii Tangutskogo gosudarstva* (Moscow: Nauka, 1968).

Kyzlasov, L. R., *Istoriia Tuvy v srednie veka* (Moscow: Izdatel'stvo Moskovskogo universiteta, 1969).

Lattimore, Owen, *High Tartary* (Boston: Little, Brown and Co., 1930).

Laufer, Bertold, "Loan Words in Tibetan," *T'oung-pao* 17 (1916), 403–552.

"The Early History of Felt," *American Anthropologist* 32 (1930), 1–18.

Sino-Iranica: Chinese Contributions to the History of Civilization in Ancient Iran, repr. (Taipei: Ch'eng-wen, 1967).

Jade: A Study in Chinese Archaeology and Religion, repr. (New York: Dover Publications, 1974).

von Le Coq, Albert, *Buried Treasures of Chinese Turkestan* (Hong Kong: Oxford University Press, 1985).

Ledyard, Gari, "Two Mongolian Documents from the *Koryŏ Sa*," *JAOS* 85 (1963), 225–38.

Legget, William F., *Ancient and Medieval Dyes* (Brooklyn: Chemical Publishing Company, 1944).

Lelekov, L. A., "O simvolizme pogrebal'nykh oblachenii (zolotye liudi skifo-sakskogo mira)," in A. I. Martynov and V. I. Molodin, eds., *Skifo-Sibirskii mir: Iskusstvo i ideologiia* (Novosibirsk: Izdatel'stvo Nauka, Sibirskoe otdelenie, 1987), 25–30.

Litvinskii, B. A., "'Zolotye liudi' v drevnikh pogrebeniiakh Tsentral'noi Azii (opyt istolkovaniia v svete istorii religii)," *Sovetskaia etnografiia*, no. 4 (1982), 34–43.

Liu Ts'un-yan, "Traces of Zoroastrian and Manichaean Activities in pre-T'ang China," in his *Selected Papers from the Hall of Harmonious Wind* (Leiden: E. J. Brill, 1976), 3–55.

Liu Xinru, *Ancient India and Ancient China: Trade and Religious Exchanges, AD 1–600* (Delhi: Oxford University Press, 1988).

"Silks and Religions in Eurasia," *Journal of World History* 6 (1995), 25–48.

Silk and Religion: An Exploration of Material Life and the Thought of People (Delhi: Oxford University Press, 1996).

Liu Yingsheng and Peter Jackson, "Chinese-Iranian Relations, III, In the Mongol Period," *Encyclopedia Iranica* (Costa Mesa, California: Mazda Publisher, 1992), vol. IV, 434–36.

Lobachëva, Nina P., "Clothing and Personal Adornment," in Basilov, *Nomads of Eurasia*, 111–26.

Lockhart, Lawrence, "The Relations between Edward I and Edward II of England and the Mongol Īl-khāns of Persia," *Iran* 6 (1968), 23–31.

Loewe, Michael, "Spices and Silk: Aspects of World Trade in the First Seven Centuries of the Christian Era," *Journal of the Royal Asiatic Society*, no. 2 (1971), 166–79.

Lombard, Maurice, *Études d'economie médiévale*, vol III, *Les textiles dans le monde musulman du VIIe au XIIe siècle* (Paris, the Hague and New York: Mouton, 1978).

Lopez, Robert S., "Silk Industry in the Byzantine Empire," *Speculum* 20 (1945), 1–42.

"China Silk in Europe in the Yuan Period," *JAOS* 72 (1952), 72–76.

Lubec, G., *et al.*, "Use of Silk in Ancient Egypt," *Nature* 362 (March 4, 1993), 25.

Lubo-Lesnichenko, E. I., "Nekotorye terminy dlia shelkovykh tkanei v drevnem Kitae," *Trudy gosudarstvennogo Ermatizha* 5 (1961), 251–56.

"Velikii shelkovyi put," *Voprosy istorii*, no. 9 (September 1985), 88–100.

Kitai na shelkovom puti: *Shelk i vneshnie sviazi drevnego i rannesrednevekogo Kitaia* (Moscow: Vostochnaia literatura, 1994).

Mair, Victor H., "Dunhuang as a Funnel for Central Asian Nomads into China," in Gary Seaman, ed., *Ecology and Empire*: *Nomads in the Cultural Evolution of the Old World* (Los Angeles: Ethnographics Press, 1989), 143–63.

"Mummies of the Tarim Basin," *Archaeology* 48/2 (1995), 28–35.

Mayor, Adrienne, "Guardians of the Gold," *Archaeology* 47/6 (1994), 53–59.

Mayor, Adrienne and Michael Heaney, "Griffins and Arimaspeans," *Folklore* 104 (1993), 40–65.

McCulloh, John M., "The Cult of Relics in the Letters and 'Dialogues' of Pope Gregory the Great: A Lexicographical Study," *Traditio* 32 (1976), 145–84.

McNeil, William H., *The Rise of the West* (University of Chicago Press, 1963).

Meiss, Millard, *French Painting in the Time of Jean de Berry*: *The Boucicault Master* (Kress Foundation Studies in the History of European Art, no. 3; New York and London: Phaidon, 1968).

Melville, Charles, "The Chinese Uighur Animal Calendar in Persian Historiography of the Mongol Period," *Iran* 32 (1994), 83–98.

Merserve, Ruth I., "The Inhospitable Land of the Barbarian," *Journal of Asian History* 16 (1982), 51–89.

Micklewright, Nancy, "*Ṭirāz* Fragments: Unanswered Questions about Medieval Islamic Textiles," in Carol Barrett Fisher, ed., *Brocade of the Pen*: *The Art of Islamic Writing* (East Lansing: Kresage Art Museum, Michigan State University, 1991), 31–45.

Miller, Christopher L. and George R. Hamell, "A New Perspective on Indian-White Contact: Cultural Symbols and Colonial Trade," *The Journal of American History* 73/2 (1986), 311–28.

Miyasita, Saburo, "A Link in the Westward Transmission of Chinese Anatomy in the Later Middle Ages," *Isis* 58 (1967), 486–90.

Molchanova, O. T., "Zheltye tsveta v altaiskom onomastike," *Turcologica, 1986* (Leningrad: Nauka, 1986), 192–201.

Moorey, P. R. S., "Some Ancient Metal Belts: Their Antecedents and Relatives," *Iran* 5 (1967), 83–98.

Mostaert, Antoine, "A propos de quelques portraits d'empereurs mongols," *Asia Major* 4 (1927), 147–56.

"Le mot *natigay/načigay* chez Marco Polo," in *Oriente Poliano* (Rome: Instituto Italiano per il Medio ed Estremo Oriente, 1957), 95–101.

Moule, A. C., *Christians in China before the Year 1550* (London: Society for Promoting Christian Knowledge, 1930).

Munkuev, N. Ts., "Novye materialy o polozhenii mongol'skikh aratov v XIII–XIV v.v.," in Tikhvinskii, *Tataro-Mongoly v Azii i Evrope*, 413–31.

"O dvukh tendentsiiakh v politike pervykh mongol'skikh khanov v Kitae v pervoi polovine XIII veka," in *Materialy po istorii i filologii Tsentral'noi Azii* (Trudy buriatskogo kompleksnogo nauchno-issledovatel'skogo instituta, vol. VIII; Ulan Ude, 1962), 49–67.

Munro, J. H., "The Medieval Scarlet and the Economics of Sartorial Splendor," in N. B. Harte and K. G. Panting, eds., *Cloth and Clothing in Medieval Europe: Essays in Memory of Professor E. M. Carus-Wilson* (London: Heineman, 1983), 13–70.

Murra, John V., "Cloth and its Function in the Inka State," in Weiner and Schneider, *Cloth and Human Experience*, 275–302.

Nadeliaev, V. M., *et al.*, eds. *Drevnetiurkskii slovar* (Leningrad: Nauka, 1969).

Needham, Joseph, *Science and Civilization in China* (Cambridge University Press, 1965–1969), vols. I and II.

Clerks and Craftsmen in China and the West: Lectures and Addresses on the History of Science and Technology (Cambridge University Press, 1970).

"China's Trebuchets, Manned and Counterweighted," in Bert S. Hall and Delno C. West, eds., *On Pre-Modern Technology and Science: A Volume of Studies in Honor of Lynn White, Jr.* (Malibu, California: Undena Publications, 1976), 107–45.

Nekliudov, Sergei Iu., "Zametki o mifologicheskoi i fol'klorno-epicheskoi simvolike y mongol'skikh narodov: simvolike zolota," *Etnografia Polska* 24/1 (1980), 65–94.

Newton, Stella Mary, *Fashion in the Age of the Black Prince: A Study of the Years 1340–1365* (Woodbridge, Sussex: Boydell Press, 1980).

"Tomaso da Modena, Simone Martini, Hungarians and St. Martin in Fourteenth Century Italy," *Journal of the Warburg and Courtauld Institutes* 43 (1980), 234–38.

Noonan, Thomas S., "Rus, Pechenegs and Polovtsy: Economic Interaction along the Steppe Frontier in the Pre-Mongol Era," *Russian History* 19 (1992), 301–27.

Norman, Jerry, *Manchu-English Lexicon* (Seattle: University of Washington Press, 1978).

Okladnikov, A. P., "Drevnemongol'skii portret, nadpisi i risunki na skale y podnozh'ia gory Bogdo-Uula," in S. V. Kiselev, ed., *Mongol'skii arkheologicheskii sbornik: Posviashchaetsia slavnomu XL-letiiu Mongol'skoi Narodnoi Respubliki* (Moscow: Izdatel'stvo akademii nauk SSSR, 1962), 68–74.

"Notes on the Beliefs and Religion of the Ancient Mongols: The Golden-Winged Eagle in Mongolian History," *Acta Ethnographica Academiae Scientiarum Hungaricae* 13 (1964), 411–14.

Olschki, Leonardo, *Guillaume Boucher, a French Artist at the Court of the Khans* (Baltimore: Johns Hopkins Press, 1946).

"Ölün's Chemise: An Episode from the *Secret History of the Mongols*," *JAOS* 67 (1947), 54–56.

The Myth of Felt (Berkeley: University of California Press, 1949).

Marco Polo's Asia: An Introduction to his "Description of the World" *called* "il Milione," (Los Angeles: University of California Press, 1960).

Oppenheim, A. Leo, "The Golden Garments of the Gods," *Journal of Near Eastern Studies* 8/3 (1949), 172–93.

Ōshima Ritsuko, "The *Chiang-hu* in the Yuan," *Acta Asiatica* 45 (1983), 69–95.

Pacey, Arnold, *Technology in World Civilization: A Thousand Year History* (Cambridge, Mass.: MIT Press, 1991).

Pavlinskaya, Larisa R., "The Scythians and Sakians, Eighth to Third Centuries B.C.," in Basilov, *Nomads of Eurasia*, 19–39.

Payne, Joan Crowfoot, "Lapis Lazuli in Early Egypt," *Iraq* 30 (1968), 58–61.
Pelliot, Paul, "Une ville musulmane dans la Chine du Nord sous les Mongols," *Journal Asiatique* 211 (1927), 261–79.
"Le mots mongols dans le *Korye să*," *Journal Asiatique* 217 (1930), 253–66.
"Notes sur le 'Turkestan' de M. W. Bartold," *T'oung-pao* 27 (1930), 12–56.
Notes on Marco Polo (Paris: Libraire Adrien-Maisonneuve, 1959–63), vol. II.
Petrascheck-Heim, Ingeborg, "Die Mittelalterlichen Textilfunde von Kordlar Tepe," *Archaeologische Mitteilungen aus Iran* 15 (1982), 287–305.
Phillips, J. R. S., *The Medieval Expansion of Europe* (Oxford University Press, 1988).
Piggot, Stuart, *Wagon, Chariot and Carriage: Symbols and Status in the History of Transportation* (New York: Thames and Hudson, 1992).
Pikulin, M. G., "Chingiskhan v Afganistane," in Tikhvinskii, *Tataro-Mongoly v Azii i Evrope*, 140–49.
Polos'mak, N. S., *Steregushchie zoloto grify* (*Ak-Alakhinskie kurgany*) (Novosibirsk: Nauka, 1994).
Poppe, Nicholas, *Introduction to Mongolian Comparative Studies* (Helsinki: Suomalais-Ugrilainen Seura, 1955).
"The Use of Colour Names in Mongolian," *The Canada-Mongolia Review* 3/2 (1977), 118–34.
Pritsak, Omeljan, "Orientierung und Farbsymbolik: Zu den Farbenbezeichnungen in den altaischen Volkernamen," *Speculum* 5 (1954), 376–83.
Pulleyblank, Edwin G., *The Background of the Rebellion of An Lu-shan* (London: Oxford University Press, 1965).
de Rachewiltz, Igor, "Some Remarks on the Ideological Foundations of Chingis Khan's Empire," *Papers on Far Eastern History* 7 (1973), 21–36.
"Muqali, Bōl, Tas and An-t'ung," *Papers on Far Eastern History* 15 (1977), 45–55.
Rall, Jutta, "Zur persischen Übersetzung eines *Mo-chüeh*, eines chinesischen medizinischen Textes," *Oriens Extremus* 7 (1960), 152–57.
Raschke, Manfred G., "New Studies in Roman Commerce with the East," in Hildegard Temporini, ed., *Aufstieg und Niedergang der Römische Welt* (Berlin and New York: Walter de Guyter, 1978), vol. II, pt. 9.2, 604–1361.
Ratchnevsky, Paul, "Über den mongolischen Kult um Hofe der Grosskhane in China," in Louis Ligeti, ed., *Mongolian Studies* (Amsterdam: Verlag B. R. Grüner, 1970), 417–43.
Reinhold, Meyer, *History of Purple as a Status Symbol in Antiquity* (Brussels: Latomus, 1970).
Renne, Elisha P., *Cloth That Does Not Die: The Meaning of Cloth in Bùnú Social Life* (Seattle: University of Washington Press, 1995).
von Richthofen, Ferdinand, "Ueber die Zentralasiatischen Seidenstrassen bis zum 2. Jahrhundert n. Chr," *Verhandlungen der Gesellschaft für Erdkunde zu Berlin* 4 (1877), 96–122.
Roach, Mary Ellen and Joanne Bubolz Eicher, "The Language of Personal Adornment," in Justine M. Cordwell and Ronald A. Schwarz, eds., *The Fabric of Culture: The Anthropology of Clothing and Adornment* (The Hague: Mouton, 1979), 7–21.
Róna-Tas, András, "Felt-making in Mongolia," *Acta Orientalia Academiae Scientiarum Hungaricae* 16 (1963), 199–215.

"Preliminary Report on a Study of the Dwellings of the Altaic People," in Denis Sinor, ed., *Aspects of Altaic Civilization* (Bloomington: Indiana University Press, 1963), 47–56.

"Böz in the Altaic World," *Altorientalische Forschungen* 3 (1975), 155–63.

Ronsdorf, Braun, "Gold and Silver Fabrics from Medieval to Modern Times," *CIBA Review* (1961–63), 2–16.

Ross, E. Denison, "Fresh Light on the Word 'Scarlet'," *Journal and Proceedings of the Asiatic Society of Bengal* 4 (1908), 403–04.

Roux, Jean-Paul, "Quelques objects numineux des Turcs et des Mongols, I, Le bonnet et la ceinture," *Turcica* 7 (1975), 50–64.

La religion des Turcs et les Mongols (Paris: Payot, 1984).

S. P. M. H., "Jade Shroud Found," *Archaeology* 49/3 (1996), 28.

Safi, I. M., "Fresh Light on the Ghaznavids," *Islamic Culture* 12 (1938), 189–234.

Sahlins, Marshall D., "Poor Man, Rich Man, Big Man, Chief: Political Types in Melanesia and Polynesia," *Comparative Studies in Society and History* 5 (1962–63), 285–303.

Sarianidi, V. I., "O velikom lazuritovom puti na Drevnem Vostoke," *Kratkie soobshcheniia Instituta arkheologii* 114 (1968), 3–9.

"The Lapis Lazuli Route in the Ancient East," *Archaeology* 24/1 (1971), 12–15.

"The Treasure of the Golden Mound," *Archaeology* 33/3 (May–June 1980), 31–41.

Sayre, Pamela G., "The Mistress of the Robes – Who Was She?," *Byzantine Studies/Études Byzantines* 13 (1986), 229–39.

Schafer, Edward H., *The Golden Peaches of Samarkand: A Study of T'ang Exotics* (Berkeley: University of California Press, 1963).

Schlegel, G., "Hennins or Conical Lady's Hats in Asia, China and Europe," *T'oung-pao* 3 (1892), 422–29.

Schlumberger, D., "Le palais ghaznévide de Lashkari Bazar," *Syria* 29 (1952), 251–70.

Schneider, Jane, "Was There a Pre-Capitalist World System?," *Peasant Studies* 6/1 (January 1977), 20–29.

"Peacocks and Penguins: The Political Economy of European Cloth and Color," *American Ethnologist* 5 (1978), 413–47.

"The Anthropology of Cloth," *Annual Review of Anthropology* 16 (1987), 409–448.

Schurmann, Herbert Franz, *Economic Structure of the Yuan Dynasty* (Cambridge, Mass.: Harvard University Press, 1967).

Seiler-Baldinger, Annemarie, *Textiles: A Classification of Techniques* (Washington: Smithsonian Institute Press, 1994).

Serjeant, R. B., *Islamic Textiles: Material for a History up to the Mongol Conquest* (Beirut: Librairie du Liban, 1972).

Serruys, Henry, "Remains of Mongol Customs in China during the Early Ming," *Monumenta Serica* 16 (1957), 137–90.

"Mongol *Altan* 'Gold' = 'Imperial'," *Monumenta Serica* 21 (1962), 357–78.

Sino-Mongol Relations in the Ming, II, The Tribute System and Diplomatic Missions (1400–1600) (Mélanges chinois et bouddhiques, vol. XIV; Brussels: Institut belge des hautes Études chinoises, 1967).

Kumiss Ceremonies and Horse Races: The Mongolian Texts (Wiesbaden: Otto Harrassowitz, 1974).

Shaked, Shaul, "From Iran to Islam: On Some Symbols of Royalty," *Jerusalem Studies in Arabic* 7 (1986), 75–91.

Shakhanova, Nurila Zh., "The Yurt in the Traditional Worldview of the Central Asian Nomads," in Gary Seaman, ed., *Foundations of Empire: Archaeology and Art of the Eurasian Steppe* (Los Angeles: Ethnographics Press, 1992), 157–83.

Shavkunov, E. V., "O semantike tamgoobraznykh znakov i nekotorykh vidov ornamenta na keramike s Shaiginskogo gorodishcha," *Sovetskaia etnografiia* 3 (1972), 128–33.

Shaw, Robert, *Visits to High Tartary, Yarkand and Kashgar* (Hong Kong: Oxford University Press, 1984).

Shepard, Dorothy G., "Iran between East and West," in Theodore Bowie, ed., *East–West in Art: Patterns of Cultural and Aesthetic Relationships* (Bloomington: Indiana University Press, 1966), 84–105.

Shepard, Dorothy G. and W. B. Henning, "Zandanījī Identified?," in Richard Ettinghausen, ed., *Aus der Welt der islamischen Kunst: Festschrift für Ernst Kühnel zum 75 Geburtstag* (Berlin: Gebr. Mann Verlag, 1959), 15–40.

Singer, Charles, "East and West in Retrospect," in Charles Singer *et al.*, eds., *A History of Technology*, vol. II, *The Mediterranean Civilizations and the Middle Ages, c. 700 B.C. to A.D. 1500* (Oxford: Clarendon Press, 1956), 753–76.

Sinor, Denis, "The Greed of the Northern Barbarians," in Clark and Draghi, *Aspects of Altaic Civilization, II*, 171–82.

Skrynnikov, T. D., "Sülde – The Basic Idea of the Chinggis Khan Cult," *Acta Orientalia Academiae Scientiarum Hungaricae* 46/2 (1992/93), 51–59.

Soucek, Priscilla, ed., *Content and Context of Visual Arts in the Islamic World: Papers from a Colloquium in Memory of Richard Ettinghausen* (University Park and London: The Pennslyvania State University Press, 1988).

Spuler, Bertold, *Die Mongolen in Iran: Politik, Verwaltung und Kultur der Ilchanzeit, 1220–1350*, 4th edn. (Leiden: E. J. Brill, 1985).

Stillman, N. A., "*Khil'a*," *Encyclopedia of Islam*, 2nd edn. (Leiden: E. J. Brill, 1979), vol. V.

Stoddart, D. Michael, *The Scented Ape: The Biology and Culture of Human Odour* (Cambridge University Press, 1990).

Sudzuki Osamu, "Silk Road and Alexander's Eastern Campaign," *Orient: Report of the Society for Near Eastern Studies in Japan* 11 (1975), 67–92.

Suleimanova, Fazila, *Miniatury k 'khamse' Nizami* (Tashkent: Fan, 1985).

Sutherland, C. H. V., *Gold, its Beauty, Power and Allure* (London: Thames and Hudson, 1959).

Tainter, Joseph A., *The Collapse of Complex Societies* (Cambridge University Press, 1990).

Taylor, Romeyn, "Yuan Origins of the *Wei-so* System," in Charles M. Hucker, ed., *Chinese Government in Ming Times: Seven Studies* (New York: Columbia University Press, 1969), 23–40.

Terent'ev-Katanskii, A. P., *Materialnaia kul'tura Si Sia* (Moscow: Vostochnaia literatura, 1993).

Thompson, Georgina, "Iranian Dress in the Achaemenid Period: Problems Concerning the *kanys* and Other Garments," *Iran* 3 (1965), 121–26.

Thorley, J., "The Silk Trade between China and the Roman Empire at its Height, *circa* A.D. 90–130," *Greece and Rome*, 2nd series, 18 (1971), 71–80.

Thorp, Robert L., *Son of Heaven: Imperial Arts of China* (Seattle: Son of Heaven Press, 1988).
Tikhonov, D. I., *Khoziaistvo i obshchestvennyi stroi uigurskogo gosudarstva* (Moscow-Leningrad: Nauka, 1966).
Tikhvinskii, S. L., "Tataro-mongol'skie zavoevaniia v Azii i Evrope: Vstupitel'naia stat'ia," in S. L. Tikhvinskii, ed., *Tataro-mongoly v Azii i Evrope: Sbornik Statei*, 2nd edn. (Moscow: Nauka, 1977), 3–22.
Tintsius, V. I., ed., *Sravnitnel'nyi slovar Tunguso-Man'chzhurskikh iazykov: materialy k etimologicheskomu slovariu* (Leningrad: Nauka, 1977), vol. II.
Tolybekov, S. E., *Kochevoe obshchestvo Kazakhov v XVII-nachale XX veka* (Alma Ata: Izdatel'stvo 'nauka' Kazakhskoi SSR, 1971).
Toynbee, Paget, "Tartar Cloths," *Romania* 24 (1900), 559–64.
Trigger, Bruce G., "Monumental Architecture: A Thermodynamic Explanation of Symbolic Behavior," *World Archaeology* 22 (1990), 119–32.
Vainberg, B. I., *Monety drevnego Khorezma* (Moscow: Nauka, 1977).
Vale, Juliet, *Edward II and Chivalry: Chivalric Society and its Context, 1270–1350* (Woodbridge, Sussex: Boydell Press, 1982).
Viktorova, L. L., *Mongoly: Proiskhozhdenie naroda i istoki kul'tury* (Moscow: Nauka, 1980).
Voll, John Obert, "Islam as a Special World System," *Journal of World History* 5 (1994), 213–26.
Waida Manabu, "Birds in the Mythology of Sacred Kingship," *East and West* n.s. 28 (1978), 283–89.
Wang Penglin, "On the Etymology of English Silk: A Case Study of IE and Altaic Contact," *Central Asiatic Journal* 37 (1993), 225–48.
Wang Ping-hua, "Yen-hu ku-mu," *Wen-wu*, no. 10 (1973), 28–34.
Wardwell, Anne E., "*Panni Tartarici*: Eastern Islamic Silks Woven with Gold and Silver (13th and 14th Centuries)," *Islamic Art* 3 (1988–1989), 95–133.
"Two Silk and Gold Textiles of the Early Mongol Period," *The Bulletin of the Cleveland Museum of Art* 79/10 (December 1992), 354–78.
Watson, Andrew M., *Agricultural Innovation in the Early Islamic World: The Diffusion of Crops and Farming Techniques* (Cambridge University Press, 1983).
Watson, Oliver, *Persian Lustre Ware* (London and Boston: Faber and Faber, 1985).
Weiner, Annette B. and Jane Schneider, eds., *Cloth and Human Experience* (Washington, DC: Smithsonian Institution Press, 1991).
Wheatley, Paul, "Geographical Notes on Some Commodities Involved in Sung Maritime Trade," *Journal of the Malayan Branch of the Royal Asiatic Society* 32/2 (1961), 5–140.
Whitman, Marina D., "The Scholar, the Drinker, and the Ceramic Pot-Painter." in Soucek, ed., *Content and Context of the Visual Arts in the Islamic World*, 255–78.
Widengren, Geo, "Some Remarks on the Riding Costume and Articles of Dress among Iranian Peoples in Antiquity," *Studia Ethnographica Upsaliensia* 11 (1956), 228–76.
Mani and Manichaeism (London: Weidenfeld and Nicolson, 1961).
"Le symbolisme de la ceinture," *Iranica Antiqua* 8 (1968), 133–55.
Wittfogel, Karl A. and Feng Chia-sheng, *History of Chinese Society, Liao (907–1125)* (Philadelphia: American Philosophical Society, 1949).
Wulff, Hans, *The Traditional Crafts of Persia: Their Development, Technology, and*

Influence on Eastern and Western Civilizations (Cambridge, Mass.: The MIT Press, 1966).
Zhdanko, T. A. and S. K. Kamalov, *Etnografiia Karakalpakov, XIX-nachalo XX veka (Materialy i issledovaniia)* (Tashkent: Fan, 1980).
Zhou Xun and Gao Chunming, *5000 Years of Chinese Costumes* (San Francisco: China Books and Periodicals, 1987).
Zhukovskaia, N. L., "Mongoly," in R. Sh. Dzharylgachinova and M. V. Kriukov, eds., *Kalendarnye obychai i obriady narodov Vostochnoi Azii: Novyi god* (Moscow: Nauka, 1985), 179–87.
Kategorii i simvolika traditsionnoi kul'tury mongolov (Moscow: Nauka, 1988).

Index

CPSIA information can be obtained at www.ICGtesting.com
Printed in the USA
LVOW060407281211

261317LV00001B/1/A

9 780521 893145